Totalitarianism

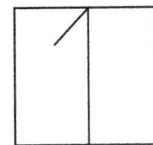 **SQUARE ONE**
First Order Questions in the Humanities

Series Editor: **PAUL A. KOTTMAN**

TOTALITARIANISM

A Borderline Idea in
Political Philosophy

Simona Forti

Translated by Simone Ghelli

STANFORD UNIVERSITY PRESS
Stanford, California

Stanford University Press
Stanford, California

A version of the first two chapters of this work was originally published in Italian in 2001 under the title *Il totalitarismo,* ©2001, Gius. Laterza & Figli, all rights reserved.

©2024 by the Board of Trustees of the Leland Stanford Junior University. All rights reserved.

No part of this book may be reproduced or transmitted in any form or by any means, electronic or mechanical, including photocopying and recording, or in any information storage or retrieval system, without the prior written permission of Stanford University Press.

Printed and bound by CPI Group (UK) Ltd, Croydon, CR0 4YY

Library of Congress Cataloging-in-Publication Data
Names: Forti, Simona, author. | Ghelli, Simone, translator.
Title: Totalitarianism : a borderline idea in political philosophy / Simona Forti ; translated by Simone Ghelli.
Other titles: Totalitarismo. English | Square one (Series)
Description: Stanford, California : Stanford University Press, 2024. | Series: Square one: first-order questions in the humanities | "A version of this work was originally published in Italian in 2001 under the title Il totalitarismo." | Includes bibliographical references and index. |
Identifiers: LCCN 2023006792 (print) | LCCN 2023006793 (ebook)
  | ISBN 9781503627505 (cloth) | ISBN 9781503637375 (paperback) | ISBN 9781503637382 (ebook)
Subjects: LCSH: Totalitarianism—Philosophy. | Democracy—Philosophy. | Political science—Philosophy.
Classification: LCC JC480 .F6713 2024 (print) | LCC JC480 (ebook) | DDC 320.5301—dc23/eng/20230215
LC record available at https://lccn.loc.gov/2023006792
LC ebook record available at https://lccn.loc.gov/2023006793

Cover design and art: David Drummond

Contents

Preface by Paul A. Kottman   vii

Introduction   1

1 How the Concept "Totalitarianism" Came to Be   8

2 From the Construction of Models to the Practice of Dissent   36

3 Philosophy in the Face of Extremes   57

4 Specters of Totality   110

Conclusion   141

Notes   147

References   149

Index   161

Preface

Just like any other science, political science requires a set of concepts—such as "monarchy" or "democracy" or "totalitarianism"—that help us to grasp political reality by classifying it. But when it comes to politics, our practices of classification are often rooted in simplistic or ideological notions of what politics is for, what politics is all about. As a result, political concepts often block us from understanding what we want to understand; or they warp our understanding—and this, too, has political consequences.

Moreover, our ways of classifying reality are not simply contested by reality itself; our ways of understanding reality—the concepts we use and our ways of using them—are also a part of the very reality we seek to understand. Political concepts do not simply descend from our passive observation of the nature of politics; we give shape to politics and political discourse by combining certain observations we make, by noticing family resemblances and differences in political life and our ways of thinking and talking about them.

So, the first-order question of Simona Forti's book is not just "What is totalitarianism?"—a query that might call for a taxonomical answer, or a "dictionary-style" entry in a glossary of political concepts. This is not because the challenge of classifying "totalitarianism" as a reality and a concept can be sidestepped. Again, political science requires concepts; classificatory ambitions cannot be simply set aside. Indeed, I believe that, in the pages that follow, Forti has offered us the best map we have of the concept of totalitarianism and its deep implications, uses, history, and controversies.

But I think that this tumbles into the true first-order question to which Forti responds in these pages: "Whence—and what is—our *need* for the concept of totalitarianism?" Put another way, "What exactly—in the difficult realities and painful experiences of the past century—continues to animate discussions of totalitarianism, urging us to use this concept, to talk in these ways?"

To suggest that we *need* the term *totalitarianism* is not simply to suggest that something essential to our political experience would, without this term, remain unnamed or inarticulate; it is also to suggest that absent this term, something essential to our collective experience, to our historical suffering and present sorrow, would be inexpressible. In this sense, this book is philosophical in scope.

Of course, it is one thing to come into possession of the words and concepts that we might need. But it is quite another to know how to *use* these concepts, such that our need for them itself is clarified, tended to, or somehow satisfied.

How are we ever to evaluate whether our concepts are being used well or if our need for them is being satisfied? How might we ever settle whether the term *totalitarianism* is anything other than propaganda or name-calling? How might we settle whether and how our use of the term is adequate, whether it helps us grasp our predicament and what we feel is urgent about it? It is to Forti's credit that such questions are the beating heart of her book.

Forti is aware that to possess the concept of totalitarianism is ipso facto to try to know how events and reflections on those events are given shape in human history. The term gives voice to a knowledge of human possibilities and of the enigmatic nature of political realities and their implications. To be able to use the term *totalitarianism* well is thus not just to be able to tell a totalitarian reality apart from an "authoritarian" or "democratic" one—as if distinguishing an apple from a pear.

"Applying" terms or concepts is hardly the only use to which they can be put. To use the term *totalitarian* is also to evaluate the possibilities that arise from its usage and, thereby, to think about difficult political realities from the inside out.

PAUL A. KOTTMAN, *Series Editor*

Totalitarianism

Introduction

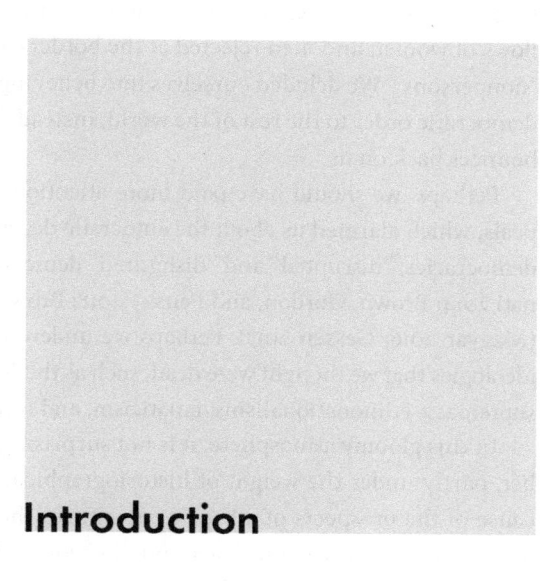

The time is out of joint—O cursèd spite!
                    HAMLET, ACT 1, SCENE 5

We are truly living in "Dark Times," when the fragile equilibriums of the late twentieth century seem to have shattered—times that Europe and the West thought they had dismissed, relegated to a past outside their geographical horizons. Yet here we are, civilized Westerners, once again facing a world that seems to have gone off its hinges, a world "out of joint"—so much so that a statement such as "The 1930s are back" cannot, unfortunately, be said to be merely rhetorical.

We see this devolution everywhere: the threat of a possible nuclear catastrophe; a war in the heart of Europe that, triggered by Russia's aggression against Ukraine, threatens to engulf the world; citizens forced to leave their countries and live as refugees; new authoritarian regimes and so-called populist regimes that no longer even bother to hide their policies of repression; a pandemic that has thrown us into insecurity and awakened forgotten dystopian fears; terrorist attacks in the centers of our capitals; flows of women and men rejected at the borders as "residual material"—as "nonpersons." We deluded ourselves into believing that we could export the democratic order to the rest of the world; instead, like a nemesis, barbarism bounces back on us.

Perhaps, we should have paid more attention to political scientists' appeals, which alarmed us about the autocratic degeneration of states, illiberal democracies, "disrupted" and "disfigured" democracies (Krastev 2014; Urbinati 2014; Brown, Gordon, and Pensky 2018; Brown 2019), and "mafia states" (Magyar 2016; Gessen 2017). Perhaps we underestimated the resurgence of ideologies that we thought were dead, such as the "Great Replacement," white supremacy, ethnonationalisms, fanaticism, and fundamentalisms.

In this gloomy atmosphere, it is not surprising that, after years of slumber, partly under the weight of historiographical controversies, partly because of the prospects of a happy outcome of the end of history, the term *totalitarianism* has come back into fashion. "Populist totalitarianism," "Islamist totalitarianism," "health totalitarianism," "technological totalitarianism," "digital totalitarianism," "media totalitarianism," "managerial totalitarianism," "neoliberal totalitarianism"—these are the most recurring locutions in our public opinions, as well as in current political theory. As much as these terms give rise to novel formulations, we do well to ask, Is the totalitarian specter hunting us once again?

Hence, my first question: how is the term being employed? Is it a generic, media-driven appropriation that merely points out the danger of a narrowing of pluralism and individual freedom, or does it attempt to recover the specific meaning of a political category belonging to the last century?

Because these two options are probably not always clearly distinguishable, we need to ask a second question: do we really need to recover this concept? Or does it instead obscure the awareness of the difference between forms of domination that, like those of the last century, saw the state apparatus as the central actor, and today's forms of power, for which, since reticular and horizontal, sources are almost impossible to locate? (Traverso 2019).

Why are the new exponents of that same culture that in the last century contested the ideological use of the term *totalitarianism* now employing it without the historical scruples of the past? Is the category of totalitarianism resilient enough to resist deconstructions, contextualizations, clarifications, and partisan uses? Is this a resilience activated anytime we feel disoriented before the new manifestations of power and violence in which we are immersed?

During the twentieth century, the notion of totalitarianism somehow responded to the historical disorientation caused by the catastrophes of the two world wars. For some, the neologism succeeded in accounting for the unprecedented novelty of what was happening. For others, it represented a Manichean linguistic machine dividing the world into good regimes (read democracies) and bad regimes (read Nazi-fascist and Soviet totalitarianisms).

If, with the end of the Cold War, we deluded ourselves into believing that we had finally overcome the phase of violent oppositions, that we had archived their simplifying and "warring" schemes, September 11, 2001, set in motion a new phase of cross-demonizations. In this book, I examine the several layers of meaning that structured, and still structure, the concept of totalitarianism. For now, it is sufficient to note that the generic use of terms such as *totalitarianism* and *totalitarian* still represent ostracizing judgments. For instance, from the beginning of the twenty-first century, Islam has been accused of fostering a theological-political totalitarianism, and the West, especially the US, has been considered a set of totalitarian regimes that mask their will to economic and political total power under false ideals of freedom and self-determination.

How can superficial and demonizing employments of this concept be avoided? How can one claim its problematic, but still useful, heuristic power in spite of those who, yesterday and today, aim at dismissing it once and for all?

First, I believe that a reconstruction of the tricky development of the concept can shed light on the different layers of meaning accruing to it over time. There is a basic definition of *totalitarianism* on which, broadly speaking, the social and political sciences agree. For the regimes of the twentieth century, totalitarianism designates a political universe in which a single party has conquered the ownership of the state and has subjugated the whole of society, both by resorting to a widespread and terroristic use of violence and by conferring on ideology a key role. On closer inspection, this meaning of the concept is not questioned even by historians, who have always been the most reluctant to admit its explanatory value. With the exception of the most radical revisionists, historians also tend to acknowledge that the great processes of transformation characterizing Europe since the Great War have produced political experiences that can be framed in this new category of political thought. If anything, to agree on whether these experiences can be defined as totalitarian has been more problematic. For instance, the debate on whether Italian fascism can be defined as totalitarian or as simply authoritarian is still open, as is that of whether Salazar's Portugal and Franco's Spain are comparable to fascism and, therefore, whether they fall under the category of authoritarian or totalitarian regimes. Moreover, was Hitler's Germany truly one of the few pure examples of totalitarianism, and was it so from 1938 or from as early as 1933? Another set of unanswered questions concerns the second half of the twentieth century: did the end of the Second World War mark the end of totalitarianism? Or, instead, did the countries of the Soviet bloc continue to revolve around a totalitarian ideal? Were some regimes in Latin America only forms of authoritarianism, or did they give rise to totalitarian dynasties? Still awaiting an answer is the question of which experience in Asia best corresponds with the totalitarian ideal. We must also consider the question of whether Stalin's regime alone has the characteristics of totalitarianism or whether the society that emerged from the Bolshevik Revolution should already be considered totalitarian.

Fortunately, this book does not, cannot, want to be a history book but only an attempt to account for the development and meaning of a term and a notion. Here, the reader will find neither a defense of the concept nor a denunciation of it. I aim to offer a genealogy and conceptual map to navigate one of the most significant and stormy debates in contemporary political theory and philosophy. The concept, initially built on the historical comparison between Nazism and Stalinism, has not only caused scandal but also strained the alleged inviolable boundaries between "right" and "left." This is one reason why no other political notion has been as controversial.

On the one hand, totalitarianism has been accepted as the only hermeneutical tool capable of endowing the most tragic side of the twentieth century with a unitary meaning. On the other hand, it has been the target of endless polemics, inasmuch as any accusation of being totalitarian has been considered the weapon of choice used by the West to delegitimize communism. Eventually, the potential ideological uses of the concept have greatly jeopardized it. For a long time, what truly counted was simply the evocative and mobilizing power of a term that, beyond its scientific status, compelled those who used it, as well as those who rejected it, to declare their political position. Thus, perhaps unlike any other concept, the content of the concept of totalitarianism, along with its potential meanings, has not been properly expressed.

In the first two chapters of this book, I have tried to reconstruct the development of the term, how the concept was articulated, and the rise of theories and interpretations attached to it. By doing so, I am convinced we can clear "the question of totalitarianism" of clichés. I think it is important to remind those who still consider the concept of totalitarianism a mere pawn on the bipolar chessboard that it has its roots in a period long before the era of East-West opposition and that not only liberal-democratic thinkers participated in its construction. The notion of totalitarianism arises, as we will observe, from political militancy but not from the West's struggle against the "Empire of Evil"; it certainly has a normative value, but it follows different paths, in no way reducible to the mere defense of liberal-democratic values. Perhaps only today is this being recognized. It is worth repeating: it is probably no coincidence that, now, those who belong to that culture that yesterday refused to use the term *totalitarianism* because they believed it to be a weapon of liberal capitalism are today among those who do not hesitate to denounce the totalitarian drifts threatening us all.

However unfair the criticism that interprets the concept of totalitarianism as an ideological instrument of cold war may be, it may help to highlight the limits of those political typologies, developed from the 1950s to the 1970s, that have led to the full affirmation of the concept, although fixing its content in a rigid and schematic enumeration of characters. Such typologies, which are mostly vitiated by an uncritical apologia of Western democracies, even though they attempt to appear as neutral taxonomic criteria, risked transforming the notion into a sterile tool that simply updates the existing list of political regimes. If the category of totalitarianism should simply describe the features of a political regime based on a presumed empirical and objective analysis, then its purpose would run out. Additionally, such first "ideal-types," which crystallized in statistical distinctions, have been followed by increasingly articulate and dynamic comparative analyses. Nevertheless, political theory and philosophy have continued to dwell on the scope and influence of this notion. This means that the questions it raises convey much more than the mere observation that the last century has witnessed the birth of a regime in which political pluralism and parliamentary institutions were suppressed. Above all, totalitarianism still proves to be one of the few available categories capable of capturing the tragic specificity of the twentieth century. After all, even current trends are brought within its semantic area. This is because such a concept, well beyond the historical configurations that have marked its birth, probably succeeds in rendering the sense of a power that by its intensity and extension aims at totality, continually transcending its boundaries and achievements.

The third and fourth chapters are devoted to political philosophers—those who, in my opinion, are keeping the debate on totalitarianism alive. The authors and interpretations that I will take into consideration represent a type of reading that some exponents of political science would promptly define as "essentialist"—that is, intent on seeking "eternal essences" and "spiritual continuities" wherein any concrete and factual element is forgone. It is true that these interpretations, often bold and sometimes even arbitrary, risk dissolving singular facts and times within philosophical genealogies conceiving it as an inner potentiality of Western politics. But the crucial question may be whether there is any difference between the historical-political employment of the expression "totalitarian regime" and the philosophical understanding of "totalitarianism" as a dynamic of power. All philosophical-political investigations move from radical and, so to speak, "experienced" questions about the epochal meaning of totalitarian realities. In other words, they aim to understand totalitarianism not only as a set of events or characteristics but also as the key figure of the power characterizing the contemporary age. Totalitarianism, in fact, is read as that extreme power experience that interrupts the continuity of a cultural, political, and philosophical tradition, questioning, at the same time, its basic assumptions.

At first, the philosophical use of the concept of totalitarianism assumed a deconstructive function. With the emergence of "radical evil," as some twentieth-century philosophers argued, the nihilistic and destructive potential contained in the very project of modern instrumental rationalism came to light: its will to power, as well as its inseparable "constructivist obsession." "Radical evil," to use Hannah Arendt's expression, shattered faith in the coincidence of reason and history; it highlighted the dark side of that hope in the possibility of achieving a political community "under the sign of the One." If there is one trait that fascism, Nazism, and communism truly have in common, it is a clear desire to affirm unity.

A philosophical understanding of the concept of totalitarianism helps to expose the groundlessness of some modern juxtapositions. It is helpful to deconstruct head-on those reassuring antitheses that oppose democracy to totalitarianism. Certain philosophical reflections teach us that one cannot oppose democracy, firmly defined in a formal and institutional identity, to totalitarianism as a political monster that assumes the convenient role of a "countertype." They suggest that, rather, we should be suspicious of those alleged impassable boundaries that separate a regime of freedom from a totalitarian system. In short, they invite us to an endless inquiry of the democratic epoch: the possibilities the latter has opened up, the gaps it fills in, the mechanisms it activates, and the "voluntary servitude" it engenders. Totalitarianism cannot be considered an external threat to democracy. In fact, it represents one of the possible answers to those questions that modernity has posed and to which democracies have failed to find solutions.

ONE

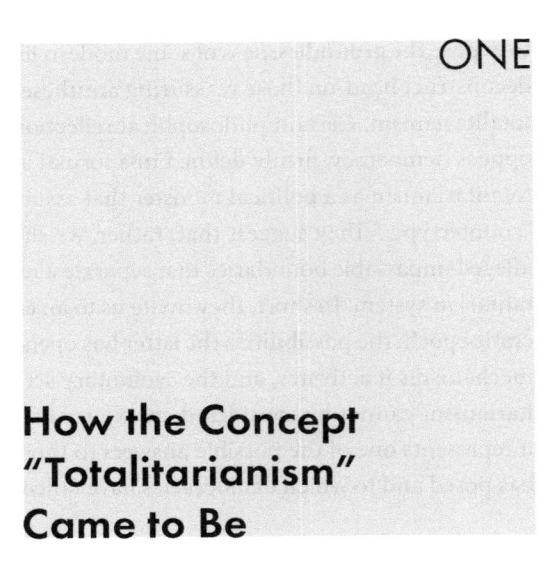

How the Concept "Totalitarianism" Came to Be

THE ORIGINS OF A NEOLOGISM

When did we start using the term *totalitarianism*? When did it become common enough to represent a new political reality? When did it become a precise concept, and when did it become a theory? To reconstruct the history of the term, we must begin with these questions, and we must leave behind, as much as possible, our historical prejudices and ideological clichés. For instance, many people still think that fascism created this word when Mussolini employed the adjective *totalitarian* to define his own regime. But although the terms *totalitarianism* (*totalitarismo*) and *totalitarian* (*totalitario*) originated in Italy, neither *Il Duce* nor any of his devoted fellows coined them. When Mussolini self-defined fascism's ambitions as "totalitarian," the term was already circulating among liberal, democratic, socialist, and Catholic opponents to the regime. Thus, Italian antifascist opposition is where these terms were coined, providing a history of political thought with the key notion to describe perhaps the most crucial historical experience of the twentieth century.

Giovanni Amendola was probably the first to employ the adjective *totalitarian* to describe the novelty of Italian politics.[1] Mussolini's government was totalitarian because it sought absolute, unchecked dominion over political and administrative life. In two articles published in 1923 in the newspaper *Il Mondo* (May 12 and June 28), Amendola defined recent administrative elections as scandals: Mussolini's party presented both the majority and the minority lists, forcibly preventing the existence of any other candidates. In Amendola's eyes, these acts were the signs of what he named "a totalitarian system"—that is, the "prefiguration of absolute domination, the complete and uncontrolled tyrannization of political and administrative life" (Amendola 1960, 102–5). Thus, the adjective *totalitarian* refers to governments that disregard the two foundations of any democracy: the rights of the minority and the rule of the majority. A few months later, the meaning of the term broadened. In November 1923, Amendola wrote, "For those who will study [the] fascist movement in the future, its prominent feature will always be the 'totalitarian' spirit, which will permit our tomorrow to greet sunrises with but the Roman gesture, just as it does not permit present days to nourish souls who do not comply with the creed 'I believe.' Such a singular 'war of religion' that has been pervading Italy for over a year does not truly offer you a faith ..., but it actually denies you the right to have your own consciousness, and, with it, your tomorrow" (193). In January 1924, Augusto Monti also used the word *totalitarian* to denounce fascist elections: "After the sudden attack on Rome and the totalitarian election in cities and regions," he wrote, "fascism is getting set to conduct totalitarian elections for the House of Parliament" (Monti 1924).

Hence, *totalitarian* becomes the adjective that effectively depicts the new direction undertaken by the fascist regime. Although initially employed generically, this term would gradually solidify into a more defined concept. In Amendola's introduction to *Atti del Congresso dell'Unione Nazionale*—published in July 1925, when the regime had already shown its true face—we find "two ways of thinking, two opposite political inspirations which negate the liberal-democratic State and seek to subvert the foundations of modern political life: communism and fascism, i.e., totalitarian reactions to liberalism and democracy." Amendola has a clear feeling that such a "totalitarian reaction" represents an unprecedented challenge for the very foundation of European politics. It is not only a dangerous change of institutional dynamics; what is at stake here is the possibility of a new social and political reality: "the paroxysmal, monomaniac[al], and extreme interference of executive power in state and social life as a whole; the overturning of normal relationships between State and Society, such that the Society serves the State, the State serves the government, and the government serves the party" (Amendola 1951, 240–42). Hence, Italian antifascists—Amendola, Sturzo, Nitti, and others—not only introduced a term and its polemic political employment. By refusing to overlap society, the party, and the state, as well as by denouncing the "total" and "totalitarian" dimension of public life, they eventually suggested a similarity between communism and fascism that, even still, represents the theoretical core of traditional theories on totalitarianism.

In this period, however, few people fully grasped the innovative potential of the adjective. Intellectuals such as Salvatorelli, Fortunato, Mosca, Ferrero, Traves, and Labriola saw the destructive force of fascism, even though they preferred traditional terms such as *tyranny*, *dictatorship*, and *despotism*. But Piero Gobetti, Lelio Basso, and Luigi Sturzo acknowledged *totalitarian* as a more effective term to describe the radical changes of the times in which they were living. They all understood how the identification of state, nation, and party ends up deifying power and its actions in an unprecedented way, destroying freedom completely. On January 2, 1925, Lelio Basso, under the pseudonym Prometeo Filodemo, published an article in *La rivoluzione liberale*, where he "created" the noun *totalitarianism*: "State bodies, such as the crown, the parliament, and magistrature, which, according to traditional theory, embodies the three powers whose will is realized by armed forces, all become instruments of one Party alone, aiming at unanimously representing the common will, the indistinct 'totalitarianism.'" Indistinct totalitarianism is the fascist state's aim to represent the entire population, thereby destroying any individual or movement that stands in its way. Fascist totalitarianism "has these principles: suppression of all conflicts for the sake of the superior good of the Nation, identified with the State, and which, in turn, is the same as the people holding power (the fascist State). This State is the Word, and its Head is the man that God sent to save Italy; he represents the Absolute, the Infallible. . . . Once these principles are established, the State can do anything: any opposition to fascism can be considered as a betrayal of the Nation, as well as any fascist crime may be justified" (Basso and Anderlini 1962, 241–42). A new order was rising, well beyond a simple political reorganization. Basso was not only aware of the depth of this change but also was as alarmed as Sturzo, who, a year earlier in the same journal, had denounced "the spirit of dictatorship that pervades Italy today" and "the new conception of State-party," which led to "totalitarian transformation of any and all moral, cultural, political, and religious force" (Sturzo 1924).

Antonio Gramsci also understood how radically new the terminological pair of *totalitarian* and *totalitarianism* was. He wanted to explain, not just condemn, the new reality of fascism. In the *Prison Notebooks*, he brought up a recurring problem concerning the new totalitarian politics: "A totalitarian policy," he writes, "attempts: (1) to ensure that the members of a particular party find in that one party all the satisfactions that they had previously found in a multiplicity of organizations, that is, to sever all ties these members have with extraneous cultural organisms; (2) to destroy all other organizations or to incorporate them into a system regulated solely by the party" (Gramsci 2007, 108). Hence, these antifascist intellectuals gradually realized the novelty of this phenomenon with its "total" objectives and consequences. The word *totalitarianism* came to be.

Meanwhile, Mussolini and the theorists of the "Nuovo Verbo" enthusiastically seized on these terms, as if the word *totalitarianism* expressed the revolutionary nature and omnipotent voluntarism that, at least from a propagandist viewpoint, characterizes fascist ideology. For this is the moment when fascism demonstrated overtly its tenacious desire to oppose liberal democracy. On June 22, 1925, *Il Duce* gave a speech to the IV Congress of the National Fascist Party exalting the totalitarian tendencies of fascism: "We brought the struggle on such a divergent terrain that we can but stand on one sole side. Moreover, we will pursue our goal, that is, our fierce totalitarian will, with even more ferocity. . . . We want the Nation to be fully fascist so that, tomorrow, to be Italian will be the same as to be fascist" (Mussolini 1956, 362). Mussolini would not go unheard. The adjective *totalitarian* began to circulate as a vague expression of fascist pride. As nationalist journalist Forges Davanzati wrote in February 1926, "Our opponents may call us intransigent, tyrannical, Dominican, totalitarian; yet these are not scary adjectives. Take these 'accusations' with pride. . . . Yes, we are totalitarian! And we want to be, from dawn to dusk. . . . We want to be Dominican. . . . We want to be tyrannical" (Petersen 1978, 115).

Thenceforth, the apologists of the fascist state tried to take the word *totalitarianism* away from the opposition to bestow on it a theoretical dignity. Giovanni Gentile wrote a series of articles, compiled into one volume in 1925, in which he intended to develop the philosophical account of the regime, all the while affirming that fascism had progressed from the "heroic and movementist" phase to the "statal" one (Gentile 1925). In 1928, *The Philosophical Basis of Fascism* for "Foreign Affairs," along with the entry "Fascismo" written on behalf of Mussolini for the *Enciclopedia Italiana* in 1929, Gentile turned the totalitarian elements of fascism into official doctrine. "The fascist concept of the State is anti-individualist"; yet, insofar as the individual coincides with the state, fascism "reaffirms the State as the true reality of the individual." The state promotes freedom if freedom is "the attribute of the real man and not of the abstract doll fostered by liberalism." This freedom belongs to an individual insofar as the individual is part of the state. "From [a] fascist's point of view, everything is part of the State and nothing human or spiritual exist[s] or is worthy out[side] of it. In this sense, fascism is totalitarian, and the Fascist State, synthesis and union of every value, interprets, enhances and develops every aspect of people's lives." Fascism is antidemocratic only if the concept of people is reduced to a numerical entity, but "the bluntest form of democracy is when the people are conceived, as they must be, qualitatively and not quantitatively, as moral and therefore as potent, coherent, true. It realizes the conscience and will of few, actually of One, and, since ideal, it tends to actualize in the conscience and will of all." Such a nation was an ethical reality, not a natural one, and the state was what gave the people their moral unity and identity. "The Fascist State is the highest and most powerful personality. It is a kind of spiritual power. It reassumes the intellectual and moral life of the individual." Thus, state power did not limit itself to guaranteeing order and institutional functioning, to ensuring that individuals can peacefully live their lives, the way liberalism did. "The Fascist State does not just give laws and found institutions but also educates people and promotes their spirituality. It wants to remake not only the forms that a human's life can assume but also the humans themselves, their characters, and their faith. So its discipline and authority have to go deep into people's souls, and dominate them unopposed" (Mussolini 1932, 835–40). What Gentile names the "Totalitarian Fascist State" is actually an extreme example of an "ethical state." This state would seek to unite the individual with democracy, the nation with the spirit of the people, authority with culture. It represents the umpteenth transformation or, maybe, distortion of the Hegelian concept, but it cannot be utterly assimilated into the totalitarian project.

This was Gentile's contribution to the international reception of the words *totalitarian* and *totalitarianism*. In the meantime, thanks to the 1926 publication of Luigi Sturzo's *Italia e Fascismo* in England, these terms entered Anglo-Saxon intellectual circles, assuming again negative connotations. They will receive one of the first academic consecrations by the entry "State" in the *Encyclopaedia of the Social Sciences*, compiled by George Sabine in 1934.

Starting in the 1930s, *totalitarian* and *totalitarianism* will be employed internationally. Paradoxically, despite having produced the neologisms, Italian fascism will not be considered a prototypical totalitarian regime in traditional theory.[2]

THE TOTAL DIMENSION OF POLITICS

If fascism claimed to be totalitarian and was accused of totalitarianism, Nazism—the ideal type of totalitarianism in the past fifty years—claimed, rather, to be an authoritarian state. But German cultural milieus, whether they supported or opposed Hitler, contribute to the development of the concept. Between the two world wars, many German intellectuals, who were still relatively sheltered from the urgencies of the political battle, reflected on the end of the Weimar Republic and, more generally, on how politics had changed in the twentieth century. Starting with the Liberal Democratic crisis, they systematically rethought the relationship between the individual and political power. A debate about the total versus the authoritarian state unfolded in Germany in the early 1930s (Faye 2003).

Many different authors participated, ranging from the so-called conservative revolutionaries—including Moeller Van den Bruck, Hans Frayer, Othmar Spahn, and Ernst Jünger—to the cautious liberal-conservative opposition to the "heterodox" Marxism of the Frankfurt School. This debate injects locutions and syntagmas into a process of intellectual circulation that will have great mobilizing force vis-à-vis the German totalitarian reality. For instance, the notion of a "total state" was meant to oppose the liberal dualism of state and society, as well as the "pluralistic corporativism" of modern politics that, according to these authors, merely mediated material interests. So the term *total state* constitutes the lexical and conceptual basis for the definition of the category of totalitarianism.

Ernst Jünger's 1930 essay "Total Mobilization" provided a characterization of totalitarianism to which subsequent scholars would amply resort to define the total state (Jünger 1993, 119–39). The Great War and extreme technological changes unleashed literally superhuman forces, opening the door to a new politics carrying out a sort of original conflict: "the Elementary." Twentieth-century politics was a process of "total mobilization," transforming people into "masses," into little gears whose sole purpose was to keep on functioning. Countries became great "metallurgical workshops," in which an individual's life gradually became the life of a "work soldier," pressured to be especially functional. Thus, technology invaded the most intimate fibers of human existence, making people available for mobilization and manipulation. Such a new "contemporary condition" figured a vague political and technological existence based on a devastating "absolute functionalism." According to Jünger, total mobilization is not the result of intentional political subjugation. Rather, the technological transformation of life produces unstoppable and structural changes that destroy the traditional ways of politics, from the comforting distinctions between state and society to representative institutions. Hence, Jünger grasps the fundamental dynamics of rising totalitarianism, going beyond both the antifascist Italians' moral criticisms and Gentile's fascist spiritualism.

Carl Schmitt would systemize Jünger's still literary thesis of "Total Mobilization" in *Die Wendungen zum totale Staat* and in *Der Hüter der Verfassung* (Schmitt 1940, 2016), both written in 1931, where he introduced the idea of the total state, lamenting the radical crisis of traditional state sovereignty. For the latter, risks disappear under the pressure of an invasive society made by different parties, which no longer serve the public interests but only individual and corporate interests. The political sphere was no longer distinguishable from the social and private spheres, and sovereign power was reduced to a technical-bureaucratic administrative system, serving a totality based on economic materialism. The state is total because weakened by social pluralism and private interests, which prevent the pursuit of real political unity and efficient decisions. Initially, Schmitt's concern was to identify the place of political decision-making to halt such disintegration and bring unity back. In an essay from February 1933, "Weiterentwicklung des totalen Staates in Deutschland" (On the Development of the Total State in Germany), the antidote to the "state that becomes total out of weakness" is the state that becomes total "out of intensity," meaning "out of quality and energy" (Schmitt 1958, ix, n. 2). Schmitt's proposal explains what happens when the state promotes unity through technology. "The State that is total out of intensity" is strong, solid, and capable of distinguishing friends from enemies, as well as impeding the formation of antistate forces.

This is the project of an extreme, but still not totalitarian, form of government. Neither were two other famous attempts at remedying the total merging of state and society: Ziegler's 1932 *Autoritärer oder totaler Staat* and Leibholz's 1933 *Die Auflösung der liberalen Demokratie in Deutschland und das autoritäre Staatsbild*. Even though these authors move from different assumptions, both invoke the authoritarian state to make the political sphere autonomous again, to hold the state responsible for its decisions and to make it return to the people their dignity.

Nazi political doctrine took possession of some assumptions of such debate on the total state and the authoritarian state—from the critique of liberalism and parliamentarism to the glorification of totality and authority. But combining them with the celebration of the Leader and of the "community of the people" (*Volksgemeinschaft*) was an ideological feature foreign to Ziegler's, Leibholz's, and Schmitt's reflections on "total" and "authoritarian" states during the early 1930s. Surely, these thinkers contributed to the creation of a political clime conducive to Nazism, and we may hold them responsible for it. We should also note, however, that these terms, at least before 1933, had not been synonymous with the totalitarian state as we see it today (Galli 1997).

Hitler's rise to power changed the meaning of the term *total*; after the führer, *total* and *totalitarian* became interchangeable. In November 1933, Goebbels called the rise of National Socialism "a total revolution" whose aim is a "totalitarian State embracing every sphere of the public to transform it" so that "people may completely modify their social relations, their relationship with the State, as well as their existential issues." Even Hitler's 1933 speeches employ the words *authoritarian*, *total*, and *totalitarian* interchangeably. For a brief period, the German words *total* and *totalitär* were used as much by the regime as by its opposers. In his essays from 1933 to 1937, Carl Schmitt redefined the very locution of the "total state" he had previously conceived (Schmitt 2001). For the *totaler Staat* must legitimize the Leader's power, since he must lead a racially homogeneous community if it aims at defeating the "totality out of weakness" of the pluralistic state. In *Der totaler Staat*, Ernst Forsthoff (one of Schmitt's pupils, a supporter of the "conservative revolution," and then of Nazism) goes even so far as to reject the state as such, hoping for a poststate form of government. Only a "unity of the people" could make politics truly total, concrete, and responsible (Forsthoff 1933). This praise of totality occurred especially in an early stage of the regime's propaganda, but it was more than just a rhetorical instrument. Such substantializing enhancement of unity indeed aims at identifying state, movement, and people, thereby suppressing the private dimension of existence, as well as the empty form of a state utterly separated from the people.

The paradigm of the total state fosters disdain for the mere institutional understanding of the state, while it exalts politics as the "cultivation" of biological forces and the celebration of a "homogeneity" that eliminates individuality. By doing so, it turned criticism of liberal-bourgeois formalism into an emphasis on racial community. Unlike Italy, what was at stake in Germany was neither the enhancement of a one-party state nor the educational function of an ethical state. In Germany, a kind of "natural communitarian right" was beginning to take shape, reducing the state to a secondary expression of an original racial community. "The State is a means to an end. Its end lies in the preservation and advancement of a community of physically and psychically homogenous creatures [. . .]. States which do not serve this purpose are misbegotten, monstrosities in fact" (Hitler 1982, 357–58). Nazi "theoreticians," along with right-wing intellectuals, generally agreed that the political relationships of the "New Totalitarianism" could not be defined on the basis of modern state doctrine.

Although aware of this, the German opposition to Nazism seemed incapable of producing a clear lexicon. For instance, Leibholz, in his 1938 essay "The XIX Century and the Totalitarian State of the Present," rejects his previous distinction between the total state and authoritarian state as—in Italy, the USSR, and especially Germany—authoritarianism was full of totalitarian presuppositions, such as an antipluralistic spirit, homogenization, and the elimination of individual autonomy. *Totalitarian, authoritarian,* and *total* are adjectives describing only one threat: the one represented simultaneously by Nazism and Soviet communism. Leibholz talks of "mass totalitarian States of an authoritarian hierarchical nature," a vague periphrasis that occurs in several German thinkers. The most important figures of the Frankfurt School (Marcuse, Adorno, Horkheimer, Kirchheimer) refer to these regimes as a kind of *total-autoritärer Staat*, a tout-court authoritarian state, for a long time (Marcuse 1934; Horkheimer 1973).

The concept of totalitarianism attempts to synthesize all these ideas, but German philosophers will continue to employ ambiguous terminology throughout the entire experience of the Nazi regime. The adjective *totalitarian*, as clearly distinguished from *authoritarian*, will become a key word of the critiques of Nazism only with the rise of the so-called traditional theories of totalitarianism and the following systematization carried out by political sciences.

THE PARISIAN LABORATORY IN THE 1930s

In the 1930s, Paris became the place to be for philosophers and political scientists involved in conceiving categories and concepts through which to grasp the novelty of totalitarianism: from the anthropological and sociological notion of *homo totalitarius* to philosophical comparisons between fascism and bolshevism. By questioning historical determinism, authors coming from various backgrounds—such as Souvarine, Aron, Bataille, Mounier— approached the so-called autonomy of the political to understand what makes totalitarian domination unique. Their interpretations of fascism and communism would be fine-tuned throughout the 1940s, thereby constituting the reference point for all successive theories.

In this regard, Trotsky's theoretical legacy is as fundamental as it is largely neglected. For Trotskyists, the diaspora explored a wide spectrum of issues: the question of Stalin's distortion of structure and superstructure, the degradation of bureaucracy to "a caste" that completely controls a helpless population, and the interpretation of Stalinism as a form of Bonapartism. In Trotsky's eyes, Stalinist bureaucracy betrayed the Bolshevik Revolution—a polemic he developed in works such as *Permanent Revolution* (1929–30) and *The Revolution Betrayed* (1936). But Trotsky promptly pointed out that such betrayal neither destroyed the revolution's socioeconomic system nor turned the bureaucracy into a whole new class. "Bureaucratic degradation" did not prevent the USSR from collectivizing its means of production. Despite the defeat of democracy and the political defenestration of the proletariat, bureaucracy is not economically independent enough to become a new dominant class. Trotsky refers to it as an "élite," a "caste" that takes advantage of its political power to acquire privileges; however, according to Marxist orthodoxy, it cannot be considered a new class. Soviet society is undermined by contradictions that ambiguously hang it in the balance between capitalism and socialism. If the rest of the world remains capitalist, then Stalinist bureaucracy will stay in power. If, however, the international revolution prevailed one day, then the Russian proletariat would overturn the "bureaucratic caste" and reinstate democracy. Hence, despite Stalin's crimes, for Trotsky, the Bolshevik Revolution gave the USSR its unquestionable socialist character since, in his eyes, there was a clear discontinuity between Lenin and Stalin that should always be accounted for.

"Heretical Trotskyists" will question these assumptions, claiming, on the one hand, the autonomy of the political dynamics and, on the other hand, the totalitarian tendency of Bolshevism. Victor Serge is probably the first Marxist who, as early as 1933, applied adjectives such as *socialist*, *caste*, *bureaucratic*, and, especially, *totalitarian* to the USSR.[3] It is a state "intoxicated with its power, for which human beings are irrelevant" and "an unprecedented form of despotism." In 1937's *Destin d'une révolution: Urss 1917–1936*, one of the most well-thought-out essays on the USSR of its time, Serge grasps a crucial aspect: that socialism's aim to rationally control humankind's destiny conceals the possibility of an unprecedented subjugation of populations. Stalin's Russia is totalitarian not only because it is a one-party regime but also because its bureaucratic caste monopolizes political, economic, and cultural power. Like Trotsky, Serge does not hesitate to define Stalin's state as a "totalitarian state" since it represents a distortion of Lenin's revolution, its nature, and its goals, which only the awakening of the working class may restore. Unlike Trotsky, however, he does not consider the nationalization of the means of production as "objectively" socialist. A collective means of production could easily coexist with capitalist exploitation, the latter restored to help the "new caste," thereby increasing statist exploitation. His verdict is clear: the USSR has become truly totalitarian, a communism akin to fascism. Although he defends Lenin's and Trotsky's good faith, Serge eventually backdates the rise of totalitarianism to the beginning of the revolution, when ideological inquisition prevailed, and labor unions were nationalized.

This is pure heterodoxy. Serge ushered in the interpretation of Soviet totalitarianism as "bureaucratic collectivism," which would be further developed by authors such as Bruno Rizzi (Rizzi 1939), James Burnham (Burnham 1941), and the Frankfort scholars. Soviet totalitarianism is neither socialist nor capitalist; rather, it is an unprecedented form of tyranny. It represents the dark destiny of a world dominated by bureaucratization and by a blind instrumental rationality. After the "Stalinian thermidor," to use Trotsky's words, self-critical Marxist reflections abandon the rigid orthodox structure-superstructure scheme to carry out more nuanced historical and sociological analyses. Even if the more determinist aspects of Marxist interpretations have been gradually dismissed, basic historicism and "historical necessity" remain. Only when heterodox thinkers question dialectic explanations of history, thereby acknowledging the importance of singular events, may "totalitarianism" eventually become a full-fledged theoretical notion.

Boris Souvarine, founder of the journal *La critique sociale*, contributed significantly to the deconstruction of orthodox Marxism. He is the forefather of a new left-wing heterodoxy intended to overcome Trotsky's legacy. His friend Simone Weil, who wrote for his journal and somehow followed a similar political path, influenced him tremendously. Souvarine innovated left-wing anti-Stalinism, as he finally questioned the rigidity of determinism. For him, Stalinism was not solely a historical phenomenon, and it was not a simple deviation from the normal path of revolutions. Stalinism was rather an "absolute experience" that can be employed as an interpretative paradigm to compare with any other historical phenomenon and to help the masses understand the novelty of the totalitarian regime. From 1925 to 1939, Souvarine's critique of communism would gradually evolve into a complete rejection. In this period, his writings deal with controversial questions destined to affect public opinion (Souvarine 1939, 1985). Here, we find one of the first theoretical inquiries into the structural analogies between fascism and communism, two forms of *"État totalitaire"* that, although moving from different ideological premises, both result in an oppressive and centralizing state; both attempt to monopolize institutions, economy, and society; and both are led by charismatic leaders. Hence, Hitler, Stalin, Mussolini, and Franco are profoundly similar. Hitler's "pathological romanticism" is, indeed, no less destructive than Stalin's strategic cynicism, whose sole political aim is "to endure" and whose alleged revolutionary zeal did not stop him from sealing pacts with Germany, "the strongest of the capitalist states." The more Souvarine distances himself from the "Marxist philosophy of history," and its will to "deny hard facts," the more his investigation on totalitarianism is more speculative than historical. For him, both totalitarian regimes end up sharing a Manichean worldview that opposes absolute Good and absolute Evil. Such rejection of dialectic as a sterile method to decipher the novelty of totalitarianism inspired other important and pioneering authors such as Aron, Bataille, Weil, Monnerot, and, to some extent, Mounier. They would all focus on the commonalities of fascist and communist politics, as well as on their ideologies.

Raymond Aron's inquiry into totalitarianism begins in 1938, when the historian and philosopher Élie Halévy publishes *L'ère des tyrannies: Études sur le socialisme et la guerre*. Let us recall that in Halévy's eyes (polemic eyes toward Marxist analyses), the twentieth century is the age of tyrannies, not because of capitalist exploitation but because of the omnipresence of politics. Such new "universal Caesarism," which marks the end of freedom, comes neither from liberalism nor from capitalism but from the First World War—"a revolution against 1789"—and from socialism, which "has always been" associated with organization and regimentation. Both of these "two socialisms" (a provocatory locution that groups fascism and communism together) are centralizing and hierarchical states that despise any legal or real limit (Halévy 1938). They both are states where a sole party, not the people, rules, thereby bestowing all power on a tyrant.

By following Halévy's work, Aron will outline, as early as the 1940s, a critique of totalitarianism destined to become the main reference for the following liberal reflections. First, he defines the concept of totalitarianism by following four strategies: (1) critiquing the determinism/teleology of the philosophy of history, which, since it denies events of any autonomous significance, minimizes the novelty of these regimes; the novelty of totalitarianism was more than just a quantitative difference compared to past tyrannies; (2) relativizing the supremacy of the economy to advocate the centrality of politics; (3) recognizing the conservative character of totalitarian revolutions against democracy; and (4) inspecting totalitarian ideologies in relation to the process of secularization. Totalitarian systems not only eliminate the distinction between state and society, as well as pluralism; they also employ ideologies that, resembling religious doctrines, offer a future salvation attainable through the ruling regime. The party promises a shining future, the redemption of humanity. The fight between Good and Evil could make people accept the most violent oppression and atrocious crimes. Unlike traditional religion, however, "secular religions" do not aim to conquer simply inner consciousness but also public actions and collective political behaviors. There are two forms of secular religion: the hyperrationalistic one, spread by communism and Marxism, and the irrationalist one, spread by Nazism. Secular religions enchanted and bound the souls of Western humankind in a time of severe crisis, when people needed to know that everything would be all right. These totalizing ideologies, which democracy can foster at any time, do not promise individual salvation and transcendence; their promises are earthly and collective. Aron also questions their promises to reconcile truth and history. Aron's approach is still halfway between philosophical interpretation and political analysis, but it will increasingly follow the latter path later on, while still remaining open to the problem of the "ideological essence" and the "exclusively modern nature" of totalitarian phenomena.

Souvarine is to left-wing heterodoxy as Aron is to liberal culture. George Bataille and Simone Weil usher in a new interpretive field. Unlike Souvarine and Aron, however, their works do not contain a specialist analysis of totalitarian phenomena. Rather, they provide a more philosophical and anthropological inquiry destined to become just as influential. Their reflection will inspire those investigations on the relationship between totalitarianism and the roots of Western culture, and their radical critiques of the state apparatus will effectively ground comparisons of soviet communism, fascism, and national socialism.

Weil and Bataille do not consider power a derivative phenomenon; rather, it is the central issue of human experience. The bravery of their heterodoxy, along with their acuteness, should receive more consideration within the scholarship on totalitarianism. By challenging Kojève's thesis on the end of history, George Bataille contrasts the idea of a pacification and reconciliation within the "absolute universal judicial system" of humanity at the "end of history." According to him, Hegelian negativity is still functioning: philosophy should not thematize reconciliation but rather ensure the survival of a nondialectical negativity. Such "unemployed negativity" is the trace of Bataille's fascination with Nietzsche, playing the latter against the dialectical reconciliation that Hegel and Marx fostered. But Bataille's view is not only philosophical; it addresses the political present in which he was living. In the early 1930s, Bataille published some significant articles in *La critique sociale*, where he harshly questions the economistic and determinist readings of the *État totalitaire* (Bataille 1970). Bataille's works dealt with the sacred, power, myths, and the "heterogeneous"—everything that could not be reduced to the rational functionality of the "homogeneous." These themes characterize his attempt to understand fascism, Nazism, and Stalinism beyond a superficial assimilation to the system of "superstructure." Like Souvarine and Aron, Bataille thinks of religion as the key for understanding fascism and communism. Religion was not a separate issue; it is utterly political. According to Bataille, totalitarianism has fed on the emptiness of constructions of modern rationalism. Fascism and communism exemplify a *"puissance impuissante,"* a will to fill the absence of an "irrecuperable Other" with political sovereignty. Capitalist-bourgeois democracies, which rationalize the cycle of production and consumption, do not respond to the needs of the "heterogeneous." If we aim at fighting against totalitarianism, then we should understand how the political sovereignty of fascisms and of Stalinist communisms is nourished by the human need for the mythical and the emotional, by the attraction of a communitarian mystic, and by the fascination with violence. Totalitarianism exploits the "heterogeneous" to captivate the masses. But Bataille concludes that neither fascism nor communism offers an authentic space for the "heterogeneous." If anything, they propose a fictional manipulation of it that fosters domination rather than freedom. Fascism, with its cult of state power, and communism, with its sentimental utopianism and its rationalization of the productive cycle, both fundamentally deny the central, autonomous role of the "political" and of the "religious." In a nutshell, totalitarianism is nothing but the fulfillment of bourgeois democracy's rationality.

Jules Monnerot criticized Bataille for his estrangement from political activism but agreed with the idea that communism and fascism prey on people's nostalgia for transcendence. This nostalgia helped totalitarian systems build their own historical myths and supported the idea of a "realized totality." Monnerot believed that communism and fascism proved the inner weaknesses of atomized, secularized democracies, which, since incapable of satiating human demand of meaning, prove to be the obvious predecessors of totalitarian regimes (Monnerot 1945; 1948, 21–37; 1949; 1968). Therefore, Bataille and Monnerot agree on how *Le problème de l'État* should be addressed. Nazism, Italian fascism, and communism all assign a mythical role to an omnipotent state.[4] "Totalitarian statolatry" realizes the exact opposite of that which liberals have wished for—that is, "less state and more society"—just as it realizes the opposite of what the labor movement promised. In such *trois états tout-puissants*, the hegemony of totalitarian power goes well beyond fostering a "restrictive state": fear becomes a widespread and normalized condition, which is the real novelty. If the bourgeois conscience, as well as communism, a modern philosophy of history, has naively sustained a peaceful vision of the future, the emergence of totalitarianism brutally contradicts such optimism. But Monnerot and Bataille disagreed on which strategies should be pursued to weaken these states. Bataille seems to believe that the end of the state may come when fear, disorientation, and pessimism are reconverted into subversive energy, whereas Monnerot believes in traditional methods of political opposition.

Although far from Bataille's libertarian-subversive solutions, Simone Weil also affirms that the materialist interpretations of totalitarianism, as well as those opposing totalitarianism and democracy, were not enough. In the articles she published in *La critique sociale* during the 1930s and, especially, in 1934's *Reflections Concerning the Causes of Liberty and Social Oppression* and 1939's *The Great Beast: Some Reflections on the Origins of Hitlerism*, we find sharp, but merciless, inquiries on the German Communist Party, Nazism, the USSR, and the Bolshevik Revolution. Collectively, these publications present a series of reflections that, at the time, many judged to be as inconsiderate as they were excessively radical since they had been written by a loyal supporter of the working class. Consider, for instance, Weil's 1943 manifesto *On the Abolition of All Political Parties*. Weil—on the basis of Nazi Germany, where one faction rules, while opposition is imprisoned—considers the elimination of political parties as the only effective way to avoid totalitarianism. Any democracy ruled by parties cannot avoid the danger that one party may destroy the democratic play from the inside. Parties are essentially forms of "crypto-tyranny" competing to emerge one above the other. Their politics mirror the law of the jungle, and any compromise hides ulterior motives of struggle. In Weil's eyes, the only possible and effective solution is Rousseau's theory of general will, where individual, or partial, motives blend with those of "collective humanity" (Weil 2014).

Trotsky criticized Simone Weil, partly for avoiding militant activism in labor unions but mostly for going beyond the boundaries of traditional Trotskyist dissent. Weil agrees that the Soviet Union had switched the old dominant class out for a new bureaucratic caste that monopolizes every source of power. But like her friend Bataille, Weil believes that the very concepts of revolution and of structural economic relationships must be radically questioned. The so-called "Russian Revolution . . . has been able to make people believe that something new is rising; the truth is that the privileges it suppresses have not existed for a long time anyway . . . and the real forces, that is, big industry, the police, the army, bureaucracy, far from having been birthed by the Revolution, have reached, thanks precisely to the Revolution, a power unknown in other countries" (Weil 2004, 69). Revolutionaries gave their blood in the name of such utopia. Moreover, as Weil claims, no revolution would ever be successful: "the word revolution is a word for which one kills, for which one dies, for which the working class runs headlong into massacre, but which has no content" (69). This is because a true "revolution (sudden overturning of powers) has never happened in history" (69). There have been only slow transformations of regimes, and "the bloody events that we call revolutions" (69) had a secondary role in them. Materialistic investigation made Marxist thinkers blind to totalitarianism, whether Soviet or Nazi.

According to Weil, this Marxist perspective leaves out the symbolic meaning of power, as well as the importance of force. Only the recognition of the central role of power and force throughout history can allow us to understand political and social oppression, just as the dynamics of production. Twentieth-century totalitarian states might appear new in terms of their intensity, instruments, and intentions, but they are not so for the logic inhabiting them—a logic of power and force that has dominated history since society was divided into people who give orders and people who follow them. The secular reality of the state was born of the even more ancient structure of oppression that the religion of power makes even stronger.

Simone Weil's theses ushered in the continuist interpretive perspective, which understands totalitarianism not only as the continuation and radicalization of modern state coercion but also as the ultimate shape of that earthly domination existing since the dawn of humanity. As early as the *Iliad*, but even more vividly in the cruel historical intrigues of the Roman Empire, one could witness the "essential evil of humanity": that substitution of means for end that power consists of. "The law of all activities that dominate social existence . . . is that one must sacrifice one's life and the lives of others for things that are truly only better ways of living. This sacrifice takes different forms, but everything comes back to the question of power." The truth of totalitarian regimes—a truth that equalizes fascism, communism, and Nazism—is contained in this very "secret of power." But this truth does not simply acknowledge a relentless thirst for power, for omnipotence. Totalitarian states end up cultivating their weakness along with their omnipotence. "The essence of power itself" contains a fundamental contradiction that prevents it from fully existing. No matter how much people are oppressed, they will never stop being essentially active, so "all victory over people holds in itself the seed of a possible defeat, unless one exterminates them." Nevertheless, extermination kills power itself as it kills its own object. These two faces of power reveal the constitutive precariousness of any power, even the totalitarian one, whose aim is nothing but extermination (Weil 2004, 60–61).

Between 1934 and 1936, a Catholic critique of totalitarianism takes shape thanks to Emmanuel Mounier. His articles for *Ésprit*—a journal, founded by Mounier himself, that brought contemporary French intellectuals together on antitotalitarian common ground—studied the "not exclusively economic and material" side of totalitarianism. Mounier agrees with other French interpreters about the substantial structural affinity between right-wing regimes and left-wing regimes when considered from a metapolitical point of view. Moving from a "communitarian personalism" that breaks both with nineteenth-century Catholic spiritualism and with optimistic faith in the institutions of democracy, Mounier attempts to revamp "the primacy of the spiritual," since its oblivion is what fostered "totalitarian illness." This disease affected fascism and Nazism, which professes a nihilistic idolatry of biology, as well as Stalinist communism, which, by realizing Marxist ideals, denies the importance of the individual, dissolving the individual within a collective (Mounier 1934a, 1934b, 1934c, 1961). Totalitarian states rose from the fall of the spiritual, succeeding in their domination because they provide answers, however false, to the "human soul's permanent need for transcendence." Communal individualism—which contests both the abstract individual endowed with the right of the bourgeoisie and the Marxist dissolution of the individual within the community—offers a "solution to the totalitarian illness" without just superficially juxtaposing right versus left but more profoundly juxtaposing democracy versus totalitarianism. Any regime in which an aristocracy of money, class, or party imposes its will on an amorphous mass is totalitarian, no matter how consensual and enthusiastic the mass support they receive may be. Stalinist communism and fascism, as well as capitalist democracies, all exemplify totalitarianism. For a true democracy is grounded not only on institutional mechanisms but also on a functional and responsible organization of all the people: a true community.

COAST TO COAST: THE DEBATE OF THE 1940s

The importance of the 1930s debates on totalitarianism, of which I have rehearsed some of the most significant stages, is still underestimated today. Although still tentative, since conceived "in the heat of the moment," these reflections constitute the theoretical basis of the following philosophical critique of totalitarianism. During the 1940s, other key works were published that preceded the "canonical" and well-known season of American political science. As much as French interpretations of the 1930s provided heterodox comparative analyses that, by stressing the structural and symbolic analogies between Nazism, fascism, and Stalinism, brought to light the breaking features of totalitarian phenomena, however, none of them truly questioned the continuity between state and totalitarianism. They all took for granted that totalitarian regimes were a form of the hypertrophic state, a political degeneration, albeit still placed within the modern state paradigm. In the 1940s, thanks to the contribution of German-Jewish authors immigrating to the United States, analyses on totalitarianism became more specialized and sector-based; terminology became more precise; and, above all, totalitarianism was no longer considered an extreme type of strong state, nor a traditional but fiercer tyranny, but rather was perceived as an actual breaking point within the continuum of Western political institutions.

This second stage of research stresses the discontinuity between totalitarianism and the modern state not so much in philosophical terms as in political-institutional ones. Authors such as Ernst Fraenkel, Franz Neumann, and Sigmund Neumann questioned fervently the image of totalitarianism as a monolith and top-down state. Even though these authors are not unanimously considered "classic theorists of totalitarianism" since their analyses lack the fundamental assumption of comparability between Nazism and Stalinism (Wipperman 1997; Gleason 1995), their contributions have been essential for the definition of the category.

Ernst Fraenkel's 1941 *The Dual State* represents the most effective inquiry questioning the totalitarianism-monolith state. Fraenkel inspects the political-judiciary structure of Nazi Germany, acknowledging the coexistence of two competing state orders and logics. It is not the struggle between state bureaucracy and party bureaucracy. Rather, it is the fact that, alongside the "normative state," which carries out ordinary legislative activity, there stands a totally arbitrary state logic that obeys a fickle and omnipotent *Führerprinzip* and employs systematic terror to break what is issued by the "state of law." The central thesis of Fraenkel's book—namely, the idea that "Martial Law provides the constitution of the Third Reich" and that its constitutional Charter "is the Emergency Decree of February 28th, 1933" (Fraenkel [1941] 2006, 3)—shows how the political sector of German public life did not even function in terms of rights. State power is not exercised according to normal judicial and administrative activity but on the basis of specially made decisions. In a state of law, tribunals control administration from the point of view of legality; in the Third Reich the police authorities control the tribunals "by arbitrary measure" (3). Hence, in Fraenkel's eyes, the expression *Massnahmenstaat* (discretionary State) represents an oxymoron that contradicts the identification of Hitler's regime as a monolithic state of order. Nazi totalitarianism abolished every constitutional and legal limitation to claim the supremacy of the political. But what is "the political"? What is the jurisdiction of the "prerogative state"? What exactly does it overstep? Fraenkel's conclusion, which resembles Schmitt's position, is that the political is whatever political instances consider as such. For there is nothing, whether economic or social, that political instances cannot intervene in. Only when political instances give up exercising their power can private and public life be regulated by the norms of traditional rights. Tribunals defend the endurance of the basic principles of capitalism. But those in power can always annul what existing law issues. Therefore, "normative States and discretional States are not complementary but rival systems" (Fraenkel [1941] 2006, 46). For Fraenkel, totalitarianism is a *"monstrum"* made of parts and contradictions conflicting with one another, which often end up exploding the rationality of the functioning state. This is not an impenetrable order of a Moloch; it is rather a state of perpetual siege. Nazi totalitarianism is not the continuation, although paroxysmal, of that political tradition revolving around the notion of state. It destroyed basic European judicial construction.

Franz Neumann's representation of Nazi totalitarianism also contests the solid image of Nazism as a political system of order. Neumann does not provide a definition of what *totalitarian* is, but he often employs the concept to characterize any system that tends to be omnipotent and all-encompassing, thereby combining authoritarianism and monopolistic capitalism. His eminently political reading of Hitlerism, however, is as "heterodox" as Fraenkel's. Often portrayed as a "polycentric disorder," a

Behemoth (F. Neumann 2009) rather than a *Leviathan*—the Hobbesian sea monster and symbol of civil war against an earthly God who stood for state order—totalitarianism nourishes itself not only with external but also with internal disorder. In a nutshell, totalitarianism is nothing but a disorder created by the overlapping of various centers of power—party, bureaucracy, army, big industry—which, in turn, multiply and overlap further so that the führer emerges as the sole arbiter among the chaos.

In the seminal 1942 *Permanent Revolution*, Sigmund Neumann also fosters the idea that totalitarianism eventually releases chaos rather than order. As war originates, totalitarian regimes, whether Nazi or Stalinist, are also their essential engine. "A constant state of war is the natural climate of totalitarian dictatorship," for it brings permanent dynamics that cannot be stopped without stopping everything (S. Neumann 1942, xi). If they want to survive, totalitarian regimes must make an utterly artificial revolution perpetual. This is what distinguishes such dictatorships from past ones. All modern demagogues have understood the need to construct their totalitarian dominion on "almost democratic" grounds, although they likewise need to destabilize the very institutions representing democracy. The core of totalitarian regimes is, thus, a permanent revolution, an inner chaos that, while distinguishing those regimes from all kinds of monocracies and autocracies, also causes their inner weakness.

In Sigmund Neumann's view, the masses are the passive and manipulable agents of these revolutions. This new political subject had become important between the two world wars, but its ascent had begun at the end of the nineteenth century. The totalitarian dictator presents himself as "a man of the people" and as the "organizer of the masses." But similar to the system he claims to represent, "the leader of the twentieth century" is actually a son of war. Many scholars—from Mannheim to José Ortega y Gasset—have already identified this new type of society, which dissolves traditional class distinctions, as perfect soil for the "new tyrannies." Hence, totalitarianism is an extreme version of the modern tendency to dissolve any form of social solidarity, any bond among groups and classes, thereby generating atomized individuals who can be easily indoctrinated and manipulated (Lederer 1940). Only a disintegrated social fabric can create a "mass man" willing to perform the most thoughtless "voluntary servitude."

In the 1930s and 1940s, various researchers, from Wilhelm Reich to Eric Fromm, attempted to understand such a new phenomenon of mass support for totalitarian ideologies. The key factors are considered to be the "psychic impoverishment" and the "social resentment" of a petty bourgeoisie having an identity crisis because of the concentric attack coming from the upper bourgeoisie and the proletariat (Lasswell 1935); a sexual repression producing weak and powerless personalities (Reich 1933); an "authoritarian syndrome" fostered by the structural authoritarianism and servility typical of traditional German families (Horkheimer 1972; Adorno 1950); and the escape from the terrifying and unbearable weight of a liberty dissolving any societal bond (Fromm 1941).

Another approach is developing: the research on the intellectual origins of totalitarianism carried out by authors such as Rauschning, Strauss, Voegelin, Löwith, Hayek, and Popper. They all investigate the totalitarian potentiality contained in the major cultural and philosophical traditions of the West. I will dwell on this in due course. At such chronological height, all the structural elements of the "totalitarian constellation" are inspected by analysis, which still follows different and disorganized directions. What they need is great conceptual synthesis.

THE ORIGINS OF TOTALITARIANISM AND ITS INNOVATIONS

First published in 1951, Hannah Arendt's *The Origins of Totalitarianism* ferries the debate on totalitarianism toward its ultimate affirmation. Unanimously considered the paradigm analysis on totalitarianism, Arendt's book has become mandatory reading. As much as *The Origins of Totalitarianism* has surely changed the debate and the very notion of totalitarianism, however, it has also provided the major synthesis of the debate developed in the previous two decades. Arendt does not simply reconstruct the historical plot of such a phenomenon but rather aims to investigate it from a more general viewpoint. She seeks a meaning that surpasses the mere reconstruction of facts. What happened in Europe during the last century? Why did it happen? What made it possible? How can we explain it? Through what categories can we understand it? And, above all, can we truly understand its nature? These are the questions subtending Arendt's inquiry.

Because of its eclectic multidisciplinary approach, Arendt's interpretative proposal immediately disoriented historians and sociologists, and it has yet to fully persuade political scientists and philosophers. Such skepticism generated a paradoxical reception that continues to create controversies: on the one hand, *The Origins of Totalitarianism* gave birth to a vast, and often partial, "Arendtian doxa"; on the other hand, it has never ceased to provoke raging reactions that question its originality and reliability.

Consider, for instance, Arendt's claim on the comparability of Nazism and Stalinism. Like some other intellectuals before her, Arendt is convinced that only Stalin's and Hitler's regimes constitute concrete historical references for the category. She invites us to focus on the structural affinities between the two regimes, which she considers more significant than their differences. These regimes represent an absolute novelty that only the neologisms *totalitarian* and *totalitarianism* may succeed in naming. Arendt is convinced of this: totalitarianism is a fact before which traditional categories of politics, law, ethics, and philosophy are lexically and conceptually powerless. What takes place in totalitarian regimes cannot be explained in terms of a simple lust for power or of illegality, immorality, and realized nihilism. It demands an altogether "innovative" explanation. Perhaps this in-depth questioning about the novelty of these regimes is what could not fully emerge in the debate preceding the publication of *The Origins of Totalitarianism*.

Despite her will to emphasize the break represented by it, Hannah Arendt is well aware that totalitarianism did not fall from the sky: it arose from a nontotalitarian world. She refuses to follow a causality model of historical explanation and presents these regimes as the explosive emersion of contradictions characterizing the modern era. There is no teleology in this: such contradictions could have remained dormant, but this is not what happened. The first two parts of the book, "Anti-Semitism" and "Imperialism," contain a sort of historiographic archaeology that tracks down the less immediately evident, but not less important, premises of totalitarianism. Such archaeology seeks the elements that shatter European state history from within, eventually leading to its abrupt interruption.

It is worth repeating, however, that it is not a matter of reconstructing the precise concatenation of facts. Arendt's genealogical/archaeological work is retrospective: once it happened, the very fact of totalitarianism enlightens the totalitarian potentiality of the events and of the ideologies characterizing the late 1800s and early 1900s. In Arendt's investigation, all the crucial moments of modern history, including the Jewish question, concern the troubling political relationship between the universalization of the nation-state and the several movements that originate within its empty form. For Arendt, the very inner structure of the nation-state is already contradictory because it contains two conflicting elements: the state, which is a rational and legal construction, and the nation, which is sort of a substantial and homogeneous community wherein *ethos* and *ethnos* overlap. If the state, at least theoretically, is to safeguard everybody's right, the nation is instead an excluding community. Only those who, in a certain territory, belong to the same ethnicity are entitled to receive full legal protection by the state. Ethnic minorities and, especially, stateless persons—the products of nineteenth- and twentieth-century upheavals—are thus excluded, thereby highlighting the contradictory nature of the nation-state. On the one hand, the state claims to be the guarantor of those individual rights considered to be grounded on natural law; on the other hand, it concretely bestows these rights only on those who possess a certain nationality by birth. Therefore—and this is the central theme of the first two parts of *The Origins of Totalitarianism*—during the twentieth century, Europe produced people "lacking homeland," uprooted people, and individuals who do not belong anywhere. They can no longer find a place in politics, becoming "mere naked human beings" who give substance to those masses who will support and nourish totalitarianism.

Arendt's harsh critique of the *fictio* of human rights does not rely on traditional and historicist arguments but rather on the predictive awareness, which is currently again topical, of the inefficacy of abstract proclamations about the universality of human rights. After the First World War, anyone who is not born a citizen, who is born without a nationality, is treated as if they are not even human. Similarly, anyone who was not German or Aryan was not even considered fully human. For Arendt, such contradictions explode with the passage from the nation-state's judicial structure to the imperialist dynamic. Not only does the principle of limitless expansion overturn the territorial principle, but the very ideals of popular sovereignty, as well as the inviolability of citizenship rights, capitulate in the face of the arbitrary method employed by the governments of conquered cities—the same methods adopted by the political pan-movements of Eastern Europe.

The imperialist movements, later followed by the Slavic and German pan-movements, would find in racism the most effective justification for such methods. In addition, when the war, along with inflation and unemployment, wrecked the old social ties, massified and isolated individuals fell prey to totalitarian movements claiming to embody the eternal truths of Nature and History. In this context, anti-Semitism and class struggle became mere instruments of totalitarian consent as they repositioned atomized individuals into a mass community. These are some of the origins of totalitarianism. But none of these elements are necessarily or inevitably totalitarian. There is no teleology or philosophy of history in Arendt's work. If anything, Stalinism and Nazism are what bring together all the decomposing elements and contradictions of modern politics, thereby revealing how potentially catastrophic such an itinerary was. Nobody could foresee totalitarianism before it happened.

The third part of Arendt's book, "Totalitarianism," analyzes the structural traits of totalitarian regimes. Arendt brilliantly synthesizes the twenty-year debate that precedes her work. She categorizes the discontinuity between state construction and totalitarianism, originally stressed by Erst Fraenkel and Franz Neumann. According to Arendt, totalitarian regimes have "exploded the very alternative on which all definitions of the essence of governments have been based in political philosophy, that is the alternative between lawful and lawless government, between arbitrary and legitimate power" (Arendt 1979, 461). We can no longer employ inaccurate locutions to express the historical novelty that is totalitarianism. We can no longer call Nazism and Stalinism tyrannies, despotisms, or dictatorships. In other words, these regimes are no longer forms of state—not even a strong, centralizing, absolute state. Far from being monolithic, the totalitarian legal and institutional apparatus is extremely flexible to ensure maximal discretion. To ensure this, the number of offices gets multiplied, jurisdictions tend to overlap, and centers of power keep getting moved around. Only the totalitarian leader and his cronies hold the effective mechanisms of power.

In Arendt's view, such unprecedented concentration of power is not an instrument for realizing specific goals, whether national or military. "The reason why the ingenious devices of totalitarian rule, with their absolute and unsurpassed concentration of power in the hands of a single man, were never tried out before, is that no ordinary tyrant was ever mad enough to discard all limited and local interests—economic, national, human, military—in favor of a purely fictitious reality in some indefinite distant future" (412). Arendt never tires of repeating that these regimes are not utilitarian. This is Arendt's first distinction between totalitarianism and authoritarianism, a preliminary distinction between true totalitarian regimes, such as Nazism and Stalinism, and authoritarian regimes, such as Italian fascism.

According to Arendt, authoritarianism is still a form of state—a strong state that makes use of the traditional methods of power and takes advantage of a means-goal rationality that, however oppressive, demands nothing more than obedience and silence. Totalitarian dynamics exceed all traditional criteria of power: when the opposition is no longer a threat, the secret police come into play, and the so-called objective enemy starts being eliminated. The latter is not an individual who intends to oppose the regime but rather an enemy by ideological definition. Totalitarian regimes aim at something very ambitious and extreme: to get rid of reality to recreate it according to their ideology. For Arendt and many other political philosophers, ideology is totalitarianism's pivotal element. But the ideological project is not simply what justifies the destruction of the judicial and legal system, their *instrumentum regni*. Arendt goes further than Fraenkel: Nazism and Stalinism do not even distinguish between legal and illegal, claiming, instead, to be the most authentic form of the law. Totalitarian law does not limit or forbid the way normal laws do; rather, it embodies an eternal law of movement: the movement of Nature in the case of the Third Reich, the movement of History in the case of Stalin. Hannah Arendt, like Hermann Rauschning and Sigmund Neumann, believes that totalitarianism is based on a perennial movement, on a perpetual revolution that destabilizes all institutions and all realities. Such incessant movement is kept up through terror, the true fuel of a regime whose whole population is potentially considered an enemy.

The very core of totalitarianism is the extermination camp, which Arendt interprets as "the laboratory" wherein the regime tests its ideological assumptions. The difference between concentration camps and extermination camps plays a crucial role in the definition: "corpse factory" is what definitely distinguishes a dictatorial regime from a totalitarian regime. In short, the extermination camp epitomizes totalitarianism, its ultimate truth, since it is the place where the true goal of the regime—that is, the modification of human reality—takes place. The concentration camp serves the purpose of proving that the human being—once defeated as a legal person, then as a moral person, and finally as a unique and singular individual—is reducible to a bundle of animal reactions that erase any trace of freedom or spontaneity. "Total domination, which strives to organize the infinite plurality and differentiation of human beings as if all of humanity were just one individual, is possible only if each and every person can be reduced to a never-changing identity of reactions, so that each of these bundles of reactions can be exchanged at random for any other. The problem is to fabricate something that does not exist, namely, a kind of human species resembling other animal species whose only 'freedom' would consist in 'preserving the species'" (438). Therefore, *Lagers* not only serve to exterminate but also to serially produce a new model of humanity. They represent the "guiding social ideal" of the regime insofar as there, like nowhere else, total domination is possible.

If totalitarian terror truly comes to life when the problem of the opposition is eliminated, then the means has become the end, and the means-end relationship can no longer explain the *ratio* of these regimes. This is the "radical evil" of totalitarianism: the distortion of all laws, all limits, and all distinctions, even that between life and death. The camps do not follow any utilitarian requirement, which is why they are so difficult to comprehend. Three steps are necessary to obtain such total dominion: (1) the killing of the judicial subject, which can be achieved either by excluding some groups of people from the law or by putting the camps beyond the jurisdiction of the judicial system; (2) the killing of moral personhood through the creation of situations where individual conscience is no longer relevant; and (3) the killing of the singularity of each person. By doing so, "the society of the dying"—"the only form of society in which it is possible to dominate man entirely" (456)—is finally established.

From the literature about the camps, which was beginning to circulate at the time, Hannah Arendt grasps the idea of extermination camps as a distinctive feature of totalitarian power. They realize a sort of tragicomic equality. This is because human beings "insofar as they are more than animal reaction and fulfillment of functions are entirely superfluous to totalitarian regimes. . . . As long as all men have not been made equally superfluous—and this has been accomplished only in concentration camps—the ideal of totalitarian domination has not been achieved" (457).[5]

The uniqueness and novelty of Nazism and Stalinism; an all-encompassing, but not monolithic, institutional structure; a core ideology aiming at expressing eternal laws of nature and history; the extensiveness of a terror that, by attempting to realize the guiding ideology, keeps up a permanent revolution; extermination camps as culmination of the eclipse of instrumental rationality—these are the main elements of Arendt's thesis, which, in turn, has been amply accused of asserting, rather than explaining, the structural analogy between Nazism and Stalinism, of making connections that are "more metaphysical" than factual, and of being excessively philosophical, not based on empirical confirmation (Forti 2006).

But as criticized as they have been, and still are, Arendt's reflections have ushered in the two main guidelines of the following debate on totalitarianism: on the one hand, there stands a so called phenomenological approach that will reject the most philosophical aspects of Arendt's analysis to focus on the actual functioning of the regime in view of the definition of a new political category. The latter will turn out to be the most influential interpretative trend within the scholarship. On the other hand, there stands the so-called, by political scientists, essentialist approach (Barber 1969), which was amply inspired by "Ideology and Terror: A Novel Form of Government," the additional chapter contained in the 1958 second edition of *The Origins of Totalitarianism*. Unlike the phenomenological approach, such a hermeneutical perspective attempted to understand the novelty of totalitarianism from a more philosophical viewpoint, thereby enhancing the most radical questions that Hannah Arendt posed in her seminal book.

The first approach, improperly defined as "phenomenological," distances itself from the philosophical aspects of the Arendtian work to describe how the regime functions. The second, no less improperly defined as essentialist, starts with "Ideology and Terror" and the most radical questions that Hannah Arendt posed.

TWO

From the Construction of Models to the Practice of Dissent

THE SEARCH FOR A TYPOLOGY: THE ANALYSES OF POLITICAL SCIENCE

The full affirmation of the concept of totalitarianism takes place during the second postwar period. But such success accompanies an indiscriminate and "journalistic" use that undermines the proper comprehension of the political phenomenon that characterizes the so-called tragedy of Europe. The adjective *totalitarian* undergoes a spatial as well as temporal extension, so that any regime that is not liberal-democratic risks being named totalitarian: from Franco's Spain to Japan before the Meiji reform.

Many political thinkers of the past have been accused of having formulated totalitarian ideas, and several institutional arrangements of past eras are considered close to totalitarian ones. For example, Plato's *Republic*, Hobbes's *Leviathan*, and the republic founded on the "general will" of Rousseau are considered totalitarian. A strong affinity with the regimes of the twentieth century is found not only in the despotism of the oriental ancient "hydraulic societies" but also in the Russia of the Czars, India of the Maurya dynasty, and China of the Ch'ing. According to other interpreters, the totalitarian germ was already incubating in the Diocletian Empire, in the Geneva of Calvin, in the first Egyptian dynasties, and in Inca societies. If the general recognition of the category is now beyond discussion, its indiscriminate application to different political experiences and intellectual elaborations risks robbing it of its explanatory value.

Academic political science proposes bringing this overly extensive use of the category back to a controlled scientific track and to distance it from those philosophical interpretations that, according to Aron's criticism of Arendt, seek "to define a regime by means of the identification of an essence" (Aron 1954)—that is, without paying attention to its actual functioning. This will lead some exponents of Anglo-Saxon political sciences to the exasperated search for a totalitarian model on the basis of an empirical and essentially quantitative analysis, which will fix the considerations developed by Hannah Arendt in taxonomic criteria that are increasingly rigid and ossified.

Although profoundly influenced by Arendt's analyses, the political approach of Carl J. Friedrich and Zbigniew Brzezinski responds to the need to fix and simplify the fluid and complex narrative of *The Origins of Totalitarianism* in a rigorous typology. In *Totalitarian Dictatorship and Autocracy*, the two authors present what is often considered the first organic attempt to reconstruct a model capable of identifying the specificity of totalitarian domination (Friedrich and Brzezinski 1956; see also Friedrich 1954). They insist on the modernity and uniqueness of the totalitarian phenomenon, whose "preliminary characteristic" consists of "being a form of autocracy based on modern technology and mass legitimation," as well as "the adaptation of autocracy to twentieth-century industrial society" (Friedrich and Brzezinski 1956, 4, 123). We may define a regime as totalitarian when it simultaneously displays six characteristics: (1) an official ideology, which must be embraced by every member of society, an ideology based on millenarianism and promising the full realization of mankind, rejecting any compromise with the existing social order; (2) a single mass party whose members not only accept the party's ideological directives unquestioningly but also commit themselves with conviction to promote the widest acceptance of the ideology. Such a party, strictly organized hierarchically, often under the control of a leader, manages the governmental state apparatus and superimposes itself on it; (3) a quasi-monopolistic control of the media and of the all forms of information provided to the masses; (4) an almost monopolistic control of the instruments of coercion and armed violence; (5)

widespread terror, exercised by secret police through physical and psychological coercion; terror that falls not only on the regime's enemies but also on entire classes and groups of the population arbitrarily; and (6) centralized management of the economy.

The combination of these factors configures a model of political society that, although constructed on the basis of the analysis of Nazism and communism, can nevertheless serve to evaluate and define different political realities, such as Italian fascism and the communist regimes of Eastern Europe and China. Although many "autocracies of the twentieth century" do not have the "purity" of Nazism and Stalinism and therefore fall outside the strictness of the model, the latter turns out to be a useful tool for defining the "degree" of totalitarianism within a political regime. In sum, totalitarianism, a unique and unprecedented phenomenon, cannot be considered extinct but must be constantly monitored. The simultaneous presence of the six characteristics gives rise to the so-called totalitarian syndrome—to which the authors will return again in 1965—which will remain, despite numerous criticisms, an obligatory passage for the following political science.

The influence of Friedrich and Brzezinski was very wide on both sides of the Atlantic. It can be traced, for example, in Raymond Aron's works from the 1950s and 1960s, where Aron reformulates the constituent factors of the "totalitarian syndrome" in a slightly modified way (Aron 1969). Unlike the two American political scientists, however, Aron demonstrates a greater theoretical-philosophical sensitivity in understanding and researching "totalitarian specificity." In these years, he reiterates the crucial importance of ideologies and their quasi-religious role in the realization of the will to omnipotence of such regimes. Moreover, in polemic with many French Marxists, Aron points out that Stalinist totalitarianism cannot be interpreted as a form of bureaucratic despotism of the twentieth century. For it should also be inspected for that element of novelty represented by the revolutionary impatience of putting the world at the service of the idea. Thus, the affinity of Nazism and Stalinism is reasserted, more specifically, their common identification of party and state. Both Nazism and Stalinism are considered to operate a *Gleichschaltung* (alignment) of all independent bodies; they both transform a minoritarian doctrine into a national orthodoxy and confer unlimited power on the police.

In the wake of Tocqueville, Aron is also convinced that totalitarian phenomena can be interpreted as the irrepressible impulse of a democracy, which, under the pressure of the impetuosity of the masses, has shattered its own representative institutions and thus killed any sense of distinction and freedom, originally "aristocratic." He refuses, however, to interpret this outcome as inevitable, just as he is adamant about maintaining distinctions between the inspirational ideas and objectives of the communist and Nazi ideologies. Although the two ideologies are comparable, they imply incommensurability between the two regimes: on the one hand, the failure of a humanitarian and rationalistic ideal to build a "new society" should be accounted for; on the other hand, the properly "demonic will" to build a pseudorace should be simply taken into consideration.

By dwelling on both the process of "detotalitarianization" of the Soviet Union and the first modeling attempts of political science, Aron progressively moves toward an investigation comparing democracy and totalitarianism on the basis of the analysis of party systems. By applying the classical one-to-many antithesis to a comparison of party systems, Aron reformulates the opposition between democratic and totalitarian regimes according to the "most recent criteria of political science." According to him, current Europe sees two opposing systems: those in which a single revolutionary party claims the monopoly of political activity and those in which several parties accept the rules of competition. The parties are now the sole and undisputed agents of political life, and the exercise of power takes place through them. Western democratic regimes are regimes in which there is a constitutional organization of the competition for the exercise of party power. In these regimes, written and unwritten norms specify the mode of peaceful competition between individuals and groups, which is normally expressed through elections.

The multiparty system, which Aron utterly identifies with democracy, is configured, from an ideological viewpoint, as a secular state wherein two principles rule: respect for competition and acceptance of compromises. If, according to Aron, this institutional mode is the only possible translation of the democratic principle, at the same time, it is the only possibility of opposition and resistance to totalitarianism. Totalitarian regimes are depicted as one-party systems, with a revolutionary character. Such a ruling party justifies its monopoly by the greatness of its ambitions, the global character of the end at which it aims. These are monopolistic regimes relying on two different sentiments: faith and fear. In short, the ideal type of one-party system is animated by a grandiose vision of the world and aims for a total transformation of society as per the assumptions of the ideology; its ambitions transcend political and institutional reality. The representation of the future society carries out a fusion between the state and society. The ideal society is a classless society or at least one without any internal differentiation of social groups.

Although rewritten with an apparently more rigorous terminology, these analyses by Aron do not diverge from his previous considerations of "secular religions." Since totalitarian regimes are defined as those in which a single party has mono-politicized political life, then, in his eyes, what is still decisive is the totalitarian will to imprint the mark of official ideology on the community as a whole, as well as the strenuous "millenarian" appeal announcing the possibility of achieving a totally pacified society.

Through the analysis of the changes that occurred in Eastern Europe, Aron conceives of a new category: that of nontotalitarian one-party regimes, which, while reserving for themselves the monopoly of political activity, do not profess an all-encompassing ideology. Thus, one-party regimes would be classified according to the degree of totalitarianism. At the same time, the latter is measured by the more or less all-encompassing character of the ideology, as well as on the basis of how blended state and society are. Therefore, the contrast is blatant: democracy is opposed to totalitarianism insofar as it is based on the peaceful regulation of competition between two or more parties and insofar as it is a representative, parliamentary, and liberal form of government.

As early as the 1960s, both the so-called totalitarian syndrome developed by Friedrich and Brzezinski and Aron's characterizations were accused of not responding to descriptive models. If anything, according to these critiques, they tend to give in to the ideological necessity of condemning communism pursued through the construction of specially made ideal types, which, in contrast, bring out the virtues of liberal-democratic societies.

Liberal journals such as *Preuves, Der Monat, Encounter, Forum,* and *Tempo presente* are targeted and accused of reiterating stereotyped and mystifying typologies without any scientific originality. From the point of view of content, these journals—the critique goes—do not truly go beyond the warning against a constant totalitarian threat. Fundamentally, they insist on confronting the West of freedom and the East of totalitarian slavery head-on; they reiterate their condemnation of neutralism and pacifism as irresponsible positions before the Soviet threat. Finally, they often lack conceptual depth, ultimately strengthening the arguments of those who reject the concept of totalitarianism.

The liberal-democratic political paradigm is not only attacked by leftist intellectuals. Its plausibility is also contested by right wing scholars of the Third Reich. The best known and most extreme example is that of Ernst Nolte, who not only radically questions *das Totalitarismusmodell* but also challenges its employment in Nazi Germany, preferring to define it as "a fascist dictatorship" (Nolte 1966, 1998). In turn, fascism, well before the "Historikerstreit" of the 1980s, is characterized by the author as an "anti-Marxist" regime—that is, as "a revolutionary reaction" to communism, "a counterrevolution by revolutionary means" against the Bolshevik Revolution (Nolte 1987).

At the end of the 1960s, a phase of radical reassessment began under the pressure of attacks from both the Right and the Left. For more than twenty years, this led to divisions and conflicts within political science. Many became skeptics regarding the validity of the concept, divided internally between those who considered the ideal-typical construction definitively outdated in the face of the disappearance of concrete historical references—Nazism and Stalinism (Curtis 1969)—and those more radical who, like Herbert Spiro, hoped for the erasure of the term *totalitarianism* from the lexicon of political and social sciences (Spiro 1968). "Totalitarianism" would have proved to be either an empty formulation, valid for an excessively wide range of regimes, or a mere philosophical interpretation ideologically influenced.

In *The Conceptual Foundations of Totalitarianism*, Benjamin Barber provided one of the most significant formulations of this position (Barber 1969). Barber gives voice to a widespread discontent among political scientists. The aura of ambiguity that has always hovered around the notion of totalitarianism would not have been dispelled even by that "phenomenological approach"—whereof Friedrich's work is emblematic—which engaged in an "objective" and "institutional" definition of totalitarianism. As much as it attempted to oppose the theoretical elusiveness and ideological emotionalism of "essentialist" interpretations—from Popper to Hannah Arendt, authors, in his opinion, were exclusively concerned with the contents and aims of totalitarian ideology—such phenomenologies of totalitarianism fell into an empty and vague formalism. In the course of two decades of investigation, the theories of totalitarianism have failed to substantively attest to the possibility of speaking of totalitarianism as a specific political organization qualitatively different from all other political forms of the past.

Barber's call to get rid of the concept is flanked by the more moderate attitude of those who, by defending the sole validity of the conceptual construction, aim to reconsider its single contents. From this perspective, no factor of the "syndrome" emerges unscathed from such revision. In particular, the following aspects have been reconsidered: the role of the leader, which tends to be downsized to a function not necessarily held by a "special individual" but rather by a clique of power or the "ruling caste" of the party (Shapiro 1972); the role of ideology, which, while remaining a distinctive trait, is less and less analyzed for its specific contents and more and more studied as an indicator of the degree of identification of the will of the people with the will of the rulers; and the role of the party, whose real autonomy with respect to state institutions and the limits of its ability to control economic and administrative processes is questioned (Huntington and Moore 1970). These authors, however, do not intend to close the debate but to readapt the ideal type to a new empirical reality on the basis of a revised methodology. Surely, as some might argue, the concept has undergone strong distortions, but it is still the only tool to describe an unprecedented regime, typical of nineteenth-century history.[1] A more accurate distinction must be drawn between right-wing and left-wing totalitarianism, but it remains undeniable— for instance, this is Karl D. Bracher's position—that the particular political modality that in the twentieth century took on the terrifying face of totalitarianism still works, more or less covertly, in numerous regimes.

If Leonard Shapiro redefines the five characteristics of the regime—the leader, the emptying of the legal order, the control over private morality, the permanent mobilization, and the mass legitimization—and if in Bracher "the seven characteristic traits of totalitarianism" carefully follow historical reconstruction (Bracher 1984; Menze 1981, 11–13), Juan J. Linz makes the political community that is not opposed to the concept take a real step forward. In *Totalitarian and Authoritarian Regimes* (1975), Linz invokes prudence in regard to distinguishing between model and theory. Moreover, he constantly acknowledges that the abstract definitions he employs are only heuristic tools that never have precise correspondence with concrete reality.

This is what makes Linz's typological theory acceptable as a criterion for distinguishing totalitarianism from other nondemocratic regimes. Thus, the definitions developed by previous political science are recalled to mark the differences between the various "sub-types" of totalitarian systems—communist, fascist, national-socialist—as well as, above all, between the different phases of their evolution. Therefore, now, the indispensable elements for judging a regime as totalitarian are (a) an ideology sufficiently elaborated to allow a legitimization that, above all, serves as an engine for the regime's mechanisms; (b) a single mass party that manages to condition, integrate, and mobilize a large part of the population; and (c) the concentration of power in the hands of an individual or a small circle of leaders who do not feel responsible to the electorate and who can be deposed only by resorting to extralegal methods. Thus, the monistic, antipluralistic character of totalitarianism tends to destroy every boundary separating state and society, and the hyperpoliticization of the social body is obtained through the cancellation of group and interest associations. Monopoly of power, single party, and ideology can give rise to different combinations, depending on the historical, social, and cultural context in which they assert themselves. Therefore, according to Linz, there is not simply one "totalitarianism" but different types of totalitarianism, and each type goes through different phases and oscillates between different inclinations, from populist to bureaucratic, from doctrinaire to elitist. Through such dynamization, the concept is substantially accepted, especially in its function as a differentiating criterion between democratic and nondemocratic regimes.

If we summarize the central theses of that part of political science that, from Shapiro to Besançon (1980), by reworking Hannah Arendt's analysis, considers it necessary to keep the concept alive, we can maintain that the following factors are constitutive of the totalitarian phenomenon. As an exclusively twentieth-century regime rooted in those processes of modernization following the paths of industrialization, technologization, and democratization, totalitarianism is usually considered consubstantial to a type of terror that, unlike normal political violence, does not simply aim to obtain submission. If it appears "absurd" and "delusional," this is because it does not seem to respond to any kind of rational necessity but to the desire to render superfluous entire categories of people who, by their mere presence, hinder the completion of the totalitarian project (Maffesoli 1979; Ferry and Pisier-Kouchner 1985). Therefore, this terror proves to be inseparable from its link with ideology. The ideological project—a true political principle of the regime—aims to restructure the present radically, eventually reconstructing it to build the new history, the new society, and the new human being. But there is something more: "ideology imposes the fiction that another reality already exists. . . . The regime is not only terroristic because it would make ideology pass from power to action but also and above all because it pretends that it is already actual" (Besançon 1980, 129). Despite its totalizing and strongly utopian connotations, once in power, ideology does not hesitate to change some of its contents in favor of its effectiveness as an instrument of domination.

So what are the necessary institutions and devices to ensure the actualization of ideology? A decisive role is played by the secret police, which, through arbitrary trials and forced confessions, perform a function that is more terrorist than preventive or repressive. But the true original contribution of totalitarian phenomena, their "masterpiece of destruction," is unanimously recognized in the concentration camp universe, programmed not as a penal institution but as a place of suspension of all forms of law. Therefore, the purpose of the camps is neither to prevent nor to punish crimes perpetrated against the regime. Rather, they pursue the definitive eradication of the social fabric through practices—from mass deportation to the spectacle of the insignificance of others' life and death—aimed at the annihilation of individual psychophysical identity. If the monistic vocation of totalitarianism corresponds not only to the will of such a regime to annex society but also, and especially, to the desire to change the totality in a way that has no precedent in history, then it is understandable why the revolution that such regimes claim to implement must be permanent. If the objective is to revolutionize the existing, this implies a huge effort toward a constantly different temporal goal. The result is the primacy of the single party over the state apparatus as the interpreter of ideology and historical laws—a primacy claimed in the name of the legitimacy received from the masses. For these reasons, the totalitarian regime combines a formalistic preoccupation with respect for public law with a substantial negligence of written law. The construction of the "new order" implies the perpetuation of disorder, in which the very notion of law is lost.

Monistic demands for total domination are primarily directed against any form of social pluralism. This is why mass society is considered the indispensable transition phase to the totalitarian project. In fact, thanks to the almost total disappearance of intermediate social groups, such a society would be characterized by direct relations between elites and nonelites, which produce a high willingness for top-down mobilization (Kornhauser 1959). Even if some interpreters are skeptical about the capability of totalitarian terror to fully destroy any form of social grouping, as well as to completely abolish social distinctions and hierarchies (Grawitz and Leca 1985), totalitarianism scholarship unanimously agrees to acknowledge that, in all these regimes, the traditional distinction between state and civil society utterly fails.

Totalitarian regimes used to produce the image of a social organization that coincides with the needs of the population. Such an image induces the conviction of a bottom-up legitimization. Nevertheless, the establishment of totalitarian regimes actually accompanies the overturning of preexisting power relations. The social system of Nazism, like Stalin's, is not a simple spontaneous product but is contextual to the realization of "political totalitarianization." If it is true that terror dissolves group solidarity and the capacity to create social ties, it nevertheless cannot lead to the total destruction of all forms of social and economic aggregation, as the early typologies maintained. In reality, terror and ideology form or reinforce specific group bonds, strictly hierarchical and organized, which bind individuals into a specific membership. Indeed, the emphasis on massification and the cancellation of the traditional distinction between state and society could make us forget the gap that nonetheless continues to exist between the political elite and an orderly society. Hence, society is crossed not only by a multiplicity of reinforced hierarchies but also and primarily by a precise contraposition between the dominant, the holders of the power of life and death, and the dominated, the victims.

ATTEMPTS ON DISTINCTIONS: AUTHORITARIANISM AND TOTALITARIANISM

Although political science has mostly accepted the neologism *totalitarianism* to express the novelty of some "extreme regimes" of the twentieth century,[2] there have been different positions for the distinction between totalitarian and authoritarian regimes. Do they represent two qualitatively different forms of politics, or are they only different degrees of a single modality? Moreover, do autocratic and totalitarian regimes stand in a relation of mutual implication, or can they undertake two different directions? How does the transition from an authoritarian regime to a totalitarian one and from it back to authoritarianism take place? These questions have occupied political science, which, in recent decades, revamped the totalitarian question, as if the authoritarianism/totalitarianism dichotomy replaced the one that, after World War II, revolved around the distinction between liberal democracies and totalitarian regimes.

As early as the end of the 1950s, political science, especially within the Anglo-Saxon landscape, dwelled on bringing order to a literature that tended often to use terms such as *dictatorial regimes*, *authoritarian regimes*, *tyrannical regimes*, and *totalitarian regimes* interchangeably. But the development of these distinctions left some crucial questions unanswered. In a world scenario experiencing, in both the East and the West, the weakening of the grip of "ideological formulas," as well as the weakening of political alternatives to the democratic model, did it still make sense to speak of totalitarianism? Was this concept still able "to stimulate adequately research in the comparative study of new forms of authoritarianism"? (Tucker 1961; Howe 1983, 89–102). It was believed that these questions could be answered by replacing the notion and the term *totalitarianism* with renewed formulas, among which one of the most "fortunate" sounded: "Revolutionary Mass-Movement Regime under Single-Party Auspices" (Tucker 1961, 283).

But even on the side of those who continue to claim the heuristic utility of totalitarianism, the new key to interpreting comparative analysis is the sharp contrast between "competitive democracies" and "monocratic systems," as well the assumption of a profound divergence, within the latter, between authoritarian and totalitarian regimes.

The first general characteristic of authoritarian systems is their residual pluralistic structure, unlike totalitarianisms, which are marked by absolute monism.[3] According to Linz, authoritarian regimes are "systems of limited pluralism whose political class is not accountable for its actions" (Linz 1997, 157). While strongly centralizing power, an authoritarian state does not succeed, and perhaps does truly intend to, in going so far as to annihilate all competing social and political groups. Thus, alongside a state that monopolizes authority and administration, elements of "a legally recognized society" survive (Stawar 1963).

Totalitarianism is driven, instead, by the will to do away with all forms of real and legal pluralism, claiming unlimited power over society. If authoritarianism is somehow the attempt to provide a strong solution to the crisis of the state, totalitarianism is nourished by that state crisis up to its extreme consequences. This means that however arbitrary an authoritarian regime may seem, it remains bound to the value of order and state sovereignty: it recognizes or reinforces the symbolic-representative role of the state.

In contrast, the totalitarian system, in addition to the kind of rhetoric employed, uses the state apparatus as a functional organ, emptying it of its sovereign prerogative and opposing it first to the movement and then to the party, which alone is bestowed with the function of representing the whole. If it is true that even authoritarian systems are almost always characterized by monopartisanship, the single party nevertheless remains in a subordinate, and not alternative or conflicting, position vis-à-vis state power (Bracher 1984, 1987).

How can a totalitarian system succeed in such an effective fusion of the political, social, and private spheres in which the state eventually survives as a mere facade? Totalitarianism does not simply seek obedience. Unlike authoritarianism, it does not settle for acting undisturbed amid the silence of its "subjects." Rather, it wants to legitimize itself through the consent of the masses. The party and its ramifications penetrate deep into society to obtain the constant mobilization of citizens, making them fully adhere to the worldview assumed by the regime. On the one hand, totalitarianism wants to—and in some ways must—bring about "a revolution of all social values and relations" by introducing a new normative and ideological system capable of coagulating the largest possible number of adherents; on the other hand, authoritarianism tends to preserve traditional values and hierarchies, making them acceptable by force, even to dissidents.

Thus, Linz proposes distinguishing between "ideology," of which totalitarian regimes are the bearers, and "mentality," to which authoritarian regimes adhere. The former is an articulated and coherent system—elaborated by intellectuals or pseudointellectuals—capable of exciting and compacting the population, as well as of creating the identification between the system and the masses; the latter is a way of thinking based more on emotional elements, often incoherent, than on logical and rational concatenations. If totalitarianism is linked to the diffusion of a new ideology claiming to be revolutionary, authoritarianism is rather essentially conservative. If totalitarianism inputs a powerful subversive charge, not only in the institutional structure (the dualism of state and party) but also in the system of values, the authoritarian perspective is rather that of a controlled management of the existing social equilibrium.

As Jeane Kirkpatrick claimed in a 1982 essay, "Traditional autocracies leave unchanged the existing allocations of economic and power resources, which . . . keeps the people in poverty. However, they worship the gods of tradition and obey traditional taboos. Such autocracies do not upset the usual rhythms of work and leisure, the usual places of residence. . . . And since the miseries of traditional life are familiar, they are bearable for ordinary people who learn to live with them. . . . Such societies do not produce refugees" (Kirkpatrick 1982, 48). It is not surprising that the description of "traditional autocracies," or "authoritarian regimes"—in contrast to totalitarian regimes—sounded to many intellectuals like a sort of indirect legitimization of some governments toward which the United States was showing itself to be very tolerant, Latin American countries in particular (Gleason 1995, 190ff).

By the end of the 1970s and throughout the 1980s, the sharp distinction between authoritarianism and totalitarianism was considered outmoded. Authors such as Michael Walzer, Robert C. Tucker, Richard Lowenthal (all in Howe 1983), and Pierre Ayçoberry (Ayçoberry 1979)—to mention only the best-known scholars—attempted to reset the question. Although they accepted the validity of the argument according to which totalitarianism represents a radical turning point in a long history of regimes without freedom, they believe that the distinction between authoritarian and totalitarian regimes—revamped by liberal and, as in the case of Kirkpatrick, progovernment authors—is now employed not only in defense of liberal regimes but also of some tyrannies, the latter tolerated insofar as they are not totalitarian. For instance, as Walzer points out, "it was never the intention of the theorists of the fifties to celebrate authoritarianism. . . . Contemporary conservatives have taken the step with calculated ease. Since authoritarian rulers aren't even touched by messianism, since they neither seek nor pretend to produce a social transformation, since all they want is to hold on to their power and prerogatives, not to exercise greater and greater power, they don't produce the terrible upheavals of totalitarian politics" (Walzer 1983, 108–9).

The implicit ideological assumption of these arguments is questioned, as well as, and even more, the theoretical weakness of an interpretation that seems to elude any temporal perspective. In authors such as Kirkpatrick, the rigid contraposition between authoritarianism and totalitarianism ignores the dynamic aspect that makes a regime a moving reality and not an eternal essence. By doing so, totalitarianism assumes the characteristics of immutability and permanence, while authoritarianism becomes a mere and unpleasant parenthesis. In contrast, according to Walzer, if some elements highlighted by "classical" analyses are to be taken seriously—as the character of permanent mobilization that totalitarian terror assumes, or the tendency to the total destruction of reality—then one cannot conclude that either totalitarianisms collapse by inevitable entropic force or they must necessarily transform themselves into something less intense.

Therefore, these remarks suggest interpreting authoritarian regimes, especially "the epigones of Soviet totalitarianism," in terms of Weber's "routinization" of charisma. Authoritarian regimes, at least some of them, would be regimes in which the totalitarian afflatus toward political utopia has lost its vigor; in which the end of time has been postponed; in which the political cause has been transformed into a career issue, into a rhetoric of obedience and into cynical and corrupt behavior. Hence, is it still necessary to envisage an absolute discontinuity between totalitarianism and authoritarian regimes, or does it not make more sense to think of "totalitarianism as the name we give to the most frightening form of authoritarian rule?" (Walzer 1983, 119).

TOTALITARIANISM AS SEEN FROM THE EAST

Walzer's question was driven not only by a precise sensitivity to historical changes but also by the intention to take into account the debate on totalitarianism and post-totalitarianism ushered in by Eastern European dissidents. Within the latter, it is possible to distinguish two different attitudes toward the concept, attitudes that characterize two different phases of "real socialism." While during the decade following Stalin's death Eastern intellectuals showed a strong aversion to the concept, from the invasion of Czechoslovakia onward, there was instead a rediscovery of this notion.

Totalitarian and *totalitarianism* enter the current lexicon, becoming the common denominators of the political writings of dissidence. In these authors the concept becomes a more philosophically oriented notion that overcomes the limits of a mere typological inquiry. During the "thawing," the question posed from the East is not very different from the one that troubled Marxist intellectuals in the West: were the unspeakable Stalinist crimes a pathological deviation of a healthy historical course, or did they represent the inevitable outcome of a political and ideological system flawed from the beginning? The answer has remained ambiguous. "Marxist humanist" intellectuals such as Kolakowski in Poland, Kosik in Czechoslovakia, the Budapest School in Hungary, and the group of the journal *Praxis* in Yugoslavia attempt to question the "system" from within, moving from assumptions that are incompatible with those of the "classical theories of the West" (Isaac 2008). They assume not only the Stalin/Lenin break—whereof Khrushchev marks the reestablishment of the "Leninist norm"—but even more the discontinuity between Stalin's theorizations and Marxian doctrine, in particular the thought of the earliest Marx (Rupnik 1984; Mueller 1998). Here, the concept of totalitarianism is employed only to be delegitimized.

Milo van Djilas's 1957 *The New Class* is a touchstone in the 1970s political debate, as it interprets communist power without abandoning some Marxian categories. The "new class," the bureaucratic class, would have confiscated political power from a largely invisible proletariat. Some scholars insist on the redefinition of the role played by ideology in a system increasingly oriented toward an advanced industrial society, wherein the old political bureaucracy, depositary of the Marxist-Leninist doctrine and proponent of an economic model based on "production for the sake of production," gives way to a technocracy fostering a new model of production-consumption (Richta 1969).

Another important contribution questioning the concept of totalitarianism is represented by the theories of "limited pluralism." Developed in the 1960s, especially by Mlynář's research group on the Prague Spring's eve, these theories aim to provide a new political model capable of institutionalizing the plurality of interest groups emerging within single-party regimes. According to this model, in the communist system, there would no longer be the Marxian-Leninist universal class, which, through the party, represents the whole of society. Rather, the Soviet Union would be involved in a process of "dislocation and dispersion of power," resulting in "limited pluralism," which would and should coexist with the formal reality of one-party rule.

While the 1960s witnessed the growth of reformist sentiments and thus a clearer rejection of the totalitarianism–Soviet Union equation, the end of the Prague Spring marked the beginning of disillusionment with Brezhnev's restoration. The impossibility of "detotalizing totalitarianism" and the "clinical death of revisionism" in Eastern Europe decided the end of "the concept of Stalinism" (Kolakowski [1971] 1978, 2005). In line with Soljénitsyne (1975), these authors deconstruct the hypothesis of the Stalinist parenthesis: Stalinism has never existed; there has only been an uninterrupted domination that remained faithful to Leninism in its essential lines; the Gulag is not an accident, and its origins in Lenin's period elevate it to a historical figure of an epoch that links communism to Nazism. The testimonies of the survivors, which reset the investigation around the link between the concentrationary universe and Marxist-Leninist ideology, revive the conceptual tool of "communist totalitarianism." This is not a return to the Western political science of the 1950s but an attempt to reformulate the concept while still fully coming to terms with the reality of the situation.

These East European authors do not search for a model or a new typology to provide a common definition of *post-totalitarianism*. Both through a more literary-philosophical approach, which sought to identify the theoretical constellation of the new ideology, and through the scientific-political intention to lay the mechanisms of power bare, they are all committed to researching the origins of the phenomenon, and they all wish to move away from the methods of Anglo-Saxon political science.

Therefore, in the panorama of Eastern intelligentsia, we do not witness that abstract and artificial opposition between "phenomenologists" and "essentialists," between political scientists and philosophers, that has been typical of the West. All dissident thinkers agree in defining the nature of the regime as an "institutionalized lie."[4] There is no writer in the 1970s or early 1980s who does not acknowledge a debt to George Orwell's *1984*,[5] read not as a literary work but as a realistic and circumstantial analysis of the mechanisms of power. No one rejects the thesis according to which a totalitarian power remains alive only if, and as long as, it manages to recreate a language that becomes a pure instrument of ideology: only through the use of a "neo-language" can a "heretical thought" be prevented. Thus, the Orwellian theme of lies and the possibility of resistance to lies become the starting point from which to reconstruct independent political thought (Havel 1985).

Once the physical liquidation of entire strata of the population by ideological terror has ceased, the totalitarian potential of a system operating on the preclusion of all independent judgment still needs to be attested. But totalitarian power is also the kind of power that destroys the very criterion of truth by transforming historical memory and manipulating information. If the truth changes according to the needs of power, the criterion of what is true and what is false is unattainable. Therefore, nobody can be accused of lying any longer. It is not a question of analyzing the mechanism of a trivial lie but of a lie that becomes the foundation of an entire system of power. In the need to destroy the past and to give linguistic expression to a new reality lies an impulse that is unhesitatingly called totalitarian (Kolakowski 1983; Šimečka 1984).

As Kolakowski points out, "A people whose memory—individual or collective—is nationalized, it becomes a property of the state that can be completely manipulated and controlled" (Kolakowski 1983, 127). Under the "regime of oblivion," as Milan Šimečka maintained, "any attempt, however limited, to preserve one's memory and hence one's freedom to think represents an act of self-preservation, and self-defense in the face of total disintegration, as well as an assertion of human dignity. Nowhere in the world," he concludes, "does history have such importance as in Eastern Europe."[6] If "the struggle of man against power is the struggle of memory against forgetting" (Kundera 1981, 3), so-called post-totalitarianism must tirelessly shape the "institutionalized lie," well aware of the fact that there is no consciousness without memory. This is what decisively binds Stalinism to the various following "thawings," which can certainly mitigate the charge of terrorist violence but cannot go so far as to dismiss the system of "regime lies," whose functions persist, even as its contents mutate.

On closer inspection, these considerations recall Milosz's positions, according to whom if "popular logocracies" are erected "by means of weapons," their preservation can be achieved "only by means of language" (Milosz [1953] 1990). If, however, during the phase of "ideocracy," an enthusiastic adhesion to lies was needed, in the epoch of the "cold ideology" (Papaioannou 1967), an "existential lie" (Havel 1985) is accepted: a set of external behaviors, which do not necessarily have to correspond to an inner faith in the mystifications of the regime. In other words, a conformist consent to the power of the rulers, or at least its silent acceptance, is sufficient. This sort of "banality of evil" sustains the regime no less than the inculcated ideology and repressive mechanisms. Therefore, the aim remains totalitarian: to conform all aspects of life, reality, and language to political power; to reduce, up to the point of destruction, every space of freedom.

Nevertheless, it is undeniable that the communist system has loosened the grip of violence and terror and expressed itself through less visible forms of repression. Mass terror, trials, and "purges" give way to mechanisms of social control by using softer instruments. The value of the concept of totalitarianism is not questioned, but it is reviewed in light of more recent sociological and political acquisitions. According to Mlynář, for instance, true totalitarianism is established precisely when the unlimited use of terror has no reason to exist any longer—that is, when subjects have completely lost their autonomy (Mlynář 1983). Heteronomy is then pursued "cybernetically," interrupting the flow of information about both the outside world and the past. Above all, however, it tolerates intersubjective relations only if they take place through circuits controlled by power. Whereas society used to be depicted as a healing body, it now increasingly resembles a corpse. Despite the shattering of specific ideological contents, ideology, that is, the "systematic deception" of information and memory, remains the heart of totalitarianism with a human face, which is always ready to take off its mask and apply the old methods (Heller 1989).

Alexander Zinoviev is more critical of the category of totalitarianism. According to him, the comparison between Nazi terror and communist terror does not work. It would work only in relation to the initial phase of these regimes, leaving the mature phase of communism completely unexplored. If the engine of national socialism is "top-down violence," then real socialisms maintain their power through a "bottom-up" mechanism (Zinoviev 1984). Communism is not a deviation of history but a natural phenomenon of the human communitarian spirit, which, however, is deprived of the counterweights of civilization: law, morality, and religion. Its coconstitutive trait is not the political conflict of state-party-society but a social mechanism of integration, "cell by cell," between microstructures and structures eventually composing the global network. Hence, communism would be the reflection of a communitarian society, wherein the cell (the factory, the institute) is the privileged means of transmission for the compactness of the whole.

Thus, is it correct to continue to speak of totalitarianism? If communist regimes resort to nationalistic and economic legitimations, would it not be better to talk of authoritarianism? After all, is the distinction between the two labels not largely based on the role of ideology? Is ideology not unanimously declared to be decomposing? Is the Soviet system still a "utopia in power," or has it become a "state-cracy" that has traded Marxism with the harshest political realism?

Although the golden age of ideology is said to be over, none of the Eastern European authors denies that it has remained, even in a so-called post-totalitarian phase, the privileged means of communication between the citizen and the power: the instrument through which the integration of the parties in the whole is pursued. This leads to the hypothesis of a duplicity of the system: totalitarian when it is to achieve internal alignment, post-totalitarian in its relations with the outside world.

Whether we speak of totalitarianism or post-totalitarianism, of "ideocracy" or "post-ideology," of "existential lie" or "cold ideology," all dissident literature attests to a strong change in the structure and mechanisms of power. The figure of the "ego-crate" loses importance, and a nomenklatura utterly interested in securing key positions in the state administration takes on importance; the irrational and terrorist violence of the Stalin era gives way to police methods that formally respect the rules in force; the "great confessions" extracted in the name of truth give way to "small interrogations" with the more modest objective of creating complicity and connivance with the system. The citizen renounces critical thinking and participation to obtain the security of a job and the possibility of a wider use of material goods in exchange. As consumer society bursts, citizens tacitly stipulate a "new contract" with the regime: by renouncing a large part of their personal freedom and the whole of their political freedom, they obtain greater security and an improvement in the quality of their life in exchange.

But from 1968 to 1989, the will to find the necessary space for dissent and opposition in the more or less deep cracks of the regime was firmly reiterated—whether emphasizing the crisis of legitimacy of a totalitarian ideocratic empire, of which the reborn Polish civil society and the Hungarian market economy would be a sign, or considering the Soviet system, together with its satellites, to be the continuation of the "old totalitarianism" with other means. All authors who identify themselves with the horizon of independent thought refute the validity of Orwellian prophecy at least on one decisive point: it is possible not to love Big Brother, and it is possible to refuse daily subjugation. Moral resistance is therefore possible.

Thus, there is a seamless shift from the field of political analysis to the sphere of an ethical project of intellectual resistance that, however revisited, retains the notion of totalitarianism as a reference. Above all, the evocative power of this term still plays a fundamental role, which, beyond its scientific status, obliges those who use it to take a stand. This is what all the dissident, political, and sociological literature of Eastern Europe does, and even more so the philosophical reflection, the latter involved in a double commitment of conceptualization and self-clarification: the understanding of the origins of communism, on the one hand, and the comparison with Western philosophy, on the other.

The attempt to go back, sometimes naively and sometimes cleverly, to the spiritual origins of communism is evident, and temptation is strong to see socialism as the result of a long march of power toward a progressive social "transparency" that in reality conveys ever greater control. Marxism transforms the ambition of state domination into a totalitarian regime and translates socialism from power into action (Kolakowski 2005). Bolshevism would be in charge of realizing the "mad communist utopia." It is therefore "the logic of an idea" that is called into question—in some cases since Plato (Chafarevitch 1975), in others only since the Enlightenment (Baczko 1981)—and that must answer for its totalitarian potential.

In this context, Patočka's reflections, which are very important within the panorama of dissidence, give voice to the most articulated attempt to trace the origins of totalitarian subjugation. Nazism and communism are not mere accidents of modernity, but they are linked, albeit in a complex and indirect way, to objectivist metaphysics (Patočka 1996). They are also the result of that crisis of European consciousness originating in the triumph of an impersonal rationality as opposed to the concreteness of the life world. Or rather, they would be unthinkable without the expansion of a technical rationality revolving around the sole criterion of efficiency, operating as a function of the combination of forces that make it possible to "take possession," "annex," and "exclude."

The dissidents' philosophical questions never take on the character of a purely intellectual quest. According to Patočka—the figure who perhaps more than any other acts as a bridge between the philosophical culture of the East and that of the West—to be pregnant, a philosophical thought must take a stand "on the front line." To go to the front is, in fact, what dissident philosophers believe they are doing through the movement of "Charter 77," on which Patočka works tirelessly and for which he is the most exposed spokesman.

For him, philosophical practice is a "dissident practice" by definition. Philosophy is not about accumulating secure knowledge but about embarking on a radical commitment. This is the only power of "the powerless," whose struggle is expressed in the attempt to "live in the truth," which does not mean believing in an objective or revealed truth but living in the very problematic nature of truth.

Philosophy is established on the basis of a "withdrawal": a withdrawal from immediate public resonance, from official circuits and ideologies; a withdrawal into spaces wrested from the grasp of the state, in the awareness that meaning is always something to be reprobated and in the determination to continue, despite the risks, the infinite search for truth. In other words, as Patočka points out, if the possibility to access meaning—that is, the world as a totality—cannot be provided by science, which renounces the totality of meaning in the belief that it can obtain knowledge of the whole, and if truth cannot coexist with religion either, which cancels the tension toward transcendence in favor of the transcendent (Patočka 1990), then a structural affinity between the philosophical spirit, the spiritual life, and the dissident attitude emerges eventually.

The call for courage by the powerless of Prague, Budapest, and Warsaw is answered by "the heroic man who does philosophy," insofar as the latter, stripped of any search for certainty, lives only in the interminable search. For the one who seeks the truth is "obliged to let grow within himself the disquieting, the irreconcilable, the enigmatic" (36), everything opposing the "order of the day," the supine acceptance of what exists, in a word, everything that no totalitarianism could accept. "Life in truth," in the philosophical perspective of dissidence in general, and particularly in Patočka's, is not, then, "an anti-political morality" (Ash 1990). Rather, it is an "impolitic" attitude that eschews politics when it coincides with totalitarianism or post-totalitarianism to relaunch the conjugation of ethics and philosophy in a heretical thought that for this very reason can become immediately political.

THREE

Philosophy in the Face of Extremes

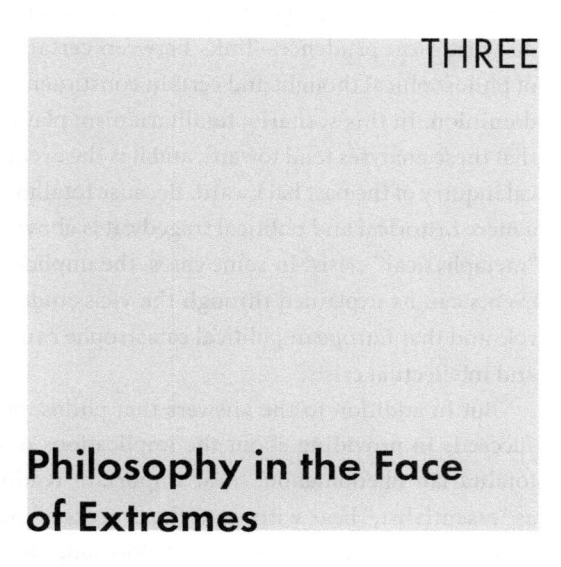

NIHILISM IN POWER

There is still another way to interpret the totalitarian phenomenon: philosophical readings that, since they are not interested in fixing the material of history in ideal types, are, rather, involved in the search for a sense of "political evil," thereby attempting to elaborate a sort of archaeology of totalitarian ideology. From the end of the 1930s, and especially throughout the 1940s, investigations into the intellectual origins of totalitarianism multiply: Gurian's and Castoriadis's "ideocracy" (Gurian 1969; Castoriadis 1973); Milosz's and Besançon's "logocracy" (Milosz [1953] 1990; Besançon 1977); Aron's "secular religions" (Aron 1944); Voegelin's "political religions" (Voegelin 2000a); Arendt's "ideological supersense"; and Inkeles's "totalitarian mysticism" (Inkeles 1969). Numerous formulas are employed to indicate that the real novelty of totalitarianism consisted of the fact that, for the first time in history, an idea, the inspiration for an ideology, became praxis.

What makes these interpretations interesting is not so much the analysis of certain ideological contents as the ability to connect the totalitarian ideological functioning to a specific way of understanding reality. In many cases, we witness the genealogical reconstructions establishing—without due historical prudence—links between certain currents of our tradition of philosophical thought and certain constituent features of the totalitarian dominion. In this scenario, totalitarianism plays a dual role: it is the focus that these analyses tend toward, and it is the event directing the philosophical inquiry of the past backward. Because totalitarianism is not perceived as a mere historical and political tragedy, it is above all assessed as a profound "metaphysical" crisis. In some cases, the implicit assumption that political events can be explained through the vicissitudes of ideas certainly plays a role and that European political catastrophe can be explained by a spiritual and intellectual crisis.

But in addition to the answers that philosophy, more or less plausibly, succeeds in providing about the implications of its own categories in the totalitarian phenomenon, these important readings, superficially defined as "essentialist," bear witness to the process of examination that the twentieth century conducted on itself. Before judging the results as inconclusive and "metaphysical" on the basis of alleged scientific criteria, we must bear in mind that this is, first of all, a phenomenon of self-reflection, a demonstration by philosophy of having been able to capture in thought the great provocations of the century—from the unprecedented and systematic destructive will of Nazism and Stalinism to the unbridled and overwhelming triumph of technology.

Even before the end of the Second World War, which represented a real existential trauma, many intellectuals attempted to explain what was happening in terms of totalitarianism. It is not only a question of making sense of what seems to be disastrous and at the same time meaningless but also of coming to terms with one's own intellectual formation. Not by chance, this hermeneutical path was ushered in mainly by thinkers of Jewish origin, who were torn away from the realm of contemplation and literally thrown into the realm of history. An entire philosophical generation underwent a real shock, responding to it not only and not always with action but also often with a sort of "metaphysical revolt." This originated those "metapolitical" readings of totalitarianism, in which events cannot be reduced to the concatenation of facts but must be examined in depth until their ontological roots can emerge.

The first philosophical interpretations, which often identify in the ideology of the regime the outcome of a nihilistic and irrationalist revolution rejecting reason and destroying its norms and values, originated in the incandescent and intellectually chaotic climate of Nazism when it was still in action. But one may already encounter readings questioning the simplified rationalism/irrationalism dichotomy to explain totalitarianism as a paradoxical fulfillment of certain rationalist premises implicit in modernity, if not in the very origins of Western thought.

Hermann Rauschning's *The Revolution of Nihilism*, written between 1937 and 1938, is probably one of the first, as well as one of the most influential, interpretations of Nazism as the outcome of a "nihilistic revolution." According to Rauschning, Nazism is not only a political phenomenon but is deeply rooted in long-standing moral and intellectual processes. From a perspective that is conservative, to say the least—Rauschning had adhered to National Socialism—the author denounces the National Socialist revolution, which at the time was heading in the direction of total nihilism, the total destruction of every law and every value of the past.

Here, nihilism is seen simply as the "nullification" of the ethical norms of tradition, as a materialistic tendency that extinguishes every spiritual impulse. National Socialism opposes an irrational and blind praxis flaunting contempt for the spirit, morality, and the sense of honor and justice to the high values of nation, order and state. "For the very reason that we acknowledge the eternal values of the Nation and of a political order rooted in the nation," Rauschning states, "we are bound to turn against this revolution, whose subversive course involves the utter destruction of all traditional spiritual standards, utter nihilism. These values are the product of the intellectual and historical unity of Western civilization of historic intellectual and moral forces. Without these, Nationalism is not a conservative principle, but the implement of a destructive revolution; and likewise Socialism ceases to be a regulative idea of justice and equity when it sheds the Western principles of legality and of the liberty of the person" (Rauschning 1972, xii–xiii).

Thus, totalitarianism, whether Nazi or socialist, proves to be an accomplished nihilism, insofar as it is a movement without an aim, a revolution for its own sake: "a permanent revolution of sheer destruction, by means of which a dictatorship of brute force maintain[s] itself in power" (xi–xii). Totalitarian politics, therefore, is devoid of values and aims, and its sole objective is the domination of the world in the name of domination. The nihilistic revolution carried out by Nazism is based on "nothingness." With nothingness as its premise, it is not possible to establish either a social order or a state but only to appeal to the empty myth of violence. However naive, Rauschning's analysis inaugurates that direction of interpretation, anything but sterile, which identifies in totalitarianism not the construction of order but the compulsion to a perennial dynamism, to that permanent revolution, which is at the same time the strength and weakness of such a regime.

Ernst Fraenkel provided a reconstruction of the cultural roots of the Third Reich, which is much more articulate than Rauschning's equation of totalitarianism-nihilism. As I noted before, Fraenkel oscillates in *The Double State* between an explanation that is, so to speak, faithful to "structural-economic" assumptions of Marxism and a reading that gives an account of the greater articulation of the "superstructure"—in this case, the Nazi and pro-Nazi philosophical-legal elaborations. The main characteristic of National Socialism, the basis of the rule of a discretionary state, is for him the total repudiation of natural law. By rejecting faith in the universalist idea of justice, by leaving the recognition of right and wrong to the sole discretion of the führer, National Socialism replaces the "humanistic values of natural law" (Fraenkel [1941] 2006, 121) with a legal opportunism established on a narrow xenophobic nationalism and a crude biological materialism. Historicist and idealist critics are not responsible for such contempt for the autonomous value of law. Against the tide of a certain Marxist vulgate, Fraenkel believes that it is illegitimate to establish direct links between Hegel's political philosophy and the legal thinking of the Third Reich. By rejecting the abstractness of rational natural law, Nazism fosters an understanding of the political based on the primacy of the enemy. It is only from this point of view that a connection with Hegel's philosophy of law can be discerned. Fraenkel claims, "To the extent, however, that National-Socialism gives a specific content to its concepts of politics (as in its racial theory and its theory of 'blood and soil'), not even the remotest relationship exists" (Fraenkel [1941] 2006, 126). Hence, neither Hegel nor any other representative of Western rationality is to be blamed. If anything, all those who, by having embraced nihilism and irrationalism, triumphantly emphasize the bankruptcy of every universal idea are to be suspected. Although he mentions Luther and Machiavelli and their supine acceptance of the "evil world," Fraenkel mainly addresses Carl Schmitt, whose "political romanticism" is said to have disguised an irrationalism arising from the cult of violence as a communitarian spirit.

Nazi culture, which forged the political construction of the Third Reich, would substantially consist of a mixture of nihilism and political mysticism: that archaic-communitarian vision that, although arose from the industrial revolution, does call for natural law but a natural law that is not rational but biologically based. In Fraenkel's opinion, this natural communitarian theory of law is revived in the National Socialist concept of "ethnic community" (*Volksgenossen*). Thus, *Mein Kampf* is not the writing of a madman but an articulation of exasperation of that doctrine for which the state is a secondary expression of the primary unity of all the comrades. An ethnic community is a biological formation that exists even if it does not have a state organization. The state is an organic phenomenon "derived" from the ethnic community understood biologically. National Socialism not only endorsed a communitarian ideology; it also "archaically" placed it in connection with the threat of an external enemy. For an ethnic community hypostatized as a value in itself presupposes the existence of an enduring enemy, whether real or imaginary, as in Nazi values, the permanent enemy replaces the absence of rational purposefulness, just as biologism and romantic mysticism replaced the rational coexistence based on the universality of law. "With this repudiation of every trace of rational Natural Law, Germany has turned her back on the community of nations which consciously adheres to the traditions of occidental civilization. National-Socialism certainly cannot be said to be—as Friedrich Engels once said of Marxian Socialism—the heir of Classical German Philosophy. It is rather its complete negation" (114). Just as it is a negation of all humanistic and rationalistic philosophical culture in general.

Fraenkel's analysis shows its own theoretical weakness in this conclusion. Is it sufficient to stress totalitarianism's utter noninvolvement in the tradition to grasp its "spiritual meaning"? Are not those readings that complicate the linearity of a path culminating in totalitarianism less mystifying, perhaps even more disturbing, for the purposes of a critical reexamination of our cultural roots?[1] These interpretations of Nazi totalitarianism as an outcome of nihilism are emblematic of the desire to reduce the totalitarian phenomenon to a sort of parenthesis, separated from a whole tradition of thought. Nevertheless, is it truly possible to circumscribe nihilism to a radical fringe of mystical-irrationalist thinkers as the sole "intellectuals" responsible for the German catastrophe? Or is it not more useful to go in search of a nihilistic mentality that is born in the most hidden folds of our own rationality?

These questions will be posed by some of the most important philosophers of the twentieth century, whose reflection is strongly influenced by Heidegger's teaching. As much as they harshly contest his political stances and the theoretical outcomes of his reflection, however, the foundation of their philosophical inquiry remains Heideggerian. Paradoxically, they remain so even when they are to think of totalitarianism—that is, the event that led them to question, sometimes drastically, their old master. I am referring to Hannah Arendt, Hans Jonas, Karl Löwith, and Günther Anders but also, to some extent, Herbert Marcuse, Leo Strauss, and Eric Voegelin. By placing themselves in the philosophical horizon opened by Heidegger, as well as by using, willingly or unwillingly, conceptual categories shaped by his existential ontology, these authors cannot separate the history of Western reason from that of metaphysics and its potential nihilistic destiny.

"National Socialism is only the most famous form of German nihilism. . . . For that nihilism has deeper roots than the preachings of Hitler" (Strauss 1941, 357). This is how Leo Strauss begins "German Nihilism," an important essay from 1941, which we may consider the starting point of his rereading of Western political philosophy in terms of a progressive nihilistic drift. According to Strauss, it is possible to identify a philosophical-political path that, by moving away from the Aristotelian objective of a "good life" pursued within the "excellent state," eventually leads to political nihilism. Such a path is imbued with a historicist mentality, the fruit of that modern culture that relativizes ultimate questions, denies transcendent reference to the law of nature, and discredits universality (Strauss [1953] 1965, 1959). "German Nihilism" clearly shows how the question of totalitarianism brings into focus the themes that will occupy the center of Strauss's philosophical research—from the significance of historicism as a "dissolution of meaning" to the recovery of classical political philosophy as resistance to tyranny.

If it is true that Nazism and Stalinism represent a new form of tyranny, which, unlike classical tyranny, "has at its disposal 'technology' as well as 'ideologies,' more generally it presupposes the existence of 'science'" (Strauss [1948] 2000, 23); however, for Strauss, it is chiefly necessary to come to terms with the intellectual and philosophical climate that allowed the affirmation of National Socialism. There is no doubt that nihilism is the background against which Hitlerism was able to develop. Nevertheless, one cannot be satisfied with a definition such as Rauschning's definition of *nihilism* as the simple destruction of all the traditional spiritual criteria. For Strauss, there is an undeniable nihilistic value operating in the German cultural and philosophical tradition itself. But German nihilism also represents a moral reaction to the ethical upheaval produced by the French Revolution—an approach that identified morality with the rights of each individual, reduced honesty to the most expedient policy, and taught to resolve the conflict between private and common interest via industry and trade. "Opposing the identification of the morally good with the object of enlightened self-interest however enlightened, the German philosophers insisted on the difference between the morally good and self-interest, between the *honestum* and the *utile*; they insisted on *self-sacrifice* and *self-denial*" (Strauss 1941, 371). This is the case of Fichte, Hegel, and Nietzsche (Strauss 1941). Even the Nietzscheanism that fascinates the more recent generation of German intellectuals wants to destroy "modern civilization" to express its own "moral protest" and return to an "ethical life" that does not know the "corruption" of a selfish, utilitarian, and mercantile modern society.

Hence, German nihilism first and foremost rejects "the prospect of a pacified planet, without rulers and ruled, of a planetary society devoted to production and consumption only" and "the very prospect of a world in which everyone would be happy and satisfied, in which everyone would have his little pleasure by day and his little pleasure by night" (360). In other words, it is a revolt against what seems to impose itself, in the name of the ineluctable course of historical reason, as the destiny of Western civilization: materialistic communism.

Nihilism is the name given to the identification of Reason and History, which has marked modern thought in general, as well as historical materialism in particular. But while rejecting the false ideal of "modern civilization," nihilistic thought, which is opposed to the ideal of historical progress, is caught in the web of the very determinism it wishes to combat. It falls victim to the false prophecies uttered by those professors who unconsciously or consciously paved the way for Hitler, Spengler, Moeller Van den Bruck, Schmitt, Jünger, and Heidegger, who promise, as a similarly ineluctable event, the birth of a new epoch. In essence, the nihilists respond to a historicism that identifies Reason, History, and Progress by hypostatizing, according to specular and contrary assumptions, the advent of a new era for which "a devastating storm" that purifies the future becomes necessary, as the proletarian revolution was for communism.

Therefore, Strauss's critique addresses both mentalities: those conveyed by rationalistic historicism and those that paved the way for national socialism. These are the two faces of the same soul, whose nihilistic impulse has come to deny reason, truth, and philosophy to dissolve them in the historical becoming. "The lack of resistance to nihilism seems to be due ultimately to the depreciation and the contempt of reason, which is one and unchangeable or it is not" (Strauss 1941, 364). By replacing Truth and Reason with the truths and reasons constantly changing in History, historicism and nihilism have opened the door to totalitarianism.

Eric Voegelin's interpretation of totalitarian ideologies is very close to Strauss's reconsideration of classical political philosophy and its ultimate questions as a barrier to the nihilistic outcomes of historicism and modern science.[2] Together with Strauss, Voegelin fostered the "rehabilitation of practical philosophy" aimed at reacting to the "scientific-valuative" understanding of human action implemented by social sciences, thereby relaunching the dignity and autonomy of a reflection questioning the meaning and the value of ethical and political action. For Voegelin, nihilism, conveyed by a historicist and processualist mentality, is to be traced back to a specific religious and philosophical current: Gnosticism.

As early as the first volume of *Gnosis und spätantiker Geist* (1934), Hans Jonas placed at the center of his philosophical research the meaning of *Gnosticism*, understood in a very general sense as the first and radical nihilistic movement in Western history. According to Jonas, Gnosticism is based on an approach envisaging self-knowledge as a means of salvation in the afterlife; on a profound distrust of the idea of a good creator and of the goodness of the creator; on the resulting dualisms between God and the world, human being and God, and human being-world; and on a devolutionary and negative understanding of creation resulting in radical acosmism. Gnosticism is especially characterized, however, by a specific "existential syndrome." Because of a total lack of confidence in God, in the Law, and in the Creation, the Gnostic man falls prey to a profound anguish. On the one hand, the historical experience of National Socialism clearly moves Jonas's reflection toward the recognition of the philosophical essence of Gnosticism; on the other hand, he attempts to highlight the risks implicit in Heideggerian existentialism. Nevertheless, Jonas never abandons historical contextualization and philological expertise. In short, he never goes so far as to interpret the nihilistic aspects of modernity as the manifestation of a perpetual gnosis that finds its extreme manifestation in totalitarianism.

Somehow, this is what Eric Voegelin will do, bestowing a political and refoundational turn on the reconstruction of the characters of Gnosticism within a much more "continuistic" and "essentialist" investigation than Jonas's. In 1938, *The Political Religions*, a seminal work for the philosophical historiography revolving around the concept of "secularization," Voegelin, who immigrated to the United States because of Nazism, set up an investigation into "political collectivisms," which will constitute the basic question of all his following thought. Therefore, the shock of totalitarianism is what pushes him, even in this case, toward a "philosophical-political archaeology" of the symbolic complexes structuring the different experiences of political order. Very different phenomena—from the religious movements of ancient Egypt to the first Gnostic currents, up to the ideology of the *Führertum*—are compared in the perspective, "still experimental," of a homogeneity between their "symbolic substrata." In his following works, Voegelin identifies in a precise Gnostic constellation the tendency to eliminate the dimension of transcendence in favor of a full immanent realization of the Christian *eschaton*, a tendency that will result in the instrumental and subjectivist rationality of modernity and ultimately be completed in totalitarianism.

In *The Political Religions*, Voegelin intends to grasp the political and philosophical implications of a "spiritual view of the renewal of the soul" aimed at "the perfection of the Christian ideal of existence" in this very world (Voegelin 2000c, 51–52). The faith in the *perfectibilitas* of human reason conveyed by Gnosticism, which goes as far as the faith in the infinite development of humanity of the Enlightenment, transits into that popular religion of the nineteenth century—that is, progress—and ends up being catastrophically reversed in totalitarian regimes. According to Voegelin, "the symbolism of the apocalypse of the empire lives on in the symbolism of the nineteenth and twentieth centuries: in three empires of Marx and Engels's philosophy of history, in the Third Reich of National Socialism, and in the fascist third Rome, following the Rome of antiquity and the Christian Rome" (52). All these forms of collectivity share the assumption that the political community must and can be reduced to the worldly dimension, whose only problems consist of questions about organization and power.

Hence, totalitarianism represents the result of a progressive negation of transcendence carried out by that "inner-worldly religiosity experienced by the collective body—be it humanity, the people, the class, the race, or the state—as the *ens realissimum*" (71). It is a sort of *mystique humaine*—unlimited faith in the work of the human being—that contrasts with the true faith. In the fully immanent symbolism, on which the ultraworldly *ecclesiae* (churches) are based—from Nazi Germany to fascist Italy—the link with transcendence is severed; the community itself is the source of its own legitimacy. "The sacral substance is the national spirit or the objective spirit, i.e., *realissimum* that lasts throughout the period, which becomes historical reality in individuals as members of their nation" (65).

Voegelin's theses have become more influential than what is usually believed, even though they have been interpreted into the extremely trivialized formula of totalitarianism as "secular heresy," of communism and Nazism as perverse substitutes of the true religion, immanentist drifts "that can be traced in various degrees of purity in medieval and Renaissance sects" (Voegelin 2000b, 180).

Likewise, Karl Löwith's reflection falls within that philosophical horizon connecting totalitarianism to the nihilistic drift of historicism and to the process of secularization of transcendence. Especially noteworthy is the denunciation of the philosophies of history carried out in his 1949 *Meaning of History*. In Löwith's eyes, such philosophies cannot be acquitted for their undeniable implication in the totalitarian tragedy. Criticized not only and not so much as ideological illusions, the philosophies of history and progress are harbingers of a specific mentality. At the basis of the idea of history as a process there stands, indeed, a precise "experience of time." A future-oriented *Zeitauffassung* marks a drastic change from the Greek and Roman concept of time.

If the ancient world remains constitutively anchored to the idea of limit—to the idea of a *kosmos* naturalistically delimited as an insurmountable horizon of mortals' *pragmata*—the modern vision of history is rather characterized by that process of universalization and abstraction that overwhelms any distinction and sense of the finite. In short, if the conception that each event in itself has its own meaning is inherent in the classical concept of *historein*, then the "future-centric" revolution carried out by the philosophies of history wants the events to have a meaning only if they refer to a temporally deferred purpose. In other words, we would have witnessed the exchange of semantic content between the terms *meaning* and *end*, for which only the general end can determine the relevance of the particular meaning. Consequently, every event holds its own justification only if it refers to an end that draws it down and that is identified in a future goal. "The very existence of a philosophy of history and its quest for a meaning," Löwith claims, "is due to the history of salvation; it emerged from the faith in an ultimate purpose" (Löwith [1949] 2011, 5). Hence, modern *Geschichtsphilosophie* represents the result of a secularization of the Christian "theology of history"; it directly descends from the presuppositions operating in the Jewish-Christian conception, which considers human events in the perspective of expectation and redemption. The great modern syntheses of the universal historical path replace "Providence" with "Progress" and God with Man as the Absolute Subject of history. The consequences of such a turn would continue to operate until the philosophical crisis of the twentieth century.

Hence, the dissolution of Europe in totalitarianism is the product of historical events, as well as of a full-fledged nihilism, in which Reason, now as one with History, abdicates its role of limit, of opposition, and of critiques of external reality. Therefore, European nihilism would represent that place of decadence and transition in which reason, by burying every humanistic-rational foundation, is now only the *flatus vocis* behind which hides the irrationality of what happens. If, on the philosophical side, Heidegger's thought is the emblem of the spiritual crisis, a crisis that is prepared with Hegel and consummated with Nietzsche, on the historical and political side, both the democratic masses engulfing the individual and, even more so, the totalitarianisms suffocating all forms of freedom are expressions of nihilism.

Thus, there is more than an affinity between Heidegger's philosophy, Schmitt's legal doctrine, and National Socialism—not so much because there is a close concordance of ideological contents between the proposals of the two thinkers and the party program but in virtue of "that radicalism with which those philosophies base the freedom of German existence on the revelation of nothingness." For Löwith, nihilism is "the disavowal of existing civilization as the only real belief of all truly educated people at the beginning of the twentieth century. Nihilism is not a result of the Great War but, on the contrary, its cause" (Löwith [1940] 1966, 10).

There is, however, a fundamental text that precedes these readings of totalitarianism in terms of realized nihilism: *Some Reflections on the Philosophy of Hitlerism*, written by Emmanuel Levinas in 1934, represents undoubtedly one of the earliest philosophical appeals, along with those by Georges Bataille and Simone Weil, to think about the radicality and incommensurability of the totalitarian event. Levinas is committed to highlighting the ontological dimension of the totalitarian phenomenon to dig deep in order to identify what is hidden behind specific ideological masks. Defined as an unprecedented attack on the human, Hitlerism, which radically contrasts European civilization and its idea of freedom, is far from corresponding to its self-depiction. "The philosophy of Hitlerism therefore goes beyond the philosophy of Hitlerians. It questions the very principles of a civilization" (Levinas 1990b, 64). Thus, it is not simply a matter of explaining a certain event or the disposition of certain actors but the *Stimmung* emerging from such phenomena.

The ontological novelty of National Socialism consists of the primacy bestowed on the experience of the body, which, in Levinas's view, corresponds in Hitlerism with the existential figures of "chaining" and "being-nailed-down," tropes of a specific way of being. The exaltation of the body, the blood and the race, the type of identification that such enchainment to the biological procures, circumscribes a way of being in the world that, with the cancellation of any possible escape into transcendence, denies any possible freedom and binds the human body to total subjugation. Hence, the heart of Hitlerism's spiritual life consists of the self-closure of the self on the dimension of the body: "The biological, with the notion of inevitability it entails, becomes more than an object of spiritual life. It becomes its heart" (69).

In short, for Levinas, National Socialism is neither a pathology of human reason nor an ideological accident. Rather, it should be understood together with the very possibility of Evil, which Western philosophy has not questioned enough. In Levinas's eyes, totalitarian evil represents a possibility contained in the ontology of being, which is traversed by the "will to be." It is a danger looming over the subject of transcendental idealism, who believes itself to be free because it bases its own foundation in itself alone.

Deprived of any possible escape from self-containment, however, it can become the correlative of "being as gathering together and as dominating" (63). Far from constituting the exclusive prerogative of the experience and ontology of Hitlerism, the "chaining" is therefore constitutive of a "mode of being" that is pleased with the closure of its own identity. In this sense, we can say that Nazi ideology is both a deformation and a nihilistic derivation of the two main and alternative currents of Western thought: subjectivistic spiritualism and materialism. The unreserved acceptance of enchainment is in fact the hallmark of contemporary society, even in its liberal version. The imprisonment in a finiteness of being, glorified as such, fosters identitarian dynamics of the crowds, as well as totalitarian leaders' delusions of sovereignty, experiences that modernity had never endured until that moment, although lying in its own ontological possibilities.

The experience of totalitarianism—we must keep in mind that Levinas was called to arms in 1939 and, taken prisoner, he remained in a concentration camp for almost the entire war—along with a reinterpretation of Jewish tradition, is what led Levinas to break with the idea that philosophical thought should have as its privileged object being, in whatever way it is understood. The totalitarian phenomenon leads him beyond ontology, beyond the history of metaphysics, which, precisely because of its inability to go beyond "horrible neutrality of the *there is*" (Levinas 1990a, 292), inevitably ends up in nihilism, wherein the Other is reduced and reconceived as the Same. This explains Levinas's choice to consider "ethics as first philosophy," as primal and irreducible to any ontology.

DIALECTIC OF REASON

On closer inspection, nihilism is not the only philosophical category called to account for totalitarianism. Under its name are hidden other conceptual constellations: from historicism to subjectivism and from secularization to immanentization. This leads us to dwell on the continuity between totalitarianism and philosophical tradition and the link between totalitarian irrationalism and Western rationalism. The suspicion is extended to the philosophical *ratio* as such, to its totalizing claim to account for the whole of reality, and to its will to orient and direct the latter on the basis of its own assumptions. Therefore, it is not only a question of pointing out the failure of philosophy in the face of totalitarianism or lamenting the negation of philosophical reason by totalitarian dominion. More radically, it is a matter of grasping the involvement of philosophy and its way of relating to reality in the logic of totalitarianism.

Not by chance, Plato, who inaugurated Western philosophical tradition, became the polemical target of many philosophical inquiries of totalitarianism. In the seminal work *The Open Society and Its Enemies* (1945), Karl Popper was one of the first interpreters to question Plato's political philosophy, the latter considered the forefather of historicism (Popper 1945). The program of the author of the *Republic*, which was later handed over to dialectical philosophies, is configured as "the first totalitarian project." To escape the cosmic law of degeneration, Plato, a "social engineer" and a "utopian," is said to have rigidified, indeed petrified, the internal articulation of the state into an autarkic and strictly classist regime. But Popper's critiques of Hegel and Marx are no less harsh than his attack on Platonic holism. If Hegel is the forefather of modern nationalism and racism, Marx, an unwitting victim of faith in the scientific nature and predictability of history, is the prophet of the advent of a classless society—a prophecy that, to come true, will consider the use of any means to be legitimate.

Every system that enunciates laws to which reality must conform is put under accusation. On the one hand, historicist metaphysics is all-powerful, inasmuch as it foresees and fosters the triumphant march of humanity; on the other hand, it is inevitably imbued with the resignation, the impotence, and the irresponsibility deriving from the irreversibility of a path that has already been mapped out since forever (Popper [1944] 2012).

Popper's genealogy goes so far as to trace the historicist roots of totalitarianism to the biblical doctrine of salvation, in which historical law and God's will are one. The same call to necessity would operate as much in Nazi racism as in communist socialization: "two [of the] most important modern versions of historicism" (Popper 1945, 7). If, in racism, the chosen people are replaced by the chosen race, in communism the chosen class does so. Both doctrines are based on the belief that historical evolution is ruled by an immutable law. Racism is a natural law of biological superiority; Marxism is an economic law of the class struggle. The program of historicist rationalism, which seeks to bring reality under a law that is both assertive and normative, can never be falsified. Therefore, the fight against totalitarianism must start from epistemological premises accounting for the criterion of falsifiability as their own principle, the only one that allows, if transposed into the political and social sphere, the realization of an open society.

Hence, the future will be open free from the threat of totalitarianism as long as "piecemeal engineering" (Popper 1945, 138), liable to falsification, abdicates prophetic omnipotence and utopian planning, thereby fostering political programs that, with a great sense of limitation and human fallibility, do not propose a revolution of totality but the gradual elimination of the worst evils. By maintaining this, Popper establishes a contrast, as frontal as it is radical, between an open liberal democracy, grounded on individual reason, and a closed society, with a high totalitarian risk, contained *in nuce* in every collectivist and artificial political conception of equality.

Although highly criticized, Popper's thesis had a great impact on the Anglo-Saxon culture since it was distrustful of continental historicism, an impact equal only to that caused by the thesis of another illustrious Austrian liberal who supported Popper's work: Friedrich von Hayek. In 1944, *The Road to Serfdom* (Hayek 1976), totalitarianism was also traced back to historicism, to that "rationalistic constructivism" especially connected to the socialist and communist vision of history. In particular, totalitarianism is to be found in the "total hostility" of socialist and pseudosocialist projects to economic freedom, as well as in their aspiration to interventionism and social planning. Only a full freedom to property can safeguard an individual's freedom from the violence and intrusiveness of totalitarianism. These freedoms find their place within an order that is no longer understood as a top-down imposition—the product of rationalist constructivism—but rather as a set of rules produced by a "spontaneous process" of cultural selection, which leads to the preservation of only those proving to be universalizable.

What is puzzling about these interpretations is the rigid dualism between liberal and market society and totalitarian society, as well as the contrast between healthy individual reason and sick collective reason. Even more puzzling is the lack of problematization of the transition from idea to reality of the totalitarian tendencies contained in the philosophical doctrines—as if Plato's *Republic* truly had something to do with the Third Reich straight away. This problem will also afflict other philosophical interpretations that will also complicate the linearity of the transition from theory to praxis.

Under the banner of the lapidary affirmation that "the whole is the false" (Adorno 2005, 30), Max Horkheimer and Theodor Adorno demystify Western rationality. Already in Horkheimer's 1942 "The Authoritarian State" (Horkheimer 1973; see also Horkheimer 2020), the distance from orthodox Marxism is as clear as the heterodoxy of a hope placed in the isolated individual, the only place left for a possible resistance to the system, to that bourgeois domination that, with mass society and monopoly capitalism, has become a totalitarian domination. The project of a possible revolution became increasingly weakened, turning revolutionary hope into the praise of the thought of having the courage to escape from the "falsehood of the whole."

In this way, the Frankfurters have begun to reinterpret totalitarianism as a destiny inscribed in the contradictions of Western rationality. National Socialism is the historical occasion that brings to the surface the deep structures of that culture, which proves to be involved, from its very beginning, in the history of domination. The coparticipation of *logos* and *Herrschaft* appears in all its fullness only in accomplished totalitarianism, whereby totalitarian domination is "transformed into pure truth," the truth according to which "the Enlightenment is totalitarian." *Dialectic of Enlightenment* constantly stresses the process of reification of reality by subjective reason, which, mystifyingly, has been presented as a progressive liberation from myth. A human-nature relationship based on that instrumental and manipulative relationship, which the Enlightenment celebrates as the exit from magic, will inevitably have repercussions on the political and social environment, as if myth abandoned nature only to reappear in society and culture. "Myth becomes enlightenment and nature mere objectivity. Human beings purchase the increase in their power with estrangement from that over which it is exerted. Enlightenment stands in the same relationship to things as the dictator to human beings. He knows them to the extent that he can manipulate them" (Horkheimer and Adorno 2002, 6).

Totalitarianism is thus articulated in many ways. It is expressed not only in the terror and violence of fascism, Nazism, and communism but also in the consumption and enjoyment of the pseudoculture of so-called "democratic" mass society. The total domination of the object by the subject, a program of that Enlightenment backdated to Homer, takes place in the "magic" of a totality in which the subject disappears into the reality of a universe of domination in which the dazzling truth of the original coappearance of reason and barbarism finally appears. The "cultural industry" is only the mild face of totalitarianism, which, without terror and blatant violence, through a feigned democratization of culture, undisturbedly trains consciences to conform to the "Whole." Hence, neither totalitarian regimes, with their explosive mixture of ideology and terror, nor late-capitalist mass societies, with their ability to homologate every expression to the system, leave any "political" and existential space for freedom. If totalitarianism, as a broadening category of the domain, is the insuperable horizon of modern politics, the exercise of freedom is entrusted to a sort of ungrounded subject capable of grasping the falsity of everything and, at the same time, the truth that "Wrong life cannot be lived rightly" (Adorno 2005, 39).

Harshly criticized by both its "supporter" and its "opponent," this reconstruction of the history of domination has been the object of countless attacks. Above all, it has been accused of a theoretical radicalism that, unable to see any alternative to instrumental and subjectivist reason, ends up turning into an apologia for the existing (Habermas 2018). This is the accusation that Habermas will make to all those deconstructive genealogies going so far as to interpret totalitarianism so radically that they eventually question our philosophical tradition as a whole.

Despite countless criticisms of this approach, the Frankfurt theory of the "universe of domination" and of "instrumental reason" remains among the dragging ideas of philosophical debate—and not only throughout the second half of the twentieth century. As we will have the opportunity to observe in the next chapter, we find it between the lines, although not explicitly mentioned, in many of the readings of recent decades that address the problem of the overpowering of technologies connected to new forms of capitalism. Certainly, the Heideggerian lament also resonates loudly in attacks against the totalitarian dangers of technology. But the legacy of the Frankfurt School has never ceased to be influential.

In Herbert Marcuse's work, the two different views opposing instrumental rationality—the dialectical, but critical, Frankfurtian philosophy, on the one hand, and the Heideggerian reading of technique as will to power, on the other—find a synthesis. The 1964 *One-Dimensional Man* becomes, not surprisingly, probably the most widely read text in the 1968 season. I am convinced that especially Marcusian ideas about the administered, technological society continue to shape today's critiques of neoliberalism and its governmental rationality. He was probably one of the earliest and staunchest proponents of the existence of a mild totalitarianism that continued to operate in advanced capitalist societies. According to him, the defeat of fascism and National Socialism had not arrested the trajectory toward totalitarianism. The powers of reason and freedom are dramatically declining in "late industrial society" (Marcuse 1964), a consumer society where the apparatus of planning and management have produced new forms of total control. Marcuse's analysis starts from the assumption of the historical rise of a technological world that overpowers and controls its subject in unprecedented ways. If the subject of metaphysical tradition was still thought of as an active agent facing a controllable world of objects, the new subject now becomes one-dimensional in that it is totally integrated into the totality of "pure instrumentality" and "efficacy." Marcusian denunciations against the triumph of one-dimensional positivity, against an instrumentalizing and monolithic technological and capitalist universe, resonate strongly in today's critiques of the soft totalitarianism represented by digital technologies, run by the new neoliberal reason.

It will be a long-lived heredity, this of the Frankfurt School, which will become a powerful general critical view once intertwined with the philosophical conclusions on totalitarianism elaborated by Arendt together with Foucauldian considerations on biopower.

As a political philosopher, Hannah Arendt is best known for having given voice to a conception of politics that reevaluates its ontological dimension. In other words, politics is configured as that sphere which, radically separated from domination and distanced from identification with the state, can finally open up to the vitality of a horizontal, plural, participatory, agonistic public space wherein the relational identity of its actors is at stake. Against a politics understood as a vertical relationship of command and obedience, conceived as a sphere in which power is exercised as an instrument to obtain certain goals, Arendt rehabilitates the noninstrumental value of plural action. Although this is all correct, interpreters rarely underline that Arendt's "autonomy of the political," as it were, is the result of an inquiry into totalitarianism, which is also philosophical.

In *The Origins of Totalitarianism*, especially in the chapter "Ideology and Terror," we have seen how it is possible to identify what we might call the "metapolitics" of totalitarianism (Forti 2006): the set of all the broadly ideological elements, not only those overtly expressed by propaganda, which give rise to the so-called "totalitarian mentality." This metapolitical configuration, along with some basic assumptions of philosophy, circumscribes a circularity in virtue of which the "totalitarian mentality," if it does not turn out to be the product of philosophy, appears to be a possibility that metaphysics has offered. Therefore, dynamics that are potentially, and not necessarily, totalitarian are sought in the Great Tradition of philosophy. In a nutshell, the metaphysical configuration of totalitarianism presents itself as a deadly combination of subjectivist delusion of omnipotence, according to which "everything is possible," and dialectical evolutionism,[3] which refuses "to accept anything 'as it is,'" to interpret "everything as being only a stage of some further development" (Arendt 1973, 464).

Totalitarian metapolitics, with its strong appeal to the power of the laws of Nature and History, aims not only at oppression but at something far more radical. In totalitarianism, "suffering, of which there has always been too much on earth, is not the issue, nor is the number of victims. Human nature as such is at stake" (Arendt 1973, 458–59). For it is a question of building a new human being from whom every trait that cannot be subsumed under a universal law must be eradicated. Thanks, above all, to the concentration camps, what was once a pure abstraction of thought seems to have become reality. That hypostasis, which played the role of collective subject in the eighteenth- and nineteenth-century philosophies of history, ceased to be a fiction in Auschwitz. In the death camps, human beings, reduced to bare biological life, truly became mere interchangeable specimens of the species. This was achieved primarily through terror, which "by pressing men against each other," by destroying the space between them, "it substitutes for the boundaries and channels of communication between individual men a band of iron which holds them so tightly together that it is as although their plurality had disappeared into One Man of gigantic dimensions" (465–66).

If the analysis of terror as an accelerator of the realization of the laws of Nature and History refers polemically to the dialectical philosophies of history, the analysis of ideology and ideological mentality seems rather to contest the very dynamics of conceptual synthesis on which the whole edifice of metaphysics stands. Both the ideological formulations of the regime and the mind that accepts and integrates them work only on the basis of logical coherence. To avert the danger of the irruption of reality, ideologies "organize facts in an absolutely logical mechanism that starts from an axiomatically accepted premise, deducing everything else from it; thus proceeding with a coherence that does not exist at all in the realm of reality." By emancipating from experience and making itself independent from the possible changes caused by real facts, "ideological thought . . . insists on a 'truer' reality, which is hidden behind perceptible things, dominating all of them, and which can only be perceived by means of a sixth sense."

The "purely negative coercion of logic" (Arendt 1973, 469–70), which in the philosophical sphere has a counterpart in that principle of identity banishing contradictions, proves highly productive in erecting an imaginary and "more real" system, wherein reality, utterly homologated to ideology, is completely deprived of its elements of disturbance. The working of totalitarianism manipulates what is given—both ideally (propaganda) and operationally (concentration camps and terror)—to such an extent that it disappears in its subsumption under the basic idea of ideology. Whether the latter is the idea of the classless society or the idea of the superior race that must rule the earth, its dynamic consists of annihilating anything that might contradict the initial assumption. For these reasons, paradoxically, only in the hell of Auschwitz, the identity of Idea and Reality, of Being and Thought, on which metaphysics from Plato to Hegel has never ceased to insist, become tragically true (Forti 2006).

This is what Hannah Arendt seems to maintain—a conclusion that, although never fully explained, seems to emerge clearly if one reads the pages of "Ideology and Terror" in light of the author's last work, *The Life of the Mind* (Arendt [1978] 1981), and some important writings on Marx. In these texts on Marx—unpublished for a long time and put in writing shortly after *The Origins of Totalitarianism* in view of a book entitled *Totalitarian Elements in Marxism* (Arendt 2002, 1994)—the connection between the critique of Western philosophy and the investigation of totalitarianism is clear. On these pages, Hannah Arendt states that she wants to go in search of the "missing link between our unprecedented situation and some commonly accepted traditional categories of political thought." In short, if with Karl Marx "for the first time a thinker, rather than a practical statesman or politician, had inspired the policies of a great nation" (Arendt 2002, 274), and in this case of a totalitarian policy, the possible totalitarian elements present in that thought must be sought out. If some traits of Marxism become crucial in Stalin's work, the accusation of totalitarianism must, in fact, be addressed to all the political philosophy preceding Marxian philosophy. In fact, according to Arendt, "to accuse Marx of totalitarianism amounts to accusing the Western tradition itself of necessarily ending in the monstrosity of this novel form of government" (276). In addition, this is precisely because Marx, despite his rebellion against philosophy, remains conditioned by the set of categories of the very tradition he wanted to subvert. Hence, if Marx "cannot be adequately treaded without taking into account the great tradition of political and philosophical thought in which he himself still stood,"[4] then one of Arendt's tasks will consequently be to highlight which of the ideas of the tradition "precipitate" into Marx's philosophical heritage and, through him, even though not because of him, are "acted out" in totalitarianism.

For Marx was not the only one who interpreted political action in terms of *poiesis*, fabrication, or domination of the object by a subject who shaped and informed it. Plato and Hobbes preceded him by far. Neither was he the only one who conceived the idea of a collective Subject wherein individuals disappear and wherein the particularity of the present is sacrificed in view of a future goal. Rousseau's General Will and, above all, Hegel's Absolute Spirit are its illustrious predecessors. Nor is the conception of a historical process that, although human-made, responds to the call of the necessary dialectical movement originally Marxian.

The real novelty, potentially totalitarian—as one may deduce from Arendt's considerations—lies in having placed these same elements within an inverted theory-practice relation with respect to the traditional one. The Marxian primacy of praxis leads concretely, so to speak, to the totalizing dynamics of philosophical constructions that, before then, had never left the realm of pure theory. It is as if Marx, by wanting philosophy to be immediately practical, had made possible the passage from a purely philosophical negation to fully fledged practical elimination. In other words, if philosophy and, with it, political philosophy are built on the exclusion of contingency, finitude, and plurality—that is, those characteristics of the human condition and of any authentic politics—the extermination camps, instead, proceed to get rid of those aspects of reality that cannot be reduced to total uniformity effectively, to identify without difference: that uniformity and identity that can only be fully realized in death.

It is not a stretch to discern a notable Arendtian imprint in some more recent interpretations of totalitarianism, formulated by philosophers who are well known and discussed in France. I am referring to Philippe Lacoue-Labarthe, Jean-Luc Nancy, and, to some extent, Jean-François Lyotard, who continue Arendt's discourse, making it speak even when it is silent about its most radical conclusions. Even for them, totalitarianism is an absolutely new event that marks the end of Western metaphysics. Thus, the "hasty . . . and usually blind accusation of irrationality" (Lacoue-Labarthe and Nancy 1990, 294) sounds banal and suspicious when referring to totalitarianism.

In contrast, there is a totalitarian logic that cannot be separated from the general logic of rationality.

If Lacoue-Labarthe and Nancy identify in the extermination camps, and more precisely in the practice of the systematic annihilation of the Jews (where "Jews" is metonymically, as also in Lyotard, the name of all those who fall outside the racially or classically fixed parameters of humanity) the *quid* that makes totalitarianism irreducible to any political phenomenon of the past, this "obvious novelty" should not be dismissed as a "pathology" of reason; it is, rather, the "unveiled truth" that our political and philosophical tradition shielded. This is because, after all, "extermination is for the West the terrible revelation of its essence." And as Lacoue-Labarthe proposes elsewhere, "if it is true that the age is that of the accomplishment of nihilism, then it is at Auschwitz that [that] accomplishment took place in the purest formless form" (Lacoue-Labarthe 1990, 37). Nevertheless, if the laws and the moral standards to which mankind has adhered for two thousand years died at Auschwitz, then Nazism should be considered the event that marks the real historical caesura that one must confront.

Nazism is equivalent to what the Greeks called a sin of hubris: it becomes the bearer of "excess." Thus, totalitarianism embodies the meaning of "epochal discontinuity": the place where time is suspended because the very continuity of our tradition stops there. If, however, such continuity could be abruptly interrupted, it is because its own dynamics paradoxically became true. Lacoue-Labarthe and Nancy do not want to establish a direct derivation of Nazi or Stalinist ideology from philosophical thought; rather, they aim to stress the fact that twentieth-century ideologies benefited from concepts and categories that proved to be highly available for their use in totalitarian politics. Therefore, philosophy is not responsible; rather, responsibility falls on "the thought that puts itself deliberately (or confusedly, emotionally) at the service of an ideology behind which it hides, or from whose strength it profits" (Lacoue-Labarthe and Nancy, 295).

Having said this, it must be acknowledged that, above all, National Socialism represented the first time where what, until then, had remained a dream—the dream of the metaphysical tradition—was put into practice. It is the subject's claim to be the ultimate foundation and the sole master of reality as a whole. This claim—which brings with it the negation of the world, of its plurality and of its constituent contingency—manifests all its truly nihilistic potential only in the death camps. As Lacoue-Labarthe writes, the "mismeasure" and the "historical caesura" marked by Nazism lie in the fact that, in it, "the infinitization or absolutization of the subject, which is at the heart of the metaphysics of the Moderns, here finds its strictly operational outcome" (Lacoue-Labarthe 1990, 70). The desire to create, on the basis of the "idea," a community considered to be the product of the constructive work of men is inseparable from this metaphysical subjectivity and its political counterpart. The theme of the city, and subsequently of the state, as a work of art, as a product of human artifice, is therefore the motif that, starting with Plato, becomes the hegemonic discourse of Western political philosophy. The fact that, during the modern age, it is perfectly combined with the philosophy of history in the German tradition, almost as if it were its natural consequence, is decisive. From the teleological perspective of historical development, to put into operation, to build, the political community means to open oneself to the need to realize what the historical process carried *in nuce* within itself.

The absolutization of the subject; "projectuality" and "artificiality" reifying humankind as a whole; the cancellation of constitutive plurality and difference of the world; the processual perspective of the philosophies of history—these are the elements that such interpretations identify as those structural traits of metaphysics, abandoning their status as pure abstractions of thought to become "monstrously" concrete in National Socialism.

Alongside, or rather together with, a philosophical archaeology of totalitarianism, Lacoue-Labarthe also traces an "aesthetic" genealogy: "Racism—and anti-semitism in particular—is primarily, fundamentally, an aestheticism" (Lacoue-Labarthe 1990, 69). In fact, there is a precise specificity of the "Nazi myth," which is not reducible to the mythical contents that the regime reproposes. It has to do with the particular "will to art" harboring in German thought: "the Nazi myth . . . is the construction, the formation, and the production of the German people in, through, as a work of art" (Lacoue-Labarthe and Nancy 1990, 303). Politics would be linked to art but to that Platonic art which condemns imitation and considers the work of art a revelation of *physis* itself. Therefore, the political subject is a matter of conforming to an "original type" to affirm its own essence. This imitative, but at the same time identitarian, process is defined by Lacoue-Labarthe as "onto-typology."

It works in idealism, in many Romantic authors, later inherited by Nietzsche, and eventually continues to guide Heidegger's work. When they think about the historical destiny of the West and the role Germany played in it, all these authors are equally convinced that the German nation must attempt to realize the model of the "Greek beginning," which is to assert its own essence and come to full existence. This same "onto-typology" would continue to operate within National Socialism. It is obvious that, according to Nazi ideology, the *physis* that needs to be reshaped is the *bios* interpreted as race. The organicity to be achieved demands that anyone who is not a "form bearer" should be expelled. Jews, more than anyone else, represent the obstacle to the realization of the millennial dream of the city as a perfect work of art.

Even for Lyotard, Jews are not only a people who recognize themselves in a specific religion; they are the emblem of what prevents the concretization of the political community as such. Thus, being Jewish becomes the figure of an irreducibility, the figure, as Adorno would have said, of the nonidentical and the nonidentifiable. In this sense, for Lyotard, unjustly known only as an advocate of postmodernity, Jews are the sign of a wound and of an unrepresentable and constant openness toward it. In short, they are the figure of a "debt," of an irreducible negativity, which Western thought wanted to forget and set aside in many ways. Not by chance, the Jewish tradition does not "say" the Law; it only transmits the duty to listen to it.

Totalitarianism revealed the desire for the *forclusion*—the desire to expel something unbearable—underlying our tradition. This outlines the task of current philosophical reflection: to investigate that metaphysical thought that does not want to deal with "unpayable debts," with unhealable wounds—in other words, a thought that does not want to bear the burden of negativity. Nazism, as well as Stalinism and every violent and terrorist attempt to cement political society into the One, would then be the hyperbolic activation of the attempt "to unchain the soul from this obligation, to tear up the note of credit, to render debt-free forever" (Lyotard 1990, 84). Once interpreted philosophically, the totalitarian society becomes the construction of a political community that wants to fully realize its project of resistance "to the intractable," that wants to forget, by making it disappear, that restlessness of what does not conform and that always threatens to affect the "being-together" (Lyotard 1990, 1991).

Thus, Lyotard's antitotalitarian critique is aimed at every globalizing project, from the identity-based and unified city—built on the negation of "dissent," of "the Jews," "of the intractable"—to the great narratives telling the itinerary of abstract historical subjects wherein concrete individuals disappear. In short, the potentiality of totalitarianism is hidden in every globalizing plan fed by the need to neutralize differences, in every hegemony of the universal that rises at the expense of the singular.

Therefore, opposing totalitarianism also means safeguarding the event in its singularity. In fact, totalitarianism tears singularity away from uncertainty to dissolve it in the Universal of Nature and History. It is necessary to leverage the contradictions that these great narratives inevitably entail:

> The "philosophies of history" that inspired the Nineteenth and Twentieth Centuries claim to ensure the passage over the abyss of heterogeneity or the event. The names which are those of "our history" oppose counter-examples to their claim.—Everything real is rational, everything rational is real: "Auschwitz" refutes speculative doctrine. This crime at least, which is real, is not rational.—Everything proletarian is communist, everything communist is proletarian: "Berlin 1953, Budapest 1956, Czechoslovakia 1969, Poland 1980" (I could mention others) refute the doctrine of historical materialism: the workers rose up against the Party. . . .—Everything that is the free play of supply and demand is favorable for the general enrichment, and vice-versa: the "crises of 1911 and 1929" refute the doctrine of economic liberalism. . . . The passages promised by the great doctrinal syntheses end in bloody impasses. (Lyotard 1988, 179–80)

We can thus identify in Lyotard's reflections two forms of totalitarianism: political totalitarianism, in the strict sense, which has reached a precise institutional configuration in National Socialism and Stalinism, and so-called postmodern, postdemocratic totalitarianism, ruled by undisputed economic and mass media domination, wherein the West persists in living. It is a "soft" totalitarianism that, like the Adornian universe of the "cultural industry," operates through the systematic reduction of the other to the same, thereby deactivating otherness through a continuous process of inclusion and exclusion, homologation and rejection.

If a full-fledged political totalitarianism denies the singularity of the event by declaring it a useless accident to dismiss, the other type of totalitarian domination, without terror and without an overt ideology, dissolves it in the network of an unceasing globalization that, devoted to perpetual innovation, is focused only on profit, on trading, and on consumption.

DEMOCRACY AND TERROR

There have been, and still are, many interpretations that read the philosophical tradition in light of totalitarian catastrophes. They end up quite often being caught in the net of that same determinism, arrogant toward the singular, that they aim to fight. From the simplest interpretations to the most articulate ones abiding by historical contingency, they all entail a critical comparison between totalitarianism and the scenarios opened up by Western modernity and its peculiar rationalism. The problem of continuity or discontinuity between modern-age and totalitarian phenomena crosses the entire philosophical-political debate, which overlooks the differences between the two totalitarian ideologies. The interest shifts toward a unitary genealogy questioning, in particular, that way of conceiving history dating back to the Enlightenment. In short, they are convinced that, as far as Europe is concerned, it is possible to reconstruct a path that goes from the glorious hopes of the Enlightenment and dogmatic faith in the omnipotence of science to Marxist messianism and Nazi veterinary philosophy (Poliakov 1987).

From Jacob Talmon to François Furet (Talmon 1952; Furet 2000, 1981), a sequence of readings finds in the scenario opened up by the French Revolution the theoretical and practical antecedent of totalitarian revolutions. The role of a political mysticism combining the belief in the One Truth with the Virtue of political action is blamed: the revolutionary zeal that transforms the actors into those instruments of violence that are ready to resort to terror to achieve the Absolute. Thus, by claiming the monopoly of an actual "armed doctrine," the self-proclaimed democratic state can identify the will of its virtuous representatives with the will of a people who is never adequate to its own ideal image and that, therefore, leads the revolution to constantly postpone its goals, thereby establishing a transitory as well as salvific dictatorship.

If Jacob Talmon eventually succeeds in establishing some common characteristics among the various revolutions, he does not manage to circumscribe the specificity of totalitarian terror. In other words, according to him, a totalitarian project lies in a precise constellation of democratic doctrine that, supported by a radical egalitarianism and an unconscious "secularization" of the *parousia*, bestows the unstoppable force of historical necessity on the will of the people.

More recently, the historian Furet provides similar considerations. Indeed, by developing a reading more philosophical than historical, he continues Talmon's legacy. According to him, the original political scene from which the totalitarian dynamics of both communism and fascism arose is to be located in the French Revolution (Furet 1995). The events of 1789, no less than 1793, are the result of an ideological drive: that of the powerful and tyrannical supremacy of the Idea over reality, of an abstract and mythical messianic promise bearing the name of democracy. In addition, if Furet does not question the liberal-democratic outcomes of the bourgeois revolution—he rather clearly separates the "liberal" moment from the "Jacobin" moment—however, he considers the revolutionary fury and virtue, since "indispensable" to the translation of the democratic doctrine into action, as what truly anticipates totalitarian dynamics.

The democratic idea aims to shape historical reality so as to homologate it to True History. This is the theoretical and practical antecedent of communism-totalitarianism, both Leninist and Stalinist, which is configured precisely as an "illusion to power": that illusion, inherited from 1789 and 1793, blinds a bourgeoisie in perennial conflict with its own values, thereby pushing it toward the revolutionary and egalitarian step.

From these genealogies, which quite easily establish continuity theories between modern democracy and totalitarianism, through obviously that powerful intermediation of socialism and communism, we can then distinguish those interpretations—recently discussed—that, also thanks to the help of the social and political sciences, have taken on a greater theoretical complexity and that cannot in any way be traced back to conservative or "revisionist" positions and that cannot even be called liberal.

Claude Lefort's work is one of these. His work undoubtedly represents one of the most original and successful attempts to rethink the totalitarian phenomenon by combining philosophical reflection and political investigation. Especially in France, the so-called Gulag effect imposed on the heterodox left a new confrontation with Soviet reality, developing a review of the classical theories of totalitarianism. In 1948, Lefort gave life to the journal *Socialisme ou barbarie*, with Cornelius Castoriadis and Jean-François Lyotard. In those years, they aimed above all to critique Trockij's thesis contained in *The Betrayed Revolution*. In particular, Lefort, Castoriadis, and Lyotard contest the assumption that recognizes the "socialist foundations of the USSR"; they reject the identification of bureaucracy with a parasitic caste and do not ascribe totalitarianism to the methods of the "degenerate" bureaucratic class alone. Far from being explained as a "deviation" provoked by the Stalinist cult of personality, Soviet totalitarianism is neither a historical sequel to Bolshevism nor a phenomenon that can be dismissed as a simple "casteocracy." Already in those years, it was interpreted as "a totally social phenomenon" (Lefort 1986a), which is related to the historical emergence of a new form of society marked by an unprecedented mode of socialization that surreptitiously reintroduced social divisions behind the screen of their denial.

The closure of the project of *Socialisme ou barbarie* in 1965 traversed a different path to the problem of totalitarianism and society in general. While Lefort's criticism focused on the concepts of revolution and organization in the 1960s, in the 1970s, he had already matured his convictions on the nonderivative character of the political and on the impracticability of overcoming social conflict. The starting point of Lefort's research is that the social cannot be understood from itself; rather, it finds the "principles of its shaping" in a place that, in a certain sense, is external to it, transcendent: the place of power. This is how his repeated claim that the political is constitutive of the social should be understood.

This "discovery," which also matured thanks to Lefort's confrontation with the work of Machiavelli, whose fundamental contribution, according to Lefort, does not have to do with the Reason of State but with the existential and irreducibly conflictual character of politics (Lefort [1972] 2012). If classical politics considers discord as an evil originating in the dominion of passions over reason, Machiavelli discovers in the opposition of two antithetical desires—that of the "great" to dominate and that of the "people" to be free—the constitutive relationship of political and social space. In other words, political society is established only by virtue of its division (Lefort [1972] 2012, 299–303). Even more, it exists and is maintained only thanks to this division. In this way, Lefort can affirm that power bestows unity on society, even without putting an end to its insuperable separateness. The rationalistic dream of a society reconciled with itself and freed from conflict is, at best, an insubstantial utopia and, at worst, a project of death, the implementation of which entails the inevitable destruction of society as a whole.

From such a Machiavellian perspective, Lefort rethinks the opposition between democracy and totalitarianism, moving far beyond the frontal opposition proposed by liberal rationalism. Any definition of democracy in formal and procedural terms proves to be insufficient. For Lefort, it is not only a specific form of government but also, more radically, a form of socialization that recognizes the legitimacy of conflict within itself. Democracy presents itself as that form of society fostering the question that the social never ceases to pose to itself. In contrast, totalitarianism is defined as a mode of socialization fostering a powerful negation of conflict, thereby unleashing a logic of identity and total domination over reality. Therefore, the two societies correspond to different conceptions and institutions of the social, two different principles of "shaping."

As a manifestation of the diversity among the spheres, as an openness to otherness, as a proliferation of multiplicity, as a coexistence of heterogeneous passions, activities and temporalities, democracy cannot but remain faithful to a "radical indeterminacy" (Lefort 1986c, 237). The dynamics of democracy—namely, the continuous demand for a nonidentity with itself (and Lefort in some cases ends up speaking of "wild democracy")—can surely spawn antidemocratic movements. This is why totalitarianism constantly threatens democracies. For it conveys the promise of a positive, substantial, and complete configuration of society, both through the enhancement of a single national datum (for instance Nazism) and through the dream of abolishing class antagonisms (for instance Bolshevism).

Hence, Lefort reassesses his critique of totalitarian domination from the point of view of "democratic invention," no longer dwelling on the various betrayals or degenerations of Marxism and communism. Despite its archaic aspects, totalitarianism is, and can only be, a postdemocratic phenomenon that extends, in a new way, some dynamics implemented by modern democracy. In Lefort's view, "totalitarianism can be clarified only by grasping its relationship with democracy. It is from democracy that it arises, even though it has taken root initially, at least in its socialist version, in countries where the democratic transformation was only just beginning. It overturns that transformation, while at the same time taking over some of its features and extending them at the level of phantasy" (Lefort [1979] 1986b, 301–2).

Surely, returning to totalitarianism entails not only a return to the theory of political regimes but also a reconsideration of the symbolic meaning of power, of its capacity "to shape human coexistence" (Lefort [1981] 1988a). In this sense, the image of the totalitarian society is the "representation" of a united, indivisible body, which must be defended against external attacks. It is as if we were witnessing a return to the images of the Ancient

Regime, in which power was incorporated in a single figure, that of the sovereign. It was a "full" place, so to speak, inseparable from the concrete body of the king (Lefort [1983] 1988b) and from its direct reference to the transcendent source of principles that legitimize the social order. In democracy, however, the place of power is "an empty place," "unrepresentable," which refers to that "emptiness" that is even more essential than the absence of the legitimating source. Power is also "unrepresentable" in the sense that its holders cannot be confused with it unless they put an end to democracy. In a democratic society, there must be an insurmountable gap between the symbolic and the real.

Like democracy, totalitarianism is a purely human society. It does not receive its order from a transcendent source but legitimizes itself on its own initiative. This is why totalitarianism cannot be confused with the ancient forms of despotism and tyranny. Unlike democracy, however, it seeks to fill the empty place of power; it strives to recompose, by eliminating the gap between the real and the symbolic, the sovereign body of the democratic people, which must be presented as united through a well-defined identity. In fact, in totalitarianism, identity and unity are inseparable: it is through the common identity that society establishes itself as one.

But it is the need for unity that grounds the obligation for each person to participate in this identity. In short, totalitarianism finds a place in the power vacuum produced by the democratic era: it uses the democratic representation of the sovereignty of the people, but while appropriating the latter, it dissolves it into the inarticulate reality of the figure of the People-as-One. The undefined figure of the citizen is replaced by that of the proletarian or the Aryan. By closing in on itself, totalitarian society takes care of its substantial identity, its integrity, and its purity. By erecting a deferred imaginary, it can project onto it any otherness threatening the negation of division. Thus, the entire totalitarian edifice rests on the phantom of a society that would overcome its internal divisions, in which every difference is bent to the need to produce unity or, rather, the appearance of unity. They will thus always be functional in the construction of the unitary body the "little men in excess" who, like Soljénitsyne, disturb, but at the same time feed, the logic of a "society without division, of a People-One," of a perfectly rational and true Knowledge" (Lefort 1976, 88–89).

Nevertheless, totalitarian society has been and continues to be troubled by the democratic revolution. To impose the separation of the "People-

One" requires the mediation of a power that detaches itself from society and forces it to merge into the image of the proletarian or Aryan people. Paradox par excellence, the indivisibility of society entails a radical division of power from society: the existence of a separate place of power as a necessary condition of the constitution of the People-One. The dynamic established by the fiction of unity is implacable: the more power proclaims the indivision of society, the more it must radicalize its separation from society to shape it from the outside. At the same time, it must also deny such a separation by affirming that it is nothing but the head of this society, of this organic totality of the One-Body. Thus, the logic of the negation of internal division leads to the logic of concentration, by virtue of which the party is the totality of the people, the proletariat is the people, the party is the proletariat, the political bureaucracy is the party, and, finally, the egocrates is the political bureaucracy, that is, the people as a whole. The representation of the People-as-One can only be that of the besieged citadel. The body can keep itself intact only at the price of the production, and of the consequent liquidation, of an enemy that threatens, like a parasite or a bacterial infection, the health of the social body.

The "totalitarian reincorporation of power" goes hand in hand with a coagulation and an emptying of the poles of law and knowledge—as if the fury of the indistinction of the One could not maintain any difference between the spheres. If it is true that there is no society without reference to the pole of power, the pole of law, and the pole of knowledge, then, insofar as it denies the articulation differentiating them, totalitarianism endangers the very existence of the social or, rather, of political society and its specific spheres (Lefort [1979] 1986b).

Unlike the static opposition between democracy and totalitarianism, in Lefort the real opposition is between "democratic invention" and "totalitarian domination" or, rather, between the latter and "that democratic revolution" sustained by a continuous questioning by democracy of its own presuppositions and that betrays itself at the moment in which it is definitively structured in a political system.

It is not a question of opposing democracy, as a political regime grounded on self-identity, to totalitarianism, as a political monster that would assume the value of a "countertype." There is no wall, either juridical, institutional, or even philosophical-cultural, that separates democracy from the totalitarian system. In contrast, far from being that monster who threatens democracy from the outside totalitarianism is the unwelcome guest that keeps on knocking at its door. It is an extreme response to the questions that political modernity poses and cannot resolve. Hence, totalitarianism is not only a modern experience, but it is, and can only be, a possible outcome of democracy. It is a form of society that reacts to the constitutive weakness of the "democratic invention," to its indeterminacy, to its openness to the void, to the event, to what is not yet, in a word, to freedom.

Marcel Gauchet's interpretations lie in the wake of these reflections. But he is also committed to thinking about "the phenomenon that dominates our century" in connection with both the birth of modern bourgeois society and Marx's thought. Fascism—a category that here refers to all right-wing totalitarianisms—would theoretically originate in bourgeois ideology, understood as the attempt to mask social division by denying the dimension of conflict connected to capital. Marx would contest this, stressing instead the need to think of the social starting from its division and to restore the value of conflict.

But Marxian thought proves contradictory, as it again ends up designing an undivided, homogeneous society freed from its internal antagonisms. "For in Marx," Gauchet argues, "it is not the real question of the conflict that is at stake . . . since this question is considered resolvable at the very moment it is posed" (Gauchet 1976, 5). According to Marxian thought, establishing the role of the class struggle in history means determining, at the same time, the necessity of its abolition. Therefore, the question of communism is the question of the possibility of "building" a society without antagonism: communism as society identical to itself and One. The construction of the totalitarian regime rests on such assumptions: the necessity of a society without division—a postulate derived from Marx.

This is why it is possible to talk about the comparability of fascism and communism, why it is not only legitimate but also hermeneutically useful to place both of them in the category of totalitarianism, as they similarly affirm the "identity of society with itself." Starting from the rejection of conflict, fascist regimes and communist society move forward step by step, united in the desire for unity and identity of society with itself, both in the form of a single political will and in the form of the convergence of the interests and aspirations of all social agents.

Moreover, for Gauchet, "it is worth risking the hypothesis" of a Bolshevik Revolution that in 1917 would have freed the totalitarian potential of bourgeois ideology to bring about the realization of the "reconciled society" (11–12). What bourgeois ideology and Marx's doctrine simply affirmed, fascism and communism want it to be, thereby making the one and homogeneous society move from the realm of pure thought to reality. In addition, to bend reality to an idea that denies it in its contingency involves extraordinary violence. Totalitarianism would be exactly that: "illusion made compulsion."

Like Lefort, Cornelius Castoriadis will also keep the problem of totalitarianism at the center of his research in all its different phases. When he broke with Marxism in the 1960s, he continued his work of philosophical-political deconstruction of totalitarianism without renouncing his political commitment "from the left." In those years, he agrees with Lefort in defining the essence of totalitarian ideology as a "revolutionary will to unification and to social transparency" and to identify at the heart of ideology the meeting point of two different vectors: on the one hand, the theorization of the perfect rationality of historical events; on the other hand, the need to achieve this rationality through the active will of human beings. It goes without saying that if truth is one and knowable, there is no reason to tolerate error. Therefore, power must be total, and every libertarian and democratic claim is only a sign of human weakness and fallibility (Castoriadis 1975, 315–39).

In *Devant la guerre* (1981), Castoriadis questioned his own earlier positions that made Soviet totalitarianism an "ideocracy" (see also Castoriadis 1986). The phase of classical totalitarianism was to be succeeded by the epoch of a new totalitarianism, which he now refers to as a "statocracy." Ideology would no longer be the sole determining and homologating source of any individual or collective behavior but an instrumental appendage, rhetorically and cynically flaunted. In its first phase, totalitarianism referred to a specific metaphysical foundation expressing itself in the will to create "the new man." Power was embodied in a party, and Stalin was the sole representative of the totality and of the party as a whole. Despite the use of terror against the majority of the population, despite the enormous material deprivation that devastated daily life, there was a total and committed adherence to the ideas propagated by the ideology of the regime. An "ideocratic" totalitarianism prevailed, mobilizing the present in view of the future of the whole society.

From the will to realize the new society and the new man, we would have moved to a purely military image of the world, which is built on mere relations of force: "a military society wherein the excesses of terror have given way to a simple administration of repression." The result would be a "statocracy," in which every project of society to be realized is replaced by "brute force for brute force . . . force in the service of nothing" (Castoriadis 1981, 289).[5] Not only would an ideology, an "ideocracy," no longer be in power, but there would no longer be any ideas at all: in this way, "the most complete divestiture" would take place. In post-Stalinist totalitarianism, where the idolatry of power relations stands out, the destruction of language goes hand in hand with the destruction of meaning and beauty. This is not simply the "new man" of the first ideological phase of communism but a sort of homunculus without qualities and without desires recalling Zinoviev's *homo sovieticus* and Heller's ant man.

In describing the passage from "ideocracy" to "statocracy," Castoriadis takes into account the debate on totalitarianism and post-totalitarianism that we saw beginning in the 1970s among Eastern European dissidents. He, however, compares himself especially with a Heideggerian analysis of fulfilled nihilism. Hence, the critique of every unitary ontology, insofar as every ontology has in itself a political root, and every politics is linked to certain ontological presuppositions. Even though he agrees with Habermas in holding firm to a political-emancipatory horizon and in seeking a new form of praxis freed from the constraints of techne, with this ontological questioning, Castoriadis proves to be, much more than Lefort, close to Heidegger's thought.

If classical totalitarian domination corresponds with a subjectivist and historicist metaphysics, with its desire to make rationalist constructivism and historical necessity march together, post-totalitarianism seems to correspond to the ultimate epoch of metaphysics. This is fully realized in the "will to will" expressed in the "planetary" dimension of technology. If, until Nietzsche, the will to power was exercised as the "will to something," with the latter, who marks the transition between the nineteenth and twentieth centuries, the will no longer turns to an end but only to itself, thus becoming the "will to will." The becoming world of this latest figure of metaphysics is technique, understood in a broad sense as purely instrumental rationality, for which every end is but a means.

In a world in which all autonomy of ends has disappeared and where the only goal is the increase of domination for the sake of domination, the loss of meaning and the planetary proliferation of conflicts are inseparable. In short,

Castoriadis identifies in the statocratic USSR, and no longer in the ideocratic one, the paroxysmal fulfillment of a metaphysical conception of the world that leads to the "will to will" as an unprecedented form of planetary imperialism. On an institutional level, all this implies a reversal of the respective positions occupied by the army and the party. Where the party used to stand, now the Russian army stands; that is the sole foundation of the party's power. In such conditions, the possibility of a new kind of war opens up, a war that has no more goals but to affirm itself: the war of accomplished nihilism.

Even for Foucault, the totalitarian catastrophe is located in light of that enlightenment, which has transmitted to us the democratic universal subjects such as Man, the Nation, and History. It is true that Foucault is commonly acknowledged as the inventor of the classic formula according to which "power is everywhere"—a power that not only intersects the different social, linguistic, religious, and political spheres but also crosses various ages and different institutional experiences. But he is also the careful genealogist who knows how to trace, on a background of persistent continuity, the emergence of differences marking the leaps and bounds between various epochal hegemonies. Thus, if relations of power and knowledge characterize the development of Western modernity, there are specific modes of production and "regionalization" of these knowledge-powers that bring about modifications within the modes of subjection.

What is surprising in his thought is, on the one hand, the almost total absence of explicit references to totalitarianism and, on the other hand, an almost obsessive omnipresence of total domination. It is as if all Foucault's analyses converged in a unitary archaeology that strives to bring to light the *raisons d'être* of Auschwitz and of Kolyma, as if Foucault's texts had no other goal than to bring our attention to the catastrophes of modernity.

Even so, one of his courses given at the Collège de France in 1976–77, entitled *Society Must Be Defended*, contains Foucault's most direct confrontation with totalitarianism. Here, Foucault intends to reconstruct "the birth of state racism," emphasizing the overturning that occurs in the relations of power with the birth of modern states. As he points out, in the era of classical statehood, "the right of life and death was one of sovereignty's basic attributes" (Foucault 2003, 240). But this form of power, as the right of life and death, is basically exercised "on the side of death."

In the nineteenth century, a new technology of power emerges: "the emergence . . . of biopower, of the technology of power over 'the' population as such, over men insofar as they are living beings. It is continuous, scientific, and it is the power to make live. Sovereignty took life and let live. In addition, now we have the emergence of a power that I would call the power of regularization, and it, in contrast, consists in making live and letting die" (247).

It is precisely the birth of biopolitics, inseparable from the development of human sciences, of that new form of knowledge that makes the human being an object of investigation. From here on, politics turns to the human being as a living being, as a biological body, and to humankind as a "global mass," determined by those processes that are typical of biological life: birth, death, reproduction, and disease. Far from focusing exclusively on discipline, with the entry of bare life into the field of visibility of politics, power is carried out under the banner of "optimization," of the "maximization" of the biological. It is not simply a matter of ensuring a firm grip on individual bodies and on the collective body of a population. It is not simply a matter of watching over them. It is not simply a matter of making them functional and of conforming them to the rational rules of the new productive apparatus and the norms of the new social rationality. Much more generally, it is a matter of "investing life from side to side"—that is, taking charge of the process of birth, mortality and longevity.

In short, "From the eighteenth century onward (or at least the end of the eighteenth century onward) we have, then, two technologies of power which were established at different times and which were superimposed" (Foucault 2003, 249). On the one hand, there stands a disciplinary technique that produces individualizing effects by focusing on the body, manipulating it as the center of forces that must be made both useful and docile. On the other hand, there is a technology focused not on the body but on biological life; it is "a technology which brings together the mass effects characteristic of a population, which tries to control the series of random events that can occur in a living mass" (249). The state becomes the manager of the population through practices such as medicalization and assistance. Power, now coextensive with the entire social surface, presents, as never before, a reticular and capillary form preventing the possibility of tracing the point of crystallization to identify the source, as was possible for the classical figure of sovereignty.

Late modernity witnesses a particular reconfiguration of the relations of power. Biopower is distinguished from classical state sovereignty by its encompassing character, which addresses the "productivity" of life, thereby pushing the concern for death to its margins. According to Foucault, the decisive turning point occurs when biopower inscribes racism in the mechanisms of the state. Here is where Foucault's analysis unintentionally crosses Arendt's investigations, especially those contained in the "Imperialization" section of *The Origins of Totalitarianism*: "It is . . . at this point," Foucault writes, "that racism intervenes. . . . It had already been in existence for a very long time. However, I think it functioned elsewhere. It is indeed the emergence of this biopower that inscribes it in the mechanisms of the State. It is at this moment that racism is inscribed as the basic mechanism of power, as it is exercised in modern States. As a result, the modern State can scarcely function without becoming involved with racism at some point, within certain limits and subject to certain conditions" (254). This is because racism especially represents the way in which, within the framework of that power that has taken over life, it becomes possible to separate what is to live and what is to die.

Through racism, power can treat a population as a mixture of races and can subdivide the species into subgroups. In short, it can fragment, arrange into a hierarchy, and establish breaks within a biological continuum, which has become its new object. It can also put into operation, in a completely new and "biological" way, a warlike relation: "'If you want to live, the other must die. . . . The more inferior species die out, the more abnormal individuals are eliminated, the fewer degenerates there will be in the species as a whole, and the more I—as species rather than individual—can live, the stronger I will be, the more vigorous I will be. I will be able to proliferate'" (255). In other words, death, or rather putting to death, is admissible within biopolitics not if it tends toward victory over the adversaries but if it pursues the elimination of the biological danger—if, therefore, it aims at strengthening the species or race. "In a normalizing society, race or racism is the precondition that makes killing acceptable. . . . Once the State functions in the biopower mode, racism alone can justify the murderous function of the State" (256; see also Ternon 1995; Dumont 1995). Far from being the expression of a simple mutual hatred between races, but also irreducible to a political operation that would like to channel into a mythical opponent the hostilities that run through the social body, the specificity of modern racism is linked to a technique of power, not so much to an ideological content. "So racism is bound up with the workings of a State that is obliged to use race, the elimination of races and the purification of the race, to exercise its sovereign power" (Foucault 2003, 258).

In Foucault's perspective, therefore, Nazism and "state socialism" have become the paroxysmal development of the mechanisms of biopower, well established since the eighteenth century. Disciplinary power and biopower: all of this ran through and sustained Nazi society to the extreme. "No society could be more disciplinary or more concerned with providing insurance than that established, or at least planned, by the Nazis. . . . However, this society in which insurance and reassurance were universal, this universally disciplinary and regulatory society, was also a society which unleashed murderous power, or in other words, the old sovereign right to take life" (Foucault 2003, 259). But both the state leadership and, somehow, the whole of society are involved in this overregulatory power. Indeed, the practice of denunciation potentially endows anyone with the power of life and death.

The originality of Nazism consists of the fact that it made the two powers, which had never before been so completely overlapping, absolutely coextensive: the sovereign power to kill—to the extreme of anyone being able to kill anyone—and the biopower that cultivates, protects, and organizes life:

> There was, in Nazism, a coincidence between a generalized biopower and a dictatorship that was at once absolute and retransmitted throughout the entire social body by this fantastic extension of the right to kill and of exposure to death. We have an absolutely racist State, an absolutely murderous State, and an absolutely suicidal State. A racist state, a murderous state, and a suicidal state. The three were necessarily superimposed, and the result was of course both the "final solution" (or the attempt to eliminate, by eliminating the Jews, all the other races of which the Jews were both the symbol and the manifestation) of the years 1942–1943, and then Telegram 71, in which, in April 1945, Hitler gave the order to destroy the German people's own living conditions.
>
> The final solution for the other races, and the absolute suicide of the [German] race. That is where this mechanism inscribed in the workings of the modern State leads. (260)

Here is where Foucault's analyses become relevant for a theory of totalitarianism, even if sui generis (see also Brossat 1996; Agamben 1998, 1999).

Foucault does not claim that only Nazism adopted the extreme logic of biopolitics as the extremization of a bourgeois capitalist statehood. In a rhetorically dubious way, but actually without the slightest reservation, he does not hesitate to say that the socialist state and socialism in general are also "racist."

Because racism is not a doctrine, it is not an ideological content but the discourse that the circuit of power pronounces to trigger itself. It is the ignition of a device of forces that must produce identity functionality and eliminate the obstacles, real or presumed, of an otherness, often constructed ad hoc. "Socialism has made no critique of the theme of biopower, which developed at the end of the eighteenth century and throughout the nineteenth; it has in fact taken it up, developed, reimplanted, and modified it in certain respects, but it has certainly not reexamined its basis or its modes of working" (Foucault 2003, 261). Whether it wanted to eliminate the state or to strengthen it to better bring it down, socialism has never questioned the conditions of biopower. Thus, not an ethnic racism but an evolutionary racism—which distinguishes between the normal and the mentally ill, between revolutionaries and saboteurs, and which, in any case, works at full capacity in discriminating between those who must die and those who must live—has organized the total management of biological life. "Whenever a socialism insists, basically, that the transformation of economic conditions is the precondition for the transformation, for the transition from the capitalist State to the socialist State (or in other words, whenever it tries to explain the transformation in terms of economic processes), it does not need, or at least not in the immediate, racism" (262). Whenever, instead, socialism is forced to stress the problem of struggle, the struggle against the enemy, the elimination of the enemy within capitalist society itself, "racism does raise its head," because it is the only way in which socialist thought, "which is after all very much bound up with the themes of biopower" (262), can rationalize the murder of its enemies.

Hence, Nazism and socialism are assimilated once again and certainly not in an author who cherishes the glorious and postwar liberal triumph of the Westernization of the world, but in the perhaps more acute, certainly more merciless, critic of those mechanisms of power that cannot be dismissed either as a reflection of structural relations or as a product of the oppression of state apparatuses on individuals.

In the midst of a widespread, capillary, mostly unbreakable power, totalitarianism manages to draw its own original profile. Totalitarianism, in the Foucauldian interpretation, is the paradox of a society that for the first time manages to combine war, murder, the function of putting to death, and the protection of life, with an intensity and capillarity never seen before. Foucault teaches us that power, and even more so the total domination of "state racism," is not just something that looms over us from above, preventing us from participating at every level. Rather, it is also something that lives with us, in our lives and "in our flesh," that bends us to the docility of voluntary servitude.

These readings surely refer to the problem of an "unscrupulous" and "slack" use of the concept of totalitarianism. Especially in Lyotard and Foucault but also in Horkheimer, Adorno, Nancy, Lacoue-Labarthe, and in some ways even in Arendt, are the "final solution" and the Gulag truly processed as a break, as a point of no return? Or, despite the declarations of intent, are they rather "acquitted" as terminal moments of a process that has always been "guilty"? Auschwitz, as a unique and singular event, runs the risk of finding itself de facto reuniversalized through formulas that see the Jews as the paradigm of the West's annihilating passion. In other words, the Shoah, like the trials in Moscow, are always on the verge of being reduced to the condition of mere symptoms.

We must therefore be vigilant in the face of the danger of immersing the particularity of an event in an analysis that makes Plato's *Republic*, the goddess Reason, and biopower interact on the level of ideas. In other words, the continuistic excesses of these philosophical operations can certainly offend the memory of those who died in a gas chamber and who, by their misfortune, did not simply suffer the "offenses" of a life busy with work and consumption or the vulgarity and invasion of the cultural industry. For the social sciences, for political science, and for history, which constantly want to teach us that reality is more complex than the "universe of domination," that totalitarian regimes are not the realization of a metaphysical hypothesis, philosophical interpretations of totalitarianism are tainted by determinism and teleologism, are vague and inconclusive, and, because of their lack of rigor, prove to be irrational and therefore irresponsible.

This accusation commits an injustice. One should not talk of irrational and irresponsible readings but of investigations that, driven also and above all by ethical imperatives, as well as by a desire for understanding, react in the face of the paradoxicality of a phenomenon that can never be fully explained with the simple attitude of analytical clarification. Sure, they pay the price for the contradictions and aporias that deconstructive undertakings always entail: a philosophical investigation into the risks of philosophical reason; an unavoidable conceptual analysis to deconstruct the logic of the concept; the need to dismantle the metaphysical assumptions of politics; and the impossibility of dictating new principles for a new political order.

But if philosophy is aware of its insuperable limits, of the vicious circles in which it inevitably gets caught up, then we must take up its challenge, the challenge of the radical nature of its questioning—a challenge that is implicit in any thought that is not limited to the acquisition of knowledge, a challenge entailing the risk of "genealogical" continuity, of depths into which advances can sink, in brief, the risk of stumbling into those old Hegelian errors from which philosophy has been trying to escape for more than a century. Indeed, philosophical-political analysis is still essential if we are to be able to recognize in totalitarianism those tragic events, contingent and not accidental at the same time, which also call into question the structures of our tradition of thought. Only the radicality of a philosophical reflection can make us admit that total domination—however much it is conceived in continuity with nihilism, dialectical reason, revolution, democracy, and the state—has shattered, or should shatter, all the traditional parameters of criticism, something that forces, or should force, us to reread our history of civilization with new eyes.

By doing so, philosophical interpretations impose on us the urgency of safeguarding certain spaces of freedom, of removing reflection from the grip of a thought that is increasingly being asked to become univocal and productive, functional and instrumental. After all, what is that singularity invoked by Arendt and Nancy, a singularity that must be safeguarded, protected from a totalitarian threat that is always lurking? Which must be preserved, to use Arendt's words, in its uniqueness and in its constitutively plural presence? What does that "intractable" of Lyotard indicate that, like Adorno's "nonidentical," or Levinas's "Other," resists being part, instrument, moment of a logical or dialectical system?

They all indicate a point of resistance. It is no longer possible to appeal to the heroic individual, to the True Citizen who opposes power; however, it is still possible to claim the "poverty of existence" against the system, the impossible yet necessary autonomy of reflection against the reasons of history.

The philosophy of Foucault, Lyotard, Nancy, Arendt, and in a certain sense Adorno, Lefort, Patočka, Levinas, and Weil—as well as all those who have experienced the failure of great narratives and collective subjects and who have gravely and acutely thought through the dialectic of the impotence and omnipotence of reason—fights totalitarian domination from the suspended place of a thought that ethically places itself as "minimal resistance to every totalitarianism" (Lyotard 1992, 96).

THE CONCRETE POSSIBILITY OF TOTAL NIHILISM: GÜNTHER ANDERS AND THE ATOMIC BOMB

One author, more than any other, bridges the philosophical reflections on totalitarianism of the late twentieth century with those from the first two decades of the twenty-first: Günther Anders. Still grounded in the living memory of the totalitarian regimes of the 1900s, Anders is well aware that in the present and future, the risks of total domination will come in different guises. In a sense, those regimes should be "obsolete, now." In them, the will-to-nothingness was only partially expressed. Our hypertechnological societies, in his view, are instead enacting the "nihilistic promises" of the 1930s and 1940s. Only with the integral interweaving of advanced technologies, control, and destruction can totalitarianism be fully realized together with nihilism, its twin. It is our "atomic condition," which transforms the whole planet into a borderless concentration camp, that is the true totalitarianism. Torn between a Heideggerian-style apocalyptic rhetoric and a lucid confrontation with the specific objects of technological innovation, Anders seems to anticipate by decades the considerations I will discuss in the next chapter, on the hypercontrolled society.

In the coincidence of apparatus and world, the totalitarian aspiration of technology is realized to extinguish and absorb into itself every "outside," to "incorporate everything" and "unite in itself all thinkable functions, to assign to all existing things their own function, to integrate into itself, as its own functionaries, all men born within its sphere" (Anders 1980, 111). "Soft" totalitarianism no longer needs, like that of the mid-twentieth century, the systematic and brutal use of violence, since it obtains automatic and unconditional obedience by virtue of the effectiveness and efficiency of its imperceptible—and therefore more insidious—homologation device. The predatory voraciousness of technology and its need to expand endangers the very survival of the species and the entire living being. If, in fact, *homo faber*, understood in the traditional sense, had limited himself to employing portions of the world to create his own, then technique, in the age of its triumph, makes the world in its totality the instrument of its unrestrained growth. It obeys the imperative command to do everything that can be done and to complete every intended use of the product. It matters little if it involves tools, such as the atomic bomb, capable of annihilating humankind. Thus, technology is indifferent not only to the final destination of its products but also to their moral value. That is why it does not hesitate to unleash, without any scruples, its destructive potential.

It is indeed bizarre that a thinker like Anders, so attuned to the most burning problems of our present, has received so little attention in the Anglo-Saxon world. Let us therefore proceed to present, albeit too briefly, some features of his thought that are decisive for our discourse and for what is happening around us.

There is a painting by Paul Klee called *Angelus Novus*. An angel is depicted there who looks as if he is about to distance himself from something that he is staring at. His eyes are opened wide, his mouth stands open, and his wings are outstretched. His face is turned toward the past. Where we see the appearance of a chain of events, he sees one single catastrophe, which unceasingly piles rubble on top of rubble and hurls it before his feet. He would like to pause for a moment so fair, to awaken the dead and to piece together what has been smashed. But a storm is blowing from Paradise; it has caught itself up in his wings and is so strong that the angel can no longer close them. The storm drives him irresistibly into the future, to which his back is turned, while the rubble-heap before him grows sky-high. That which we call progress is this storm (Benjamin 2005).

This is the well-known ninth thesis of *On the Concept of History*, the last book Walter Benjamin wrote in 1940, a few months before committing suicide. Perhaps no philosophy complies with Klee's painting as much as Günther Siegmund Stern's, a.k.a. Günther Anders. Anders was born in Breslau (Poland) on July 12, 1902. Because of his Jewish origins, in 1933, he fled into exile in Paris with his wife, Hannah Arendt, whom he would divorce in 1937. With the worsening of antisemitic persecution in German-occupied Europe, in 1936, he eventually fled to the United States, first to New York and then to Los Angeles. The Frankfurt School considers him an outsider, "excessively Heideggerian," and Heidegger's disciples, with whom he studied, will always accuse him of being excessively focused on current events. In 1950, Anders left the United States but did not return to Germany, the land that rejected him and forced him into exile to escape certain death. He eventually settled down in Vienna (Austria), where he died in 1992.

In German, *anders* means "otherwise," "differently": Günther Stern wanted to be "different," to "think otherwise." Different from whom and what? First, from a certain professionalism that affects academic philosophy. As a disciple of Husserl and Heidegger during his studies in Freiburg, Anders contests the "esoteric" character of a philosophy accessible only for a few chosen ones. Against such an "initiated" academic philosophy, Anders will always present himself as an "occasional philosopher" who practices philosophy by combining metaphysics and journalism. He even refused a university chair in Germany, preferring instead to be a militant intellectual whose activity lies on the edge between theory and praxis. In 1958, Anders went to Hiroshima and Nagasaki to take part in the fourth international congress against bombs A and H. This is the period where he writes *The Man on the Bridge: Diary from Hiroshima and Nagasaki* (1959), and began a correspondence with Claude Eatherly, the pilot who authorized, at President Truman's orders, the dropping of the atomic bomb on Hiroshima. Later, Anders would support the opposition to the Vietnam War, take part as jury member in the Russell Tribunal, join the first big ecologist conferences, and commit to many other political initiatives.

Anders never wrote a fully fledged treatise; he did, however, author many essays, various thoughts, aphorisms, diaries, short stories, and letters. His main work, the two volumes of *Die Antiquiertheit des Menschen* [The obsolescence of man] (1961 and 1980, respectively), is indeed a collection of occasional essays (covering a forty-year period) that together attempt to define "philosophical anthropology in the epoch of technocracy" (Anders 1980, 9).[6] Inaugurated in 1929 by *Pathology of Freedom: An Essay on Nonidentification* (Anders 2009), Anders's negative philosophical anthropology lies in the wake of that German anthropological philosophy (read Gehlen and Plessner) according to which "the proper" of human beings consists of lacking a constitutive *proper* that can be defined once and for all. In other words, as Anders writes, "the fact of not being fixed on any a priori material world, of not being settled on any world, of not having any foreseen determination, thus of being indeterminate, defines man essentially (Anders 2009, 286).

The human condition is affected by uprooting and contingency; by the "shame of the origin" (Anders 2009, 288). Because a human being's position in the world is qualified by a defect, a human being does not belong to any predetermined world. Unlike nonhuman animals, whose instincts provide them with a certain stability, human beings are unstable and lack a specific behavior. Obviously, behind Anders's negative anthropology, there stands a Heideggerian notion of being-in-the-world as human beings' nonidentification with their very self. This is why Anders understands human freedom as a pathology: since the proper of human nature is the lack of a nature, human beings are led to turn to artificiality to bridge the poverty of their biology.

In their search for freedom as indetermination, human beings are always found to be unfree, constantly exposed to what Anders names the "shock of the contingent." Human beings discover their structural uprooting, their ontological difference in relation to the world, or even their awareness of constituting an excess. According to Anders, such an anthropological condition is exemplified by writers such as Rilke, Doeblin, and, especially, Kafka, who masterfully depicted the condition of being a pariah, the impossibility of feeling at home in the world. Surely, Anders's Jewish origins amply influenced the anthropology of the nonbelonging—in summary, a philosophical anthropology for human beings lacking a world.

Like Hannah Arendt, for Anders the figure of the Jew represents the diasporic condition of humankind, whose insurmountable feeling of nonbelonging is accompanied by messianism—in Derrida's world, a messianism without the Messiah (Derrida 1994, 74). As Anders writes in his 1978 essay "Mein Judentum" (My Jewishness):

> For many years, I have lived in the wait of the "not-yet" for the messianic to be established. However, on August 6th 1945, the shocking day of Hiroshima, I realized that, perhaps, not to say probably, we were all heading toward a "no-longer." This was the end of messianism. I have always tried to make Ernst Bloch "comprehend" Hiroshima, but he always refused to know. For he clearly lacks either the flexibility or the strength to carry out with me such a "Copernican revolution" from the "not-yet" to the "no-longer." We were not on the same page as he was incapable of accepting what is our current condition: to live hopelessly. (Anders 1984)

For Anders, 1945 marks a point of no return, as well as a turning point for his reflection and writing. His philosophical anthropology radicalizes further, becoming the abyssal thought of a "world without human beings." To put it differently, Anders abandons what Ernst Bloch would call "the principle of hope"[7] to embrace "the principle of despair" that afflicts the frightened sight of Klee's angel of history (Portinaro 2003).

Four breaking historical events make Anders move from a negative philosophical anthropology to a thought of "the catastrophe without redemption," of "apocalypse without Reign": the First World War and its horrors; Hitler's rise to power and the Second World War; the discovery of Nazi extermination camps; and the atomic bombings of Hiroshima and Nagasaki. The latter definitely persuaded him that a new age had begun.

According to Anders, neither philosophical anthropology, even when negative, nor the "philosophies of technology" that characterized the first half of the twentieth century are sufficient to comprehend such a new age. Anders's view was undoubtedly influenced by the "philosophies of technology" of authors such as Splenger, Benjamin, Adorno, Jünger, Jonas, and Heidegger, to list the best-known. In such authors, the philosophical reflection on technology becomes a fully fledged metaphysical question. As Heidegger claims, to think of technology is not something technical. Surely, for Anders, Heidegger was the most influential figure. Consider the 1953 conference *The Question Concerning Technology*, where Heidegger proposed that Western metaphysics is responsible for technology, as it has always identified being with the totality of beings (Heidegger 1977). For Heidegger—and Anders adheres to such conviction—technology transforms a living and vital whole in a rigid and deathly organization; technology violently devastates everything that falls under its grip. Nevertheless, Anders becomes more radical than Heidegger, and this is why, for him, the philosophies of technology became useless. The products of technological progress not only alienate human beings from their world, from their existence, but they also open up the unprecedented possibility of the complete destruction of the world and humankind.

According to Anders, the inadequacy, not to mention the "obsolescence" (Anders 1980, 128–30), of philosophical anthropology and the philosophy of technology is due to their stubborn and anachronistic anthropocentrism. They still bestow a central position in the world on human beings. As Anders claims in the second volume of *Die Antiquiertheit des Menschen*:

> Heidegger, the last person who asked about the meaning of man, was still an heir of Old Testament anthropomorphism, for he had judged the romantically arrogant role from the ontological point of view of the shepherd of Being. His thesis, a century after the appearance of *The Origin of Species*, represents the epitome of anti-naturalism in modern-day nonreligious philosophy. Evidently, man, if he is an ontological shepherd, does not belong to the flock of beings; that is, he does not belong to nature. Of course, this is just inoffensive and metaphysically comical. What is dangerous and fearsome, however, is the metaphysics of industrialism, which likewise is based on Genesis, which conferred upon man the "meaning" of being the exploiter of existence and sees the meaning of existence in being raw material for man. (2:461n20)

Thus, it seems that philosophical anthropology stubbornly prefers Creationism to Darwinism. Heidegger's metaphysic of technology is an outdated Creationism, a form of anthropocentrism that has not yet realized that "no God can save us." For Anders, however, we cannot but accept Darwin, and we can no longer consider the human being as the "shepherd of Being."

Such a "thought of catastrophe," which contemplates the complete destruction, rather than the mere oblivion, of being, discloses a radical ontological scenario on which Anders focuses in the first volume of *Die Antiquiertheit des Menschen*. According to Anders, there is an enormous gap between human beings' biopsychological equipment as rational animals and the artificial world they bring into the real world. This is what Anders names the "promethean gap" (*prometheische Gefälle*), that is, the dyscrasia between human productivity and humans' ability to foresee the effect of such productivity (Anders 1961, 267–71). Human beings are obsolete because they are not aware of what they produce, because between the ends they set and the means they employ to achieve them, there stands an immense hiatus. For this reason, human beings have become "smaller" than themselves—that is, incapable of being responsible for what they produce.

Unlike Heidegger, Anders does not invoke humans' thinking, as human beings are utterly unaware of their tragic condition. As Anders claims in his preface to the second volume of *Die Antiquiertheit des Menschen*, "Today, anyone who still proclaims the 'transformability of man' (as Brecht did) is a figure from the past, since we are transformed. In addition, this transformation of man is so fundamental that anyone who still speaks today of his 'essence' (as Scheler still did) is a figure from the distant past" (Anders 1980, 24–25). The triumphs of technology and, thus, the outcomes of technological progress have made human beings obsolete.

In Anders's eyes, the technical possibility of the utter destruction of humankind does not represent an extreme abuse of a technical potentiality that is otherwise positive. Like Goethe's *Sorcerer's Apprentice*, technology naturally tends to replace human beings (Anders 1980, 396–410). Before being destroyed and uninhabited, the "world without human beings" will be a place where humankind is not an end in itself but rather a means of feeding the industrial process. It is worth repeating, however, that this is not the dystopic drift of a betrayed utopia. This is the inescapable destiny of technological progress. As Anders reconstructs in the introduction to the second volume of *Die Antiquiertheit des Menschen* (15–33): initially, with the introduction of mechanization, the first industrial revolution caused the obsolescence of human beings; then, the second industrial revolution carried out the shift from the production of goods to the production of needs; finally, with the third industrial revolution, such transition from obsolescence to subjugation results in destruction. The third industrial revolution is the age that produces the instruments for the destruction of humankind, the instruments of complete apocalypse. The third industrial revolution introduced the atomic bomb into this world and, with it, the concrete possibility of nihilism.

In light of Hiroshima and the possibility of atomic apocalypse, for Anders the complete catastrophe is looming, inevitable. This is an earthly apocalypse, however—a Last Judgment that brings no salvation. Despite his catastrophism, Anders still thinks within an eschatological frame. For he considers the time he lives in as the "end of times" or, better, as the "end time." But this "thought of the end," which is often obsessive, diverges from traditional eschatology and apocalypse.

The "end time" is the nuclear age: the apocalypse without Reign. Unlike Jacob Taubes, Hans Jonas, Walter Benjamin, and all the other authors who wrote about eschatology, Anders outlines a "negative eschatology," an "anti-eschatology" that contemplates annihilation. For Anders, the future is already over. Jonas's call for the "imperative of responsibility," which still attempts to metaphysically deduce the moral obligation to preserve the world for future generations, is worthless—as if the notion of life as self-affirmation of being could still inspire in us the absolute duty to contrast the nonbeing. Bloch's principle of hope is even more naive: in Anders's eyes, at this point, calling for hope is ridiculous. After August 6, 1945, the very categories of "possible" and "free will" became pure abstractions, outmoded metaphysical delusions—in other words, ghosts.

If traditional eschatology has always carried out a mystical leap into Gnosticism, in contrast, Anders remains firmly anchored to immanence. Nevertheless, is Anders's thought truly hopeless? Does it truly renounce assigning a task, a goal, to such obsolescent humanity? I think that, in Anders, the only and effective chance for hope lies in a negative ethics that "says no" to the existing state of things. For Anders, the destiny of humankind, an escapable destiny, is clearly self-destruction, and, therefore, our task does not consist of changing it but rather of delaying it as much as possible. Humankind's bitter victory will be nothing but the postponement of such destruction.

Anders's negative ethics rises from the scandal of our not being scandalized by the scandal, from our blindness before the imminent apocalypse. Anders's negative ethics condemns a world that has made positive ethics phony and impossible, for it is not a matter of defining what is good and what is evil but of acknowledging that the very normative question of good and evil is obsolete. For Anders, if evil, as a moral notion, still makes sense today, it does so only in terms of "being blind before evil," the evil of concrete nihilism.

This finally leads me to elucidate the reasons that motivated me to include Günther Anders in a book on totalitarianism. Recent events have persuaded me, indeed, of the necessity to highlight the topicality of a reflection on our present age that, in spite of all its limitations, has been excessively neglected, not to say forgotten. We recently started to fear the atomic risk again, as if it were an ended past we thought would have never returned, when it actually was a dormant possibility before which we have been, as Anders claimed more than forty years ago, completely and deliberately blind. After all, the atomic arsenals that today, under serious threats that are not "bluffs," have returned to scare us contain mostly the same warheads that Anders feared in his time.

Perhaps his catastrophism, surely technophobic and somewhat moralistic (not to say irritatingly prophetic), has been simply debunked by decades of the celebratory rhetoric of atomic deterrence. But Anders himself, in a brief but biting essay in his second volume of *Die Antiquiertheit des Menschen*, reminded us how naive, ideological, and especially dangerous the distinction between "right hands" and "wrong hands" is. Atomic bombs are never "in right hands." They stay there, still, ready to be used: "'To have' is already 'to use.'... The amorality consists not only of the fact that they were used, but in their possession" (Anders 1980, 334). This is because the atomic bomb that has been used once and, like any "possibility" that becomes real from that moment on, the only impossible thing is its impossibility. The atomic bomb is not a "bluff."

In February 1959, Günther Anders conducted a seminar entitled *The Moral Implications of the Atomic Age* at the University of Berlin. At the end, students asked him for a short text that could serve as a basis for further discussion. Anders dictated twenty-three "theses," later published as "Theses for the Atomic Age." I believe that these theses represent a sort of "rulebook" of his negative ethics. I will summarize its key points:

1. *Hiroshima as World Condition.* Every place is potentially another Hiroshima. From August 6, 1945, we "became, at least *modo negativo*, omnipotent; but since, on the other hand, we can be wiped out at any given moment, we also became totally impotent" (Anders 1962, 493).

2. *Ethics of Respite.* By now, our existence can be only defined in terms of "respite," as "not yet being nonexisting." We "still" exist in light of our imminent "nonexisting." Hence, the only possible answer to the question "how should we live?"—and here Anders's ethics betray their negative character to provide us with normative hints—is to never end the time of the time, to keep on postponing the inevitable annihilation. "We must do everything in our power to make The End Time endless" (494).

3. *The Totalitarianism of Atomic Power.* In Anders's eyes, atomic warheads are not mere weapons. Atomic power is rather a total condition. Yet, unlike Jaspers and Strauss, for Anders, we cannot invoke "deterrence" to defend our free world from the totalitarian threat. In the atomic age, the traditional political distinction between "friends" and "enemies" utterly failed, not because we all became "friends" but because the very notion of "enemy" is now meaning-

less. The only real enemy threatening us is atomic annihilation; the only real totalitarianism is the atomic condition, which transforms the whole planet into a borderless concentration camp.

4. *The Inconceivability of Nothingness.* The human animal is incapable of conceiving nothingness. We can only conceive a determined negation, but for our mind, the catastrophe is inconceivable, and we cannot truly think of the nonbeing. This is a structural limitation that prevents us from imagining and foreseeing something that goes beyond what we perceive. Here, Anders's negative ethics provides us with another normative hint: to not rely on perception but to practice our imagination. Currently, in the atomic age, we human animals are "inverted utopians" (496). Unlike traditional utopians, who cannot realize what they imagine, we cannot imagine what we have produced.

5. *The Promethean Gap as Moral Condition of Today's Humanity.* Currently, the main dualism affecting the human condition is no longer the spirit-matter distinction but rather the discrepancy between our capacity for technological production and our capacity to imagine the ultimate purpose of such production. This causes what Anders names, in contrast to the psychological notion of subliminal (the stimulus too small to produce any reaction), the "supra-liminal" (497): an unbridgeable distance between the products we created and the inconceivability of what they may cause, something so wide that it provokes no reaction. For Anders, the "supra-liminal" is our inability to perceive any moral responsibility toward the effect of our products as they take place on such a wide scale that they no longer "touch" us. To press a button and incinerate a city is a "job," a detached "triggering" (500)—as if the atomic age had made even the "banality of evil" outmoded. If anything, the atomic age should be considered the age of the "banality of nihilism."

6. *Imagination as the Organ of Ethics.* Adolf Eichmann is no longer an ethical ideal-type. For Anders, Eichmann has become an all-encompassing anthropological paradigm concerning each of us, none excluded. Eichmann's self-deception is now humankind's self-deception. We all live within the *Promethean gap.* This is why,

for Anders, imagination, despite its structural weakness, is the sole faculty with which we are left to connect our moral consciousness to the truth, to reality, to ethics. Surely, in this struggle against the inevitable end, perception is no ally: it is rather "'false witness,' in a far more radical sense than Greek philosophy meant when warning against it" (497).

7. *The Courage of Fear.* Extending our imagination means acquiring "the courage to be frightened." As Anders claims: "'Expand the capacity of your imagination' means, concretely, to 'increase your capacity to fear'" (498). Without such fear, the fear before the imaginative representation of nothingness, we will never be able to halt the final catastrophe. This is not a paralyzing fear but a fear as principle of action, as the driving force of ethics.

It is quite surprising that Günther Anders does not constitute a key reference for the current debate on the Anthropocene. Notions such as the "Promethean gap" or "the courage of being frightened" would surely be of help to understand the catastrophic scenario toward which we are relentlessly going.

Among the threats of the "third industrial revolution" are not only the extermination camps and atomic destruction but also climate change, the new "nothingness" that we cannot truly imagine. No previous generation has ever witnessed such disproportion between the effect of human activity and the environment. In addition, as if it were not enough, beside the environmental crisis we have just started to undergo, the nightmare of nuclear holocaust has returned to torment our tranquility-seeking consciousness. This is why we still need the antidote of Anders's negative ethics. How would he define current climate deniers? And what would he say about those who, in the face of new nuclear weapons tests and new atomic crises, continue not only to invoke the "pacifying" character of deterrence or to take the rationality of policy makers for granted but even consider the employment of "tactical nuclear weapons" as a "lesser evil," as a minor-costs nuclear detonation? He would, once again, define all of them as blind people in the face of apocalypse.

I think that Anders may be not entirely right, however. I do not think that deniers truly deny. Currently, everybody knows; everybody is aware of the destructive consequences awaiting us. We know that we cannot stop what we have set in motion. Somewhere in our mind, we possess such knowledge, even those who triumphally deny and diminish. For they are simply not interested in saving this world, our world—as far as we know, the only world we have been given. As Anders suggested, they do not know how to find in a possible fear, in their awareness of the inevitable end, the courage to be frightened.

FOUR

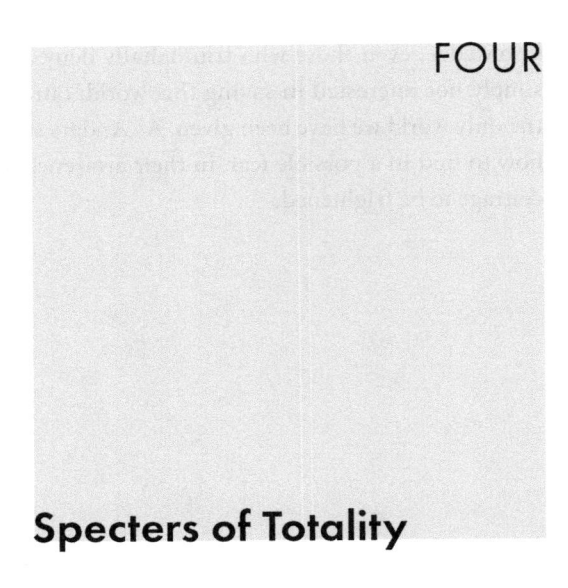

Specters of Totality

INVERTED TOTALITARIANISM AND DEMOCRACY INCORPORATED

From the earliest occurrences of the term to sophisticated philosophical discussions, what undoubtedly emerges is that the concept of totalitarianism, rooted in the tragedies of the two world wars, has been one of the most contested ideas in the political lexicon. As I noted in previous chapters, it generally refers to a type of regime that is extreme in its repudiation of freedom and liberties. Conceived out of the similarities supposedly shared by Nazism and Soviet communism—Stalinism in particular—totalitarianism was thought of as a regime with deep, radical ambitions. Its main objective is to rule totally unhampered by legal restraints, civic or social oppositions, organized pluralism, or party competition. Unlike authoritarianism, totalitarian political oppression aims at refashioning human reality itself. The radical nature of its purposes persuaded political theorists and historians that totalitarianism represented a new form of government rather than merely an extreme version of tyranny or despotism.

Before proceeding, it might be useful to briefly recall what political scientists have considered the peculiar characteristics of a totalitarian regime. To be truly totalitarian, a form of government should combine the following traits: (a) a revolutionary ideology that expresses faith in the necessary laws of history, announcing the destruction of the old order and the birth of a radically new and purified one; (b) a mass party structure headed by a charismatic leader who claims infallibility and demands people's unconditional devotion to his personality; (c) a chaotic displacement of offices and roles to ensure rivalry and, therefore, dependence on the real site of power; (d) a collective economic system (capitalist or state socialist) intended to direct productive forces toward the regime's autarchic and militaristic goals; (e) total control of mass media, and with that, the formulation of a set language designed to prevent ambivalence and complexity; (f) perpetual mobilization of the population through wars, struggles, or purges; (g) the pervasive use of terror by secret police to isolate, intimidate, and align all those whom the regime deems menacing; (h) the centrality of an "objective enemy," that is, the pursuit and elimination not simply of real opponents but also of categories of people deemed guilty of wickedness in virtue of certain qualities such as race or descent. Crimes against the state need not have actually been committed by the person accused of them; and (i) the concentration camp as a laboratory of totalitarian domination, where conditions under which human beings become fully malleable are subject to constant experimentation. The concentration camp is also a slave-labor system existing side by side with a racial and/or class-oriented policy of genocide.

Historians, as I have mentioned, have repeatedly criticized the typological rigidity of political science's characterization of totalitarianism. While the image constructed of Nazi horrors and Stalinist domination can count as a reference, they argue, it is important to revise that historical reality in light of the intrinsic problematic nature of the category. For example, so called totalitarian regimes are flexible and capable of mutation. They are not monoliths but rife with competing, opportunistic cliques scrambling for power.

On the one hand, despite criticism, for many proponents of twentieth-century liberalism, the concept of totalitarianism has been an essential hermeneutical tool. On the other hand, for Marxists, who could not accept the similarity between Nazism and communism, totalitarianism has been nothing but an ideological attempt to quash communism. As Abbott Gleason has pointed out, totalitarianism constitutes an ideological weapon of a particular kind of Manichaeism that has divided the world into good liberal democrats and evil communists (Gleason 2005). In short, controversies put the concept to rest for about a couple of decades.

It is in the early years of the new millennium that, somewhat surprisingly, the idea of totalitarianism comes back to the fore, used, on the one hand, to fight the "war against Islamic terror" and, on the other hand, to sharply criticize neoliberal globalization. Once again, the concept has been employed to establish Manichean oppositions, dragging with it even philosophical reflection, from which we would expect a more complex approach. It is as if another demonization mechanism has found, in the fear of Islamic terrorism or in the opposition to the transformations of capitalism, a new engine to eliminate the differences, the intrigues, and the folds that reality always opposes to the process of abstraction, challenging the understanding to go deeper and deeper. Once again, the specter of Nazi horrors is evoked as a borderline idea by which to measure and evaluate the current political situation.

From the hypothesis of the 9/11 attack as a Jewish plot to the idea that Islam means in itself hatred and destruction, even shrewd intellectuals fell into the theoretical trap that clearly divides the heroes of justice from the bearers of chaos. At the beginning of the third millennium, the world is thus once again divided between the "axis of evil," denounced by those who embody the absolute values of democracy to be exported, and the unredeemable corruption of the West. There is a part of the world to protect and a part of the world where the enemy must be destroyed. On the one hand, Islam is a theological-political totalitarianism (Macdonald 2007; Tibi 2007; Burleigh 2010; Hodge 2016); on the other hand, the West is a set of disguised totalitarian regimes (US first) that masks its will to political and economic power under false ideals.

From Agnes Heller to André Glucksmann, many philosophers adhere to the radical version of the theorem of civilization against barbarism, publicly warning us that, with Islamic terrorism, nihilistic totalitarianism is back again in all its strength (Heller 2002; Glucksmann 2002). According to this scheme, modern Islamism is a radical movement that aspires to planetary dimensions. Its goal is to destroy the West and re-Islamize all Muslim countries. Since every authority and duty emanates from God alone, Islamism's watchword is pure and unconditional submission. This is why Islamist language overflows with millenarian images of struggle, merciless destruction, and sacred terror. Bent on purifying the world of Zionism, liberalism, feminism, and crusaders' hegemony (US), Islamist ideology represents a culture of nihilism, terror, suicidal martyrdom for the cause, and mythological appeal to a world about to be reborn. "Muslim totalitarianism," this reasoning states, demonstrates the capillary, totalizing organization of its Western precursors. Islamist militants combine the conspiratorial anti-Semitism of the Nazis, for whom they maintain a nostalgic admiration, with the pan-territorial ambitions of Bolshevik internationalism. The archaic will to reestablish the hallowed caliphate, pursued with all the means that modern technology provides, is consistent with a political theology that combines archaism and technology, the same "reactionary modernism" of earlier totalitarian movements.

Without distinguishing within the enormous Islamic universe the differences of currents, schools, beliefs, and customs, from September 11, the mere enunciation of the word *Islam* impedes the debate and channels it toward the commonplace notion that Islamic fundamentalism is totalitarian insofar as it attempts to permeate and constrain individuals' lives completely, abolishing all boundaries between the multiple spheres of existence (Finkielkraute 2013).

In contrast to the demonization of Islamic totalitarianism, there stand those who consider the US a totalitarian regime. September 11, 2001, becomes the symbol through which a crucified nation justifies its dastardly deeds. In the name of suffering endured during and after the Twin Towers attack, the US considered itself legitimized to suspend key articles of its Constitution, decree a state of emergency, betray international treaties, and illegally detain prisoners. In critics' eyes, the ideology expressed within the National Security Strategy of the United States issued in 2002 is nothing more than a will to power that uses the martyrdom rhetoric of terrorist attacks for multiple functions: the sacralization of the body politic and its leader, preventive war, and the imperial and coercive expansion of democracy to a criminal corporate economy. Nazi Germany still represents the totalitarian paradigm through which understanding the actions of a superpower, namely the US, whose foreign policy is invasive and aggressive, justifies preventive war as a matter of official doctrine and represses opposition at home.

In my opinion, Sheldon Wolin's 2008 *Democracy Incorporated: Managed Democracy and the Specter of Inverted Totalitarianism* is the work that, more than any other, revamped the philosophical-political question of totalitarianism. With this book, Wolin, one of the greatest historians of political thought in the US, a radical left-wing intellectual who never conforms to Marxist mainstreams, ushered in a new season of debate on totalitarianism, redefining the guidelines identifying what is, or might be, totalitarian currently.

According to Wolin, Western, especially US, governments and corporations attempt to gain power over populations through propaganda and the suppression of critical thinking, supporting economic-centered ideologies that consider democracy unnecessary, an obstacle to progress. This tendency is what Wolin names "inverted totalitarianism." Wolin does not employ the term *totalitarian* superficially, but knowingly. He talks of totalitarianism "to illuminate tendencies in our system of power that are opposed to the fundamental principles of constitutional democracy" (Wolin 2008, ix). Wolin's thesis does not portray neoliberal politics as a mere repetition of Hitler's Germany or Stalin's Soviet Union. His inquiry, more theoretical than historical, attempts to make the reader aware of those totalizing power dynamics that arose from the tragedies of the two world wars and that still oppose the fundamental principles of constitutional democracy. In other words, Wolin's view makes totalitarianism's chameleonic nature explicit:

> Far from being exhausted by [totalitarianism's] twentieth-century versions would-be totalitarians now have available technologies of control, intimidation and mass manipulation far surpassing those of that earlier time.
>
> The Nazi and Fascist regimes were powered by revolutionary movements whose aim was not only to capture, reconstitute, and monopolize state power but also to gain control over the economy. By controlling the state and the economy, the revolutionaries gained the leverage necessary to reconstruct and then mobilize society. In contrast, inverted totalitarianism is only in part a state-centered phenomenon. Primarily, it represents the *political* coming of age of corporate power and the *political* demobilization of the citizenry. (ix-x)

Even if such a new form of totalitarianism takes advantage of the authority and the resources of the state, its dynamic strength is given by the symbiotic relationship between traditional government and the "system of 'private' governance represented by the modern business corporation" (xiii). The state and corporations have become the main sponsors of technoscientific *potentates*. Such a combination–this is Wolin's main idea—results in unprecedented totalizing tendencies that question the very idea of limit, whether political, intellectual, ethical, or economic. According to Wolin, as the boundaries between politics, market, and technoscientific control fail, along with the concentration of technoscientific powers in the hands of corporations, the very foundations of truth and reality are put into question.

The transformation of the United States into a "superpower" and an imperial force has been set off by a specific event: "If the burning of the German Parliament (Reichstag) in 1933 produced the symbolic event portending the destruction of parliamentary government by dictatorship," Wolin argues, "the destruction of the World Trade Center and the attack upon the Pentagon on September 11, 2001, were a revelatory moment in the history of American political life" (4). Not by chance, the symbolic centers of financial power and military power were attacked at the same time.

The event of 9/11 allowed the US to obtain citizens' consent to carry out unjust and unlawful practices. By leveraging a reinvigorated religious fanaticism and a superpower imperialistic ideology, the *Patriot Act* bestowed innocence on a whole series of aggressive policies directed both outward (territorial expansion) and inward (suspension of fundamental articles of the Constitution). "Axis of Evil," "weapons of mass destruction," "civilization against barbarism"—these phrases were part of a new political grammar that made 9/11 the myth through which the United States transfigured into a "superpowerful" geopolitical entity. As Wolin claims, "Inverted totalitarianism, the true face of Superpower, represents a blend of powers that includes modern as well as archaic ones. It comprises the business corporation . . . and the systematic conversion of new scientific knowledge into new technological applications, especially military ones" (61).

What makes such a mixture totalitarian? For Wolin, a totalizing drive inhabits each of these powers: a "presumption of virtually limitless development" that governs any aspect of society. If democratic power is characterized by a sense of the limit, "inverted totalitarianism" distorts politics under the aegis of a constant drive for expansion. Politics is monopolized by powers that "supersede their own previous limits and are totalizing in the sense that infinity, or the persistent challenging of the constraints of existing practices, beliefs, and taboos, rather than simple superiority, is the driving force" (62). In other words, "inverted totalitarianism" systematically establishes the conditions that facilitate the expression of the will to totality by eliminating any form of intermediation and interference. According to Wolin, the Bush administration satisfied all these preconditions, as "it succeeded in systematizing and exploiting a dynamic complex of powers already existing. Its principal elements include the state, corporate economic power, the powers represented in the integration of modern science and postmodern technologies, a military addicted to technological innovation, and a religious fundamentalism that is no stranger to politics and markets" (62).[1]

But the present is not the only chronological horizon of Wolin's analysis. In *Democracy Incorporated*, he also inspects deeper contradictions inhabiting American democracy from the very moment of its foundation. If the recent rise of "inverted totalitarianism" has been possible, it is because "American democracy has never been truly consolidated" (xi). The political system of the United States is undoubtedly animated by the intent to ensure freedom and welfare for the majority of the people, but from the very beginning, its institutional organization has never intended to renounce the heavy premodern burden of elitism, "the political principle which assumes that the existence of unequal abilities is an irrefutable fact" (162). As Alexis de Tocqueville had already pointed out in 1840's *On Democracy in America*, the principle of political representation is perennially haunted by the risks of being overturned into the instrument of legitimation of a government that stands as the "guardian" of a population, as active and capable in private affairs as passive and lascivious in the exercise of its political rights and duties.

The security issue imposed by the World Trade Center bombings, however, has made the institutional contours of this "benevolent despotism" (81) increasingly authoritarian and repressive, whose strength, as Hobbes showed, is directly proportional to the number of liberties that citizens spontaneously alienate in the name of their safety. In other words, when combined with fear, technology, and neoliberalism, political apathy eventually becomes the device through which a democratic government can exert unprecedented control over the population. Unlike "traditional" totalitarianism, inverted totalitarianism does not aim to bring masses into its totality. Rather, inverted totalitarianism indulges and encourages people's tendency to withdraw into the private sphere, thereby leaving the "public" in the hand of new elites' will to totality. Inverted totalitarianism does not kill democracy. Inverted totalitarianism "manages" democracy.

Wolin's work seems to chart the routes followed by the most recent inquiries on totalitarian specters reawakened by neoliberalism: the securitarian drive and the production of fear; the disappearance of politics caused by the suffocating power of corporations; the potentially total control emerging from an indiscriminate employment of technology; and the alarming manipulation of reality. These will be the guidelines of the following debate. Even if not always dependent on Wolin's analysis, during the last two decades, philosophical and political theory scholarship massively warned us of the new threats of "inverted" or "perverted" totalitarianism. It is interesting that the alarm about a return of totalitarianism comes now from precisely those who, in the cultural context of the second half of the last century, would have rejected the concept, finding it unusable because of its anticommunist and opportunistic bias. Today, totalitarianism is the widespread economic governance that suffocates any possibility of autonomy for politics.

I do not agree with the apocalyptic character that some analyses bestow on new capitalism as a form of impersonal and all-powerful domination. I do not think that today's total domination is succeeding in jeopardizing what in "classical" totalitarianism was still possible—that is, internal resistance.[2] I must acknowledge, however, the undeniable totalizing tendency of a business-centered worldview that is becoming so hegemonical that even the most radical and provocatory diagnosis of "totalitarian management" appears plausible (Deneault 2013).

Governance is the term that better describes the new reality we live in. Introduced at the end of the 1980s to claim the necessity of managing public institutions in compliance with the demands of private corporations, it expresses today's new art of politics, a nonpolitical politics that is deprived of true democratic legitimation. What is truly alarming is not only the fact that, in a regime of governance, corporations and finance are the main political actors, but their working principles are being elevated to public leading principles to which the whole society must conform. What we were still able to name "public space" at the end of the twentieth century is currently being destroyed by the "capitalist production of space" (Saladdin 2019, 13)—a "flat space" utterly exposed to an instrumental logic of production and control.

Yet not all critics of today's forms of domination think we are living in a new totalitarianism that concedes no way out (Brown 2019). Wolin himself acknowledges the existence of "demotic moments" that can "revitalize" democracy despite inverted totalitarianism seeming to prevail. As he writes in *Democracy Incorporated*, "Any prospect of revitalizing democracy in America should not assume that we can start afresh. It is not morning in America. The first step should be to reflect on the changes of the past half century that have distorted the cultural supports of democracy and eroded its political practices while preparing the way for a politics and political culture favorable to inverted totalitarianism" (Wolin 2008, 238). I believe that the prime task of a critical philosophy is to "name" what endangers our societies. It would otherwise be an abstract normativism for "beautiful souls."

TO MAKE LIVE AND TO LET DIE: BIOPOLITICS, THANATOPOLITICS, AND NECROPOLITICS

Perhaps, rather than talking of forms of totalitarianism, it would be more appropriate to focus on totalizing dynamics that harbor totalitarian risks. These are dynamics that the political philosophy of the second half of the twentieth century detected and on which we must not stop focusing our attention, even though we relate them to a reality that is utterly different from that of the period of the two world wars.

Not very "cautious" in his comparisons, Giorgio Agamben has led contemporary philosophical debate to reassess the Foucauldian theme of biopower in light of the perspective of "thanatopolitics." With 1995's *Homo Sacer* and 1999's *Remnants of Auschwitz*, he indirectly, but unequivocally, dragged biopolitics into a reconsideration of a totalitarian specter that continues to hunt our contemporary societies. Totalitarianism is in general the political system that makes life a "bare life": the ultimate outcome of a relation of domination that produces the so-called *homo sacer*, an individual who can be killed without committing homicide. According to Agamben, even if Foucault is the one who introduced the question of biopower, he did not dwell on the nexus between thanatopolitics and bare life, which was instead developed by Hannah Arendt.

Although Arendt never employed terms such as *biopower* or *biopolitics*, comparing her thought with Foucault's is sound and fruitful (Forti 2015). For both authors, power oversees not only an individual's life and death but also the vital process of the whole society and population. "Biopolitics" is not a historical category. First and foremost, it is a heuristic tool to stress the crucial discontinuity within the continuum of Western power. When the object of politics becomes life in its biological dimension, when political power addresses the biological meaning of existence, and when political strategies invade the very body of individuals, as well as the population, then power relations change radically.

Both Arendt and Foucault attempted to reflect on the complex relationship of continuity and discontinuity that connects the modern form of biopower—the power that manages life also in its biological aspect—with the brutal genocides that characterized the twentieth century. They both see Auschwitz and Soviet camps as the extreme pathology of power but also as the paroxysmal accomplishment of a politics that has elevated life to a universal category endowed with an absolute value. What are the consequences? There are "worthy" lives, and there are lives that are not worth living. This is the working logic of genocidal mentality: if the life of a certain population is to flourish and be worthy, then it is necessary to destroy all those lives—semblances of life—who are believed to endanger the health of the social body.

I think that the biopolitical approach—despite its occasional disagreements—is the most effective philosophical lens through which to inspect the continuities and the discontinuities between the twentieth century and our present. Most often from this approach, totalitarian dynamics are still in motion, even if they employ different methods and turn to violence in a more economical way than "classical" ones used to do. Surely, twentieth-century totalitarianism marked the peak, the maximum completion, of a politics that, in the name of life, overturns itself in the pure sovereign right to give death; however, even if low-intensity, such overturning of biopolitics in thanatopolitics, which decides who deserves to live and who can be let to die, still takes place today. Thus, the threat of totalitarianism returns, explicitly or implicitly, to orient the sharpest philosophical interrogations on contemporary biopolitical disasters, from Judith Butler to Giorgio Agamben and from Roberto Esposito to Achille Mbembe.

For instance, Achille Mbembe talks of "necropolitics" to describe modern politics of sovereignty and governmentality, which, far from having been defeated during the wars of the twentieth century, is now driving Europe to "decomposition," a Europe that does not intend to reflect on the historical contradictions inhabiting its own values (Mbembe 2019). In a few years, "necropolitics" has become the main concept to indicate the persistence of the reifying and lethal "colonialist way of thinking" harbored in the very heart of the West, which progressively tends to reduce life to brute matter. Mbembe recalls several perspectives we have encountered thus far: Arendt's analyses on imperialism; extermination camps and stateless people; Foucault's inquiries on biopower and the racist state; Agamben's notion of the state of exception; and Fanon's writings on colonialism. By combining all these authors, Mbembe emphasizes the indissoluble bond between a politics safeguarding life and the most overwhelming and arbitrary manifestation of domination—that is, to expose parts of populations to death. Necropower is that form of social and political power that, through explicit and implicit practices, exposes some groups or members of the population to death, thereby reactivating the totalitarian dynamic par excellence: the separation within humankind not simply between friends and enemies but rather between "persons" and "things." This dynamic justifies the possibility of dominating and destroying the latter. Modern colonial governments represent the foundational moment of such violent and repressive action on space and bodies. Colonialism classifies, hierarchizes, confines, and segregates, depriving a part of a population of its own life up to social and political, not to say real, death.

Unlike Arendt and Foucault, Mbembe assumes the figure of the "colony" as a paradigm of total domination over bodies; however, like Arendt and Foucault, he reaffirms the centrality of biopower and the modern modality of domination and control over individuals in the name of the population's vitality. Modern times overflow with examples: political terror during the French Revolution, slavery, the massacre of Native Americans, work and extermination camps, apartheid, and so on. The totalitarian dynamic that discriminates between worthy lives and rejected lives works permanently so that, in the name of necessity and exception, "death-worlds" continuously emerge in the midst of social-political spaces devoted to the maximization of life. Such a position resembles Judith Butler's theses, especially the dramatic separation between lives worthy of being mourned for their individuality and belonging and anonymous lives that are neither worthy of being remembered nor mourned (Butler 2004).

For many influential political philosophers, the COVID-19 pandemic has been the litmus test that irrefutably highlights such discriminative dynamics, revealing once again how simplifying the sharp opposition between totalitarianism and liberal democracy can be. Market economy, assumed as supreme and total value, unconditionally rules, dismantling institutions and welfare (Butler 2022; Stiegler 2021), as well as destroying climate, environment, and the animal world. This means deciding, even though not intentionally, which lives should be saved and which can be sacrificed. Although at low intensity, as Butler claims, a necropolitical plan is being overtly carried out in compliance with the death drive thriving at the heart of the capitalist machine (Butler 2022, 53). Therefore, talking of "the health of the market" is not a naive "metaphor" since the economy needs to drain individual bodies' health, especially that of the most fragile ones, to remain "healthy." Diagrams and statistical forecasts determine the acceptable level of infections, hospitalizations, and deaths. Below a certain threshold, the market economy takes off again. In this way, some people's death must be tolerated to enhance the lives of those who remain alive. Butler is not maintaining at all that totalitarianism is back through medical science, tracking, technologies, numbers, curves, and calculation; she acknowledges how indispensable they are. Rather, she thinks that they graphically portray a different form of violence and death that is not managed by the sovereign power. It is a subtle and indirect form of sanitary violence, mirroring the physiological pace of ordinary life. Racism and discrimination continue to operate, deciding on those who can afford to remain confined to work safely from home and those who instead must expose their body to the risk of infection for the sake of the economy. If the health of our world coincides with the health of the economy (finance and market), then, as Butler maintains, moral responsibility becomes the responsibility to loosen restrictions, thereby deciding on those categories of human lives that must "come back" to work to be productive. Thus, some communities, not by chance those most exposed to the aggressivity of the capitalist mode of production, are completely deprived of the right to health.

As usually happens in neoliberalism, all these dynamics are irresponsibly silent by the celebration of the sacrality of individual freedom. In an absolutized individual's eyes, movement restrictions appear as unbearable and outrageous crimes against freedom. By doing so, the right to freedom is the same as the right to harm others.

Hence, "to make live and to let die" is no longer a sovereign decision responding to a will to extermination. It is, rather, a systemic play imbued with racism, exclusion, and fragmentation of the population, which, in the name of the absolutization of the economy, exposes irrelevant bodies to malady and death. Biopower becomes an effective carrier of necropolitical practices. After all, according to Butler, neoliberalism and the obsessive affirmation of individual freedom pave the way to necropolitics. Individual absolute freedom is not only delusional but also politically destructive because it denies the common vulnerability that makes us all interdependent.

According to Roberto Esposito's analysis on the self-immunity dynamic, the denegation of our interdependence causes an explosion of individual lives (Esposito 2022). Once again, we refuse to acknowledge how mutually implicated our lives, our bodies, are, both from a social-political viewpoint and from an environmental one. Life depends on the organization of such interdependency. In other words, the COVID-19 pandemic unmasked what cruel inequalities produce: violence, discrimination, exclusion, and death.

Many authors remind us that just as nobody is innocent before totalitarianism, nobody is immune once it finishes. Murderous migration managements, "borderizations" of water and territories, new apartheid, exploitation of raw materials, sanitary discriminations—these are the specters of totalitarianism that constantly worry contemporary reflections on biopower. It is as if, for them, such a regime that arranges humankind into hierarchy is even still, as it was during the twentieth century, the political-metaphysical transcendental that facilitates the reduction of the environment and people to brute matter, to "stuff" to be exploited.

In other words, the drive to optimization of life that overturns in power of death continues in today governmentality.[3] As Foucault's works from the early 1980s had already glimpsed, biopolitics within neoliberal societies of the West differs from that of "classical" totalitarian regimes. The social powers in which we are immersed succeed in controlling our lives and directing our behavior not by limiting or impeding our freedom of movement or by imposing prohibitions and regimentations.

Currently, sovereign power no longer decides who to make live and who to let die. We are witnessing the radical fragmentation and proliferation of powers claiming the right to regulate our life. Without imposing transcendent norms, they manage the protection of life by fostering the performance of "normal" and "physiological" behaviors aimed at enhancing the wellness of the population. The more we entrust birth, death, and malady to the power and knowledge of life sciences, the more life and death seem to us as something that we can control. The critics of neoliberal biopolitics rightly maintain that an imagination imbued with the idea of optimizing life is necessary for the mutual empowerment of, on the one hand, medical science and biotechnologies and, on the other hand, the demands of capital accumulation (Rose 2007; Cooper 2008).

But I do not believe that it is only the greed of neocapitalism that feeds our biopolitical condition. There is something in us, and in our symbolic order, deeper than that. The symbolic order and the social imaginary are historical "a priori" stratifications of meaning, individual and collective, that act on all the implicated subjects, especially when they are unaware of it. It is a totality of norms that drive people to reproduce their assumptions and content, even if nobody is forced to comply. For instance, how many private institutions, associations, and public actors are being mobilized in the name of the absolute and delusional ideal of "Perfect Health"? Today's "Hyper-Humanity" corresponds with a human ideal potentially immortal in its singularity. This is no longer a politics of the collective body but rather a challenge to overcome the constitutive limits of human existence—a challenge so radical that yesterday's posthuman ideal seems nothing but the legacy of an "obsolete humanity." It is a dreamlike culture of ever-expanding possibilities, a social imaginary that aims at overcoming current capabilities, inhibitions, and constraints—as if we were compelled to live as best we can, valuing and actualizing to the fullest all the potentials we have been given. In light of these implicit imperatives, our core values become our faith and our hope in a limitless life in which nothing is left unexpressed.

Modern Western democracies have undoubtedly provided us with countless opportunities for self-realization. Personally, I do not intend to question either the achievements of "civilization" or the politics of health and protection. Rather, it is a matter of questioning the collateral effects of such a positive social imaginary. For we endlessly seek something that, whether we like it or not, strengthens the powers on which we depend—something deeply rooted in us, something that responds to our prime passions. I am talking of the desire to persist and the will to always be more vital. Our contemporary "you Ought" demands exactly the kind of self-assertion that the "moral law" was meant to prevent. The new imperative in the West exhorts us to maximize our biological life first. We could even rephrase the categorical imperative as follows: "Make the improvement of your life the absolute and universal law of your conduct." Hence, once compelled to an infinite project (maximizing life can be but a never-ending endeavor), we have neither the time nor the space to perceive and judge the external reality that, since often painful, calls us to political change.

Post-Foucauldian political philosophy believes it is capable of detecting the insidious, and potentially totalitarian, dialectic between the absolute promotion of life and the production of death. In this perspective, the securitarian paradigm is a key figure for contemporary theories of governmentality.

According to Giorgio Agamben, a "health terror" is now at stake. His analysis of the containment strategies carried out during the early stages of the COVID-19 pandemic moves from an extreme critique—in my opinion, excessive, not to say misleading—to this sort of religion of health that characterizes contemporary biopower. In Agamben's eyes, the pandemic revealed the hegemonic power of those dominating powers that absolutize health, security, and science. His theses are so radical that they not only establish a continuity between the racial hygiene of Nazi totalitarianism and the governmentality of the COVID-19 pandemic but also claim that the pandemic—"whether it is real or simulated" (Agamben 2021, 8)—was actually an excuse to spread "health terror," thereby establishing a permanent state of exception that completely transformed the state of law. "For decades now," Agamben writes, "institutional powers have been suffering a gradual loss of legitimacy. These powers could mitigate this loss only through the constant evocation of states of emergency, and through the need for security and stability that this emergency creates" (11).

For Agamben (and others), the history of the twentieth century clearly shows, especially since the rise of Nazism in Germany, how the mechanism of the state of exception is what permits the transformation of democracy into a totalitarian state. For years now, not only in Italy, he argues, the state of emergency has also become an ordinary technique of governance. By means of emergency ordinances, the executive power replaced the legislative power, thereby abolishing the doctrine of separation of powers that defines democracy. But, as Agamben argues, freedom has never been as limited as it was during the pandemic, when it underwent an unprecedented restriction that neither fascism attempted to carry out. People were confined in their homes, deprived of any social relation, and reduced to a mere condition of biological preservation. "This barbarity," Agamben claims, "does not even spare the dead: those who die are being deprived of their right to a funeral, their bodies instead burned" (Agamben 2021, 38). In other words, Agamben's hypothesis is that the world of bourgeois democracies, established on rights, parliaments and division of powers, is gradually being replaced by a new despotism that, as for the pervasiveness of controls and the termination of any political activity, "will be worse than the totalitarianisms we have known thus far" (42). While Nazi Germany needed to deploy an explicitly totalitarian ideological apparatus to achieve such domination, the transformation we are witnessing today "operates through the introduction of a sanitation terror," which requires a monolithic media apparatus to spread the gospels of the "religion of health." Agamben concludes, "What, in the tradition of bourgeois democracy, used to be the right to health became, seemingly without anyone noticing, a juridical-religious obligation that must be fulfilled at any cost" (9). "Biosecurity" is the governmental dispositif resulting from the combination of the new religion of health and the state of exception of state power. It is probably the most effective device that the West has ever known. The experience of the pandemic showed how inclined to accept unprecedented limitations to freedom human beings are once their health is endangered.

The "security state" that the war on terrorism and the "axis of evil" legitimized, and whereof Sheldon Wolin warned us about its totalitarian potentialities, is today transformed by Agamben into a governmental paradigm established on the war against anything threatening our health. For him, this proves how biological preservation is the sole value of Western and Westernized societies—the "bare life" for which we relinquish any other value and freedom: from social and sentimental relationships to work and politics. Bare life, along with the fear of losing it, does not unite human beings; rather, it blinds and separates them, as any individual is exclusively seen as a potential carrier of an infection to avoid at any cost.

Agamben's diagnosis resembles Arendt's position on the deterioration of social bonds that grounds totalitarianism. In fact, for Arendt, the perfect ingredients that pave the way to totalitarian regimes are isolation; terror; atomization and, at the same time, massification; and the inability to perceive freedom as a space of participation. There is no doubt that Giorgio Agamben sharply grasped the important transformation of contemporary biopower. Although I disagree with almost everything in his analysis of the pandemic, I do subscribe to the crucial assumption he believes to be one of the grounds of our critical times: societies value nothing more than biological life (Agamben 2021, 19). It is a crucial question for the comprehension of power relations in today's democracies. How did it happen that, in the name of biosecurity, we became able to endure almost anything?

As crucial as the issue is, Agamben's extremism ends up eluding the complexity of such a question, thereby assuming the form of a sort of apocalyptic announcement of the end of times. It is as if the pandemic had been the excuse to make us used to living under the regime of a permanent curfew that does not aim at defending us from an external and recognizable enemy but from an enemy that lives in our houses, even inside us. In other words, Agamben portrays a civil war of all against all and against ourselves, whose capillarity surpasses even the paranoid desire for control of classical totalitarianism.

From Jacques Derrida to Peter Sloterdijk and Alain Brossat, contemporary political philosophy has often considered the paradigm of biopower a paradigm of immunization. According to this perspective, twentieth-century totalitarianism eventually exposed the majority of the population to a death right because of the paranoid search for immunity from pathogenic agents, be they enemy races or counterrevolutionary classes. Roberto Esposito, who wrote probably the most elaborate works on this topic, applied the categories of his seminal reflection on the immunity-community relationship (Esposito 2008, 2009, 2017) to the physical and political hazards of the pandemic. In 2022's *Immunità comune: Biopolitica all'epoca della pandemia* (Common Immunity: Biopolitics in the Age of Pandemic), Esposito dwells on the risks coming from securitarian politics that tend to be excessive. He acknowledges the potentially totalitarian outcomes of a state community that, in the name of individual and collective health, pushes its mechanism of immunization to the fullest. With the COVID-19 pandemic, immunization has become real, literally physical immunization. Any doctor knows that an immune system whose functioning becomes excessive may run into autoimmune pathologies; likewise, a society led by biopower constantly risks imploding. In other words, Esposito acknowledges the dialectic between affirmation and negation, between the limitations safeguarding life and the restrictions to freedom that such limitations entail. In a society, actually a whole planet, devastated by a "real" virus, the fragile dialectic between immunity and self-immunity, between affirmation and negation, risks being devastated as well.

The equilibrium between protection and compulsion of life is fragile and unstable. The pandemic brutally revealed all the ambivalences and contradictions of the demand for immunization. So-called experts, sophisticated technologies, lockdowns, tracking, monitoring—these are insidious practices recalling the always more realistic totalitarian dystopias.

After all, such danger inhabits the very process of immunization, which is necessary for the preservation of life. We need to carefully watch to ensure that the need for immunization does not establish outrageous inequalities. Our thinking must remind us that the protection of some should never correspond to the extreme exposition and vulnerability of others. This is the engine of the thanatological machine of biopower: the separation between lives that must be defended because worthy to be lived and lives that are not worthy to be lived and, therefore, not worth defending. We are again facing the risk that biopower may ultimately overturn itself in necropower. This is a risk extremely more concrete and real than a pandemic considered as an *ad hoc* imaginary construction to better dominate us.

HYPERCONTROLLED SOCIETIES

New technologies represent the ultimate totalizing veer undertaken by our societies. Scholars unanimously agree on this, both those who, like Agamben, believe that the state of exception will, emergency after emergency, increasingly strengthen and discriminate and those who, like the critics of neoliberal governmentality, are convinced that platform capitalism and the society of algorithms will reduce any citizen to an object at the service of marketing and data mining. In any case, new technologies are today's most targeted totalitarian ghost.

The management of the COVID-19 pandemic has hastened the process of integrating digital technologies fined-tuned over recent decades into governance practices. Such technologies may trigger mechanisms of power aimed at adjusting behaviors by means of software increasingly preying on and totalizing citizens' lives. The bonds connecting technology, business, and politics usher in a new form of totalitarianism that concentrates all technoscientific powers in the hands of those who monopolize data mining.

I do not intend to dwell on the question of whether the totality that the so-called digital governmentality aims at corresponds to a "totalitarian totality" or whether another kind of "politically innocent" drive toward totality is at stake. Rather, I want to highlight how reflections on the "society of digital control" went well beyond the mere description of how the new technopolitical universe works microphysically and macrophysically.

If anything, they denounce the affirmation of a polished "captological" ability to determine the total "protocolization" of life.[4] Hence, unlike what Deleuze preconized, we are not only living in a "society of control." We, mobile and volatile subjectivities, are not simply enduring a form of reticular and rhizomatic domination. It is no longer sufficient to read new technologies through the lens of Foucault's governmentality—that is, as securitarian technologies concerning the biological aspects of populations. Although Deleuze and Foucault constitute essential references, theories of digital totalitarianism have constantly revised and updated traditional theories on the society of control. Our society is, in fact, a "hypercontrolled society."

Western societies are becoming, in a sort of run-up to the Chinese model, hypercontrolled societies where the new form of domination rests on "algorithmic governmentality" (Rouvroy 2013; Berns and Rouvroy 2012). Despite the diversity of perspectives, all these interpretations have the same polemic objectives: a government of processes and people nourished by raw data and metadata that flow across every aspect of human life and a government that modulates and stimulates communication to anticipate and forecast social relations and individual behaviors. Obviously, the greater the circulation of data flows, the greater the intensity and precision of control. According to Bernard Stiegler, whose complex approach cannot be reduced to a mere lamentation, control occurs "at the speed of light," nourished by the personal data that users themselves produce and publish, thereby providing material for the anticipatory calculation of behaviors (Stiegler 2015).

Shoshana Zuboff's *The Age of Surveillance Capitalism* (2019) is probably the most important critical work on this topic. With the locution "surveillance capitalism," Zuboff describes the new economic order arising from a fraudulent mutation of capitalism where an unprecedented concentration of wealth, knowledge, and power has been taking place. Surveillance capitalism threatens democracy by imposing its dominion on market societies. Zuboff does not simply outline abstract and drastic theses on hypercontrolled society. She accurately analyzes data, transformations, and policies concerning especially big tech corporations such as Amazon, Google, Microsoft, and Facebook (now Meta). Here, however, I will focus on the philosophical aspects of Zuboff's data analysis, locating it within the wider perspective of "inverted totalitarianism," in that for her the engine of surveillance capitalism is its obsession with totality. This is because, first of all, it carries out a sort of totalizing capitalist expropriation that gives birth to a new age of panoptic surveillance. Zuboff summarizes the "wider project of surveillance capitalism and its original sin of dispossession" with "six critical declarations" expressive of the true spirit of big tech corporations:

1. We claim human experience as raw material free for the taking. On the basis of this claim, we can ignore considerations of individuals' rights, interests, awareness, or comprehension.
2. On the basis of our claim, we assert the right to take an individual's experience for translation into behavioral data.
3. Our right to take, based on our claim of free raw material, confers the right to own the behavioral data derived from human experience.
4. Our rights to take and to own confer the right to know what the data disclose.
5. Our rights to take, to own, and to know confer the right to decide how we use our knowledge.
6. Our rights to take, to own, to know, and to decide confer our rights to the conditions that preserve our rights to take, to own, to know, and to decide. (Zuboff 2019, 174)

Zuboff argues that we have been so fascinated by the innovations and the vibrant results of Big Tech that we have become blind to its totalitarian aggressivity and invasiveness. These twenty-first-century invaders do not ask permission; they simply proceed, undisturbed by means of fake practices of legitimation such as cynical, obscure, and not-understandable consent forms.

Like Wolin, Zuboff constantly compares "classic totalitarianism" from the twentieth century with current surveillance capitalism. Currently, to chase totality means obtaining as much information as possible to make machines work as precisely as possible. This is an "instrumentarian power"—that is, the power of governments and corporations to use technology and infrastructure to achieve the widest and most certain forecast of users' behaviors. It turns people into "instruments" that are used in predictable ways to achieve the government's and corporations' goals (Zuboff 2019). Yet surveillance capitalism not only registers and tracks behavior; it also addresses and manipulates it. According to her, we are facing a totalitarian power whose effects are even more totalizing than those achieved by classic totalitarianism. It can do so thanks to what she names the "Big Other": a digital apparatus of permanent and computational connections that, as never before, constantly monitors, computes, addresses, and modifies human behavior (Zuboff 2015).

Even though "classic" totalitarian regimes and new instrumentarian power are historically different, they share the same will to totality. If the former employed violence, terror, and ideology to shape a totalitarian political condition, the latter "reduces human experience to measurable observable behavior while remaining steadfastly indifferent to the meaning of that experience" (Zuboff 2019, 353–54). This is what Zuboff names "radical indifference," a "form of observation without witness" that makes digital detachment the foundation of surveillance capitalism's violence:

> Instrumentarianism's radical indifference is operationalized in Big Other's dehumanized methods of evaluation that produce *equivalence without equality*. These methods reduce individuals to the lowest common denominator of sameness—an organism among organisms—despite all the vital ways in which we are not the same. From Big Other's point of view we are strictly Other-Ones: *organisms that behave*. . . . There is no domination of the soul that displaces all intimacy and attachment with terror—far better to let a multitude of relationships bloom. Big Other does not care what we think, feel, or do as long as its millions, billions, and trillions of sensate, actuating, computational eyes and ears can observe, render, datafy, and instrumentalize the vast reservoirs of behavioral surplus that are generated in the galactic uproar of connection and communication. (354)

From Günther Anders (1961) and the many post-Heideggerian authors, to more recent critiques of social media and algorithmic governmentality (Vaidhyanathan 2021; Fillimowicz 2022), the idea that technological totalitarianism is so successful that it does not need to resort to violence and physical constrictions is widespread, so much so that it is in danger of becoming a kind of empty lamentation. Of course, there are original and interesting points of view. Among them, despite some excessively extreme and abstract claims, Zuboff's work provides us not only with a very detailed analysis of big tech dominion but also with unsettling examples of how data mining has been, or could be, employed to carry out political repression. In the West, the total surveillance at which new capitalism aims is not yet addressed, as in China, to the neutralization of dissent. For now, a hyper-controlled society fulfills economic goals and market demands. To do so, surveillance capitalists have conceived a terrifying worldview. They want society to emulate machines' learning, and industrial societies are modeled on the methods and the discipline typical of factories' production lines.

According to this view, instrumental power should replace social trust, and the Big Other would put certainty in place of human relations. The power aiming at totality considers democratic institutions an impediment. Laws, regulations, rights and duties, norms and private contracts—all the traditional limitations to the market are now under attack.

The comparison between the twentieth-century totalitarian regime and the new totalizing drive of the twenty-first century constantly recurs. Even though surveillance capitalism represents an unprecedented form of total power that, thus far, does not commit violence to our bodies, our attention should be, and should have been, the same that we would have had toward a classic form of totalitarian regime. "Will we suffer the same lack of foresight as those who could not comprehend totalitarianism's rise, paralyzed by the sheer power of Big Other and its infinite echoes of consequence, distracted by our needs and confused by its speed, secrecy, and success?" (Zuboff 2019, 370).

The dangers of surveillance capitalism are unprecedented, so they cannot be contrasted with the usual practices of political resistance. It is worth repeating that, for Zuboff, what is at stake currently is the evolution toward a total domination caused by a never-before-seen concentration of power and knowledge. It is the rise of the new social order of an information civilization. They can name practices differently, justifying them in various ways, but means and ends will always be the same: datafication, instrumentalization, connection, communication, and constant and all-encompassing computation of any animate or inanimate thing, as well as of any kind of process, be it natural, psychological, chemical, IT, administrative, or financial. What happens in the real world is constantly tracked by phones, cars, streets, houses, shops, bodies, trees, buildings, and cities to feed the virtual world, where data are transformed into previsions that fill the always more copious pages of the shadow text.

Even though what we learned from the experience of past totalitarian regimes cannot save us, their historical reference still constitutes, for Zuboff, a negative guiding idea that helps to measure the totalitarian gradient of the present: totalitarianism aimed at reconstructing human species through the double mechanism of genocide and "soul engineering." Surveillance capitalists' instrumentarian power does not pursue extermination or brainwashing. It does not need to be violent, as it has at its disposal more refined and pervasive means to modify behaviors. There is no need either of training or of spiritual conversion or of ideologies to which our conducts should conform. Instrumentarian power, Zuboff states, "does not demand possession of each person from the inside out. It has no interest in exterminating or disfiguring our bodies and minds in the name of pure devotion" (Zuboff 2019, 338). Surveillance capitalism draws data from our bodies and our blood, but it does not need to get its hands dirty. It does not mean to frighten, to harm, or to kill. In other words, it is utterly indifferent toward the motives and meanings behind our actions. Surveillance capitalism wants measurable and profitable data, not the unquantifiable distresses of our souls.

Yet surveillance capitalism is surely as unsettling and frightening as classic totalitarianism was for its victims and witnesses. It has been difficult to understand this new species of domination given that it came into our lives disguised under astonishing technologies and catchy rhetoric. After all, this is the nature of power in the age of surveillance capitalism: to act in disguise to elude individuals' consciousness. By doing so, without suspending democracy, instrumentarian power replaces individuals' freedom with the manipulating knowledge of the Big Other, sociality with certainty. Surveillance capitalism does not oppose democracy head-on, but it erodes it from within, devouring those human potentialities, such as people's self-awareness, that are fundamental to democratic life. Totalitarianism was the transformation of the state into a project of total domination. Instrumentarian power and Big Other are, instead, signs of the transformation of the market into a project of total control, something inconceivable before the rise of digital technologies and the logic of surveillance capital accumulation. Such new power resulted from an unprecedented convergence: "the surveillance and actuation capabilities of Big Other in combination with the discovery and monetization of behavioral surplus" (Zuboff 2019, 358).

Critics of hypercontrolled society acknowledge unanimously how our mind is being totally captured by those technologies that condition our behaviors. If, for Shoshana Zuboff, the power striving for totality follows a top-down trajectory that, from the Big Other, hits the base of a social pyramid where citizens are reduced to mere carriers of information, for other interpreters of "soft totalitarianism," new total forms of power follow a twofold direction.[5]

Consider Byung-Chul Han, a South Korean philosopher teaching in Germany, whose works—somewhere between pop philosophy, critical theory, and philosophical manifestos—at least in Europe, represent one of the key references on the society of total control. According to Han, we are not only mobilized from above; we are not mere passive and receptive consumers of external information. We are also active senders and producers. As he maintains in his *In the Swarm* (2013): "It used to be that the masses could organize in parties and unions that were animated by an ideology. Now, the masses are falling apart into crowds of individuals—in other words, alienated, digital hikikomori who do not participate in discourse or constitute a public sphere" (Han 2017a, 65). Today's topology of digital connection is not a web of real contacts and relational intersections. It is rather a whole thing of "narcissistic islands of egos" (46). Unlike what used to happen in "classic totalitarianism," currently, total control is carried out not through spatial and communicative isolation but through the promotion of hyperconnection and hypercommunication. A society of total control comes true when its citizens lay themselves bare and confess not because they are forced to do so but because they are pushed to exhibit themselves. It is a society of performance leading to isolation. Everybody produces and spreads information, thereby pushing all others to participate and to be transparent as much as they can.

Hence, conformism is engendered despite our delusion of being a free agent who can decide whether to participate. For neoliberal power knows how to exploit freedom; it takes advantage of everything that is part of the practices and the expressive forms of freedom, such as emotion, game, and communication. Exploiting someone against that person's will is not as efficient and profitable. In contrast, the exploitation of freedom is highly profitable. Such a new regime, more affirmative and seductive than repressive, is committed to sparking positive emotions to exploit them. It encourages rather than forbids. It does not hinder the subject's sphere of action;

rather, it promises to "enrich" it. "The neoliberal imperative to perform," Han argues, "transforms time into working hours. It totalizes a belabored temporality. Breaks represent only a phase of the working day. Today, we know time only as time for working. So this temporality follows us not only on vacation but even when we sleep" (33).

Digital devices produce a new slavery or, better, an unprecedented totalitarian compulsion. If they are so effective in exploiting us, it is not only because they transform every place into a workplace by accelerating the circulation of capital but also because they foster permanent communication and connection, thereby disclosing the collective unconscious.

Once again we find the idea that the efficiency of neoliberal soft totalitarianism is not due to terror and violence but to the fact that it shapes itself on the human psyche. It does not indoctrinate us, and it does not impose duties and prohibitions on us. Neither does it want us to be silent. It rather constantly calls us to communicate, share, participate. *Like* is its motto. While we consume and communicate, while we "like" what we think our preferences are, we voluntarily subject ourselves to dominating relationships. Neoliberalism is a catchy capitalism that, formally and substantially, is not as paternalistic as nineteenth-century capitalism. Neoliberalism does not need to be commanded; it dominates by creating addiction.

Constant video surveillance and tracking surely induce the sensation of being observed by the gaze of a "Big Other." This is what the panoptic effect consists of. But by resorting to Deleuze's 1990 *Postscript on the Societies of Control* (Han 2017b, 21), Han contests any inquiry on today's totalitarian drive established on Foucault's reading of the Benthamian panopticon. For we are not living in a regime that divides and separates space, imprisoning and disciplining bodies. Even though surveillance is total, current forms of relationship and production are mobile, flexible, and hostile to any sort of limitation.

By confusing, not to say overlapping, disciplinary power with biopower, Han questions Foucauldian theories on biopolitics in a way that is not convincing to me. According to him, biopolitical control concerns only external factors, such as reproduction, health, and mortality. It does not penetrate into the psyche of the population. Neoliberal capitalism is not interested in what is biological, somatic, or corporal in the first place. Rather, it has discovered how productive the human psyche can be. Such a "psychopolitical" turn is a consequence of the immaterial and incorporeal forms of production of today's capitalism. Neoliberal capitalism does not produce material objects but immaterial goods, such as information and programs. The body as a productive force is no longer as central as it was in the disciplinary society of biopower: to enhance productivity, not only are corporal resistances to be overcome, but physical and mental processes are to be optimized.

Today's totalitarianism is surely a new form of panoptic hypersurveillance in terms of digital surveillance that observes and records. Nevertheless, it establishes neither a disciplinary society nor a biopolitical, thanatopolitical, or necropolitical society, but rather a "society of psychopolitical transparency." The true aim of totalizing drive is collective psyche, not the body of population. This is the key point of Han's critique of new total power. Psychopower is far more effective than biopower because it controls and influences the body from within. In Han's eyes, Foucault and all the interpreters of contemporary domination in terms of biopower do not understand, as Bernard Stiegler did, the importance of the hegemonization of psychical space (Han 2017b, 28–29). Agamben himself, who thought of having taken Foucault's theory one step further, also failed "to approach the technologies of power in the neoliberal regime in meaningful fashion" as today's *homines sacri* "have not been shut out of the system—they have been shut into the system" (Han 2017b, 26).

In my opinion, it is true that the biopolitical approach of strict Foucauldian observance sometimes runs the risk of not considering the psychic effects of new forms of power. What Han seems to overlook, however, is what, from Foucault to Butler, has been largely considered the true totalitarian vector of a biopolitical society: the distinction between worthy lives and unworthy lives. Surveillance devices surely attempt to capture the totality of the population and its psyche, but while doing so, they constantly establish hierarchies that discriminate between lives that are worthy of protection and mourning and unworthy lives that can be let die in complete indifference.

Han's reflection echoes an oft-repeated opinion in the contemporary debate on soft totalitarianism: the idea that the pervasiveness, the velocity, and the efficiency of digital communication is dramatically modifying our relationship with reality, be it that among people and that with the real as such. By implicitly recalling Baudrillard and Debord, Han claims that "digitality radically restructures the Lacanian triad of real, imaginary, and symbolic. It dismantles the real and totalizes the imaginary." Digital devices provide points of access to a virtuality that is constantly nourished by a hypertrophic imaginary, thereby shielding us from the irruption of reality and undermining "our ability to encounter and work with negativity" (Han 2017a, 22).

Han shares with many critics of hypercontrolled society the conviction that digital media "defactualize" reality by inputting an enormous number of images. In summary, "digital culture" is basically more totalizing than the mass culture of totalitarian regimes. Digital culture goes along with a form of existence from which becoming and aging, birth and death are cancelled, making "presentism" the sole temporal dimension we can live in (Hartog 2015). The digital age—"a postnatal and postmortal era" (Han 2017a, 32)—will no longer attempt to transform reality, as it will not encounter the opposition of material things. It will only deal with immaterial information. For Han, this is the new imperative of present times: "everything must lie open, ready and available for everyone" (Han 2017a, 39).

Yet, if transparency is the essence of information, and information is pure positivity and presence, what of the real that cannot access the communication and visibility of swarms?

THE CRISIS OF THE REAL

From surveillance capitalism to pandemic dispositif, from psychopower to algocracy (government by algorithms), the hypercontrol that digital technologies can carry out produces an all-encompassing totalization of any social spheres: microphysic and macrophysic, economic and political, social and psychic, collective and individual. The massive employment of digital technologies reaches such a level of capture, extraction, and automatization that it causes a sort of total mobilization. In a world where information can always be recovered in an extremely fast way, the social system moves from trust to control and transparency. If we leave traces of every action and intention of ours, then the risk for our lives to be completely protocolled is now imminent. Big data can replace the Orwellian Big Brother.

As we have seen, this is what all those who believe that our age of surveillance and communication is a continuation of totalitarianism by other means lament. As Harcourt pointed out, such a possibility is becoming increasingly feasible because total control is pursued not through spatial and communicative isolation but rather by leveraging our desire for exposition and visibility (Harcourt 2015). Therefore, the distinction between the observer and the observed tends to fail.

These are the general considerations that all those who reflect on the great transformations occurring in digital societies seem to endorse: from the most prudent analyses to the most radical critiques for which Facebook and Google would be the secret services of a ghostly invisible hand. Without reaching such drastic and dystopic conclusions, political and social philosophy is largely worried about the eventuality that society may become a place where any of us could be the Big Brother and the prisoner at the same time. That would be the digital accomplishment of the great totalitarian cycle that started in the twentieth century. Not by chance, the main philosophical concern of Western philosophical reflection on totalitarianism is now prominently recurring: the question of the relationship between totality, truth, and reality.

Today's scholarship on this question focuses mainly on the equation that hypercontrolled society is considered to end up establishing: the integral identity between, on the one hand, what is communicable and transmittable and, on the other hand, what it is—in other words, the identity of information and being. What is not communicated and visible does not exist. The so-called IFS (Information Fatigue Syndrome) would thus involve the separation of the referent from the real. This is the ontological overturning of the society of transparency, where behind or below the intricate play of data there stand ghostly spaces.

Hypercontrolled society, from platform capitalism to the dictatorship of algorithms, not only directs behaviors to automatize them but also succeeds in making "communication flow" and reality correspond. To put it differently, the serious consequences of surveillance technology—that is, the extension of the mining logic of the market to all society—not only undermine the value of democracy but also stress constitutional fences and transform citizens into informative sources for data mining. As Giorgio Agamben pointed out, hypercontrolled society first and foremost limits "human right that is not enshrined in any constitution: the right to truth, the need for a true word" (Agamben 2021, 46):

> Humanity is entering a phase of its history where truth is being reduced to a moment within the march of falsity. That false discourse which must be held as truth is true, even when its non-truth is revealed. In this way, it is language itself, as a space for the manifestation of truth, that is being confiscated from us. Now we can only silently observe the unfolding—a true development, because it is real—of the lie. And, in order to stop this, we must have the courage to seek, uncompromisingly, the most precious of goods: a true word. (48)

Even those authors who do not agree with Agamben's conclusions on the pandemic fear a gigantic operation of falsification of truth. Behind these diagnoses echo the alarmist twentieth-century considerations on the falsity of the whole, from Adorno to Debord. Well before digital technologies alarmed some of today's most influential philosophers, philosophical reflection on totalitarianism had insisted on the power ushered by the totalitarian lie—a power that transforms, selects, and manipulates the real, made possible by the combination of technology and the ideological lie.

"Modern man—totalitarian genus—is immersed in a lie, he breathes lies, he is a slave to lying in every moment of his life" (Koyré 2017, 143). In Alexandre Koyré's *The Political Function of the Modern Lie* (1945), Koyré expressed what would become a widespread feeling about the break brought about by the totalitarian lie with respect to a "traditional" form of lie that politics has always employed. In those decades, Hannah Arendt was not the only one to be troubled about the changes that contemporary lies underwent (Arendt 1972). As I have noted, since the end of the 1960s, Eastern dissidents have tirelessly and vigorously repeated, even if with a certain naivety, that totalitarian regimes are responsible for particular "innovations." Institutional lies are one of these. Their warning did not exclusively concern communist Eastern European countries, but it also pertained to the West since, they maintained, Western countries were inscribed in the same "post-totalitarian" fate. There is no "dissident" text that does not resort to Orwell's *1984* as a hyperrealistic analysis of the actual situation.

If totalitarianisms establish themselves by means of "gunshots," they can maintain their power only by means of "language shots," gradually transforming themselves thereby into fully fledged "mass logocracies" (Milosz [1953] 1955). Any possible attempt at resistance to the regime can be prevented only through the employment of a "new-speak." Once ideological terror is over, there comes a "cold totalitarianism" that wants all autonomous judgment to be precluded. A power that demolishes the very criteria of facticity by manipulating information and destroying historical memory is as totalitarian as a regime that violently subjugates the whole society to its will to total domination. Certainly, when truth, in the sense of facticity, changes on the basis of power's necessities, then it is impossible to distinguish between what is true and what is false. The transition from normal lie to "institutionalized lie," which secures political power with the monopoly of historical and factual truths, is thus taking place. This is what connects Stalinism and Nazism to the various "thaws" that reduced their violence by perfecting the mechanism of "regime deceit," as variable in its contents as it is inflexible in its function (Kolakowski 1983; Havel 1988).

Totalitarianism seems to have inaugurated the age of performative lies. Unlike "traditional" political lies, totalitarian lies not only put to work their destructiveness but also their constructive capacity. This has nothing to do with negations and concealments of certain factual truths, which might somehow be saved. Totalitarianism breaks with a millenary ontology that has always divided the world in truth and appearance, in reality and fiction, but that has certainly not foreseen the "creative" power of lies, which were to become the very foundation for the construction of the raving political systems of our times. By providing aberrant ideological fictions with linguistic expression, they became real, thereby risking reshaping the world. By concealing "harsh facts," we came very close to destroying the texture of the entire reality.

Obviously, what was at stake was much more than the damage provoked by the deceiver's ill will and wickedness. The world's very consistence and its possible share was at stake. This means that the problem is first ontological and then political. Totalitarian regimes have dangerously walked on thin ice, running the risk of precipitating the world toward extinction, outside a sphere in which it is still possible—in spite of all the precautions and suspicions of deconstruction—to distinguish between what happens and what is told, where it is still possible to separate facts from logical constructions. These regimes have laid the foundations for the indistinction between factual and fictitious, making such a distinction ephemeral to the point of paradox. They bestow absolute primacy on deceit while endlessly manipulating reality. But they have not succeeded in burying it completely.

Nowadays, it is as if many agents have learned how to take catastrophic advantage of this confusion, potentially ending up shattering an extremely thin demarcation line into a new totalitarian game of mirror images. Currently, an enormous possibility for lies is provided by the kaleidoscopic media world, where an incessant flow of decomposed and recomposed images and data is increasingly persuading us that reality is not immediately given to us, but it is rather weighed, selected, even produced. In addition, we are carried away by the whirl of this spectacle to such an extent that we feel impotent.

But totalitarian lies still contain specific ideological content. Even without recalling Adorno, Baudrillard, or Debord, deep inside of us, we all know how increasingly inclusive and elusive, how widespread and irresponsible, the game is becoming. Without surrendering to the complaint of those who deplore a society of control that transforms everybody into passive spectators and consumers, we cannot deny that lies, communication, information, and factuality integrate with one another to the point that, in such a thick web, no possible way out for efficacious action or thought can be conceived.

We are not immersed in a lie that violates the body of those who are not committed to it. We are not impotent, passive, and conformist only out of fear and cowardice but also because the "unquestionable falsehood" (Debord 1990) skillfully organizes the ignorance of what is happening and, when needed, it can immediately consign to oblivion what one has been able to understand. Thrown into a sort of constant alternation of images and information, incapable of understanding which ones relate facts and which ones are covering and filtrating them, a truly powerful leap—probably impossible and utopian—would be needed to regain what we have been deprived of again: the experience of a factual world that resists mediatization.

Conclusion

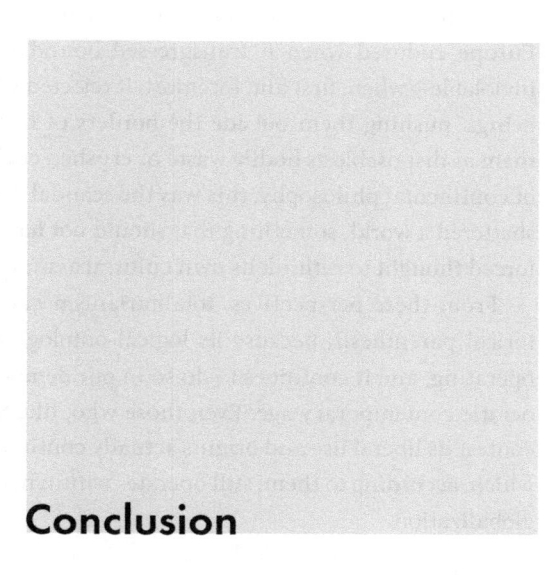

What, then, are we talking about when we talk about totalitarianism? We can say there are as many meanings as there are disciplinary fields that address such a question: history, political science, sociology, anthropology, and philosophy, among others. As I have mentioned, each selects, from its own perspective, which events or periods to give prominence, which features of the political system to highlight, which social dynamics to put under indictment, or which human behavior(s) to investigate. There is, however, one threat to which everyone wants to alert us through explorations of the concept of totalitarianism: the danger of a reality in which the regime of separation of spheres—political, public, private, technological, economic, social, intimate—seems to collapse. In other words, when pronounced, the word *totalitarianism* gives voice to the perception that a limit in the relationship between power and life has been shattered, whether political, social, economic, technological, psychological, or physical.

Perhaps, among all the disciplines involved, political philosophy has been the most effective in conveying the meaning of what many authors consider a "mismeasure." For twentieth-century philosophy, as we have seen, *totalitarianism* has named the extreme experience that a "civilized" Europe endured when it transgressed boundaries that were considered inviolable—when, first and foremost, it rejected whole categories of human beings, pushing them outside the borders of humanity and thus making them as disposable as bodily waste or crushed cockroaches. For a large part of continental philosophy, this was the scandal, the catastrophic event that shattered a world, something that should not have happened and therefore forced thought to rethink its own cultural assumptions.

From these perspectives, totalitarianism cannot be considered a historical parenthesis, because its logical-ontological *a priori* has long been operating, and it continues to do so in our democratic or, better, postdemocratic contemporary age. Even those who, like Slavoj Žižek (Žižek 2001), contest its liberal use and origins actually continue to assume such a priori, which, according to them, still operates within neoliberal and technological globalization.

Historians and political scientists have contested the value of philosophical reflections, arguing that their analyses of the totalitarian phenomenon are vague, unscrupulous, and end up dissolving historical events and political functionings into categories of the spirit. On closer inspection, all the philosophy authors that I have analyzed in this book clearly know that a philosophical interpretation is not, and cannot be, a historiographical thesis. Many know, as well, that elevating concentration camps or other concrete tragic events to the paradigm of political evil may risk confusing historical phenomena that must be safeguarded in their uniqueness. Nevertheless, if historical sciences are to validate actual events on the basis of what archives and testimonies provide, the task of philosophy consists of elaborating and drawing concepts from the muddle of events.

Hannah Arendt, Jean-Luc Nancy, George Bataille, Michel Foucault, Simone Weil, Claude Lefort, Emmanuel Levinas, Giorgio Agamben—these names (and many others could have been mentioned) represent a radical thought that wants first and foremost to provoke, thus succeeding in going beyond the concrete configuration of these regimes. As for political science, also for philosophy: totalitarianism surely designates a typology of regime opposed to constitutional, democratic, parliamentary, and pluralist forms of governments. Yet it also describes something more than political oppression, something that, more radically, has to do with the intricate, pervasive, and destructive relationships between power and human life. Therefore, at the end of this investigation, I think I can suggest the following idea: that of distinguishing between, on the one hand, the locution *totalitarian regimes* and, on the other hand, the term *totalitarianism*.

This is a controversial distinction. Some might even consider it specious. Even so, its heuristic potential is undeniable. For it would permit discriminating between the political science characterization that presumes to induce a general category from a specific historical reality and the theoretical-philosophical conceptualization that, likewise, moves from history, but not to build an ideal-type to add to the list of political regimes. In this case, the word *totalitarianism* does not refer to a specific political, institutional organization but to a configuration of power relationships that eventually determines a form of total domination, a form of dominion in which freedom—understood as possibility, indeterminateness, and new beginning—risks being completely denied. In other words, we might distinguish between two different fundamental ways of looking at totalitarian rule: as a strictly political phenomenon, which has reached a precise institutional configuration, for example, in National Socialism and Stalinism, or as a broader social phenomenon, in which power relations—not purely political—are so tightly intertwined that there is no effective space left for freedom.

It is worth repeating that the philosophical reflection on totalitarianism carried out a reconsideration of the question of power that overcame the strict dualisms grounding modern categories, such as public/private, political/social, collective/individual, and so forth. Furthermore, as political philosophy claims, the concept of totalitarianism succeeded in deconstructing oppositions, especially those that excessively simplify the different areas of the political field. I have amply examined the fact that if we take these philosophical reflections seriously, it is no longer possible to invoke comforting antitheses as, for instance, those who understand, on the one hand, fascism and Nazism as forms of right-wing irrationalist nihilism and, on the other hand, Stalinism as the ill swerve of a good, left-wing rationalist humanism. It is no longer quite so easy to distinguish between a technology of devices that track our movements to better protect and strengthen us and a society of control that uses the wiles of technology to make us submissive.

Philosophy, whether militant or not, should never work for simplification. Its practices of conceptualization and abstraction should, instead, work for the complication of established and preconceived theoretical boundaries. Philosophy is a means to inspect gray zones, aporias, and the contradictions of the past and the present. It may be difficult, perhaps even painful, to do so, but it is a duty that philosophy cannot abjure.

All the authors that I have mentioned thus far rejected the irresponsibility of an idle philosophical reflection. This does not mean, however, that they endorsed specific diagnoses on the faults of the past or committed themselves to building "corrective" projects for the future. For them, this is not the main task of thinking. We surely must "think otherwise," imagine "others'" possible politics. But our thinking must linger on the negative without rejecting it in favor of a positivity that would completely silence it. If thinking were solely normative, if it were immediately constructive to work for specific political projects, then it would result in a more or less effective technic. For the authors I have mentioned, to be responsible means also glimpsing through political and social phenomena not only the way out but also the metamorphosis of the totalitarian a priori. This totalitarianism can designate something more than a typology of a regime that stands opposite to democratic, parliamentary, and pluralistic constitutional forms.

From the second half of the twentieth century on, a large part of "continental" philosophy has conceived a hermeneutical circle that culminates with the "scandal" of thinking about the continuity between totalitarianism and Western tradition—that is, pinpointing within totalitarian logic the involvement of Western Reason and how it relates to the world. In addition to the answers that philosophy, more or less plausibly, succeeds in providing about the implications of its own categories in totalitarian phenomena, these important readings, superficially defined as "essentialist," witness the process of examination that the twentieth century conducted on itself. Before judging the results they have reached as inconclusive and "metaphysical" on the basis of alleged scientific criteria, we must bear in mind that this is, first of all, a phenomenon of self-reflection, through which philosophy has demonstrated being able to capture the great provocations of the century in thought—from the unprecedented and systematic destructive will of Nazism and Stalinism to the unbridled and overwhelming triumph of technology.

Now, the main question is, What can we still draw from these analyses if the past will surely not come back in the same way? The question of totalitarianism should be reconsidered on the basis of a very cumbersome and not unanimously accepted presupposition. Totalitarian regimes have highlighted how not only political power, but power in general—even though not evil per se, as Foucault would put it—always has a totalitarian vocation. Power is a force that constantly, almost naturally, attempts to expand its grasp on everything and everyone. The dynamics of power have no point of arrival. They have no aim, but they devour every achievement. The drive for power is thus not only limitless, but it aims at suppressing limits as such. This is why we can maintain the contemporary reflection on totalitarianism ushered in as a new, unprecedented way of thinking power. If these philosophical reflections "discovered" something relevant to power, then their legacy could help us comprehend the potential risks of contemporary dynamics.

Political philosophy has made the term *totalitarianism* a borderline idea. On the one hand, it represents a limit idea, a sort of Kantian *focus imaginarius*, on the basis of which we can detect the flaws and the dangers to freedom of our present; on the other hand, it may constitute an obsessive idea that paranoically sees specters of totality, and threats to freedom, everywhere. It is undeniable—as it becomes "extremist," tracing any event back to an overarching totalizing tendency—that the concept of totalitarianism risks going around in circles, thereby losing its distinctive grasp on reality. But it remains true that thought is nourished by provocations; it remains alive only through challenges. Reflecting on the risks of every possible totalitarianism is perhaps for political philosophy the greatest challenge.

Notes

Chapter 1

1. Recent historiographic research agrees on this. See Petersen (1978, 105–28; 1996, 15–35); Bongiovanni (1997, 23–54); and Ruocco and Scuccimarra (1996, 119–59).

2. On the discussion about which kind of regime Italy represented, see the important book by Emilio Gentile (2009).

3. Serge's 1933 testament, entitled *Everything Is Put into Question*, was originally published as *La Profession de foi de Victor Serge* in the French journal *La Révolution prolétarienne*.

4. For Monnerot, however, who anticipates Nolte's theses in many ways, the Soviet Union not only erected the perfect form of totalitarianism but served as a model for right-wing totalitarianisms.

5. Arendt's reading was amply affected by Franz Borkenau's *The Totalitarian Enemy* (London: Faber and Faber, 1940).

Chapter 2

1. See, e.g., Bracher (1984). Motivated by this same desire to rehabilitate the "scientific dignity" of the concept are the collected works of Jesse (1996); Söllner, Walkenhaus, and Wieland (1997); and Siegel (1998).

2. Some historians still reject the concept of totalitarianism, preferring instead that of fascism. A significant contribution to the debate had come from Italian scholars committed to understanding the nature of the fascist regime. On this see De Felice (1977).

3. See Almond (1956); Huntington (1970); and Kirkpatrick (1982). For one of the most articulated elaborations of the difference between authoritarian and totalitarian regimes, see Linz (1997).

4. From Zinoviev to Havel this is a recurring statement. See Kolakowski (1983).

5. The most famous of the "neo-Orwellian" books is surely Zinoviev (1979).

6. Šimečka's words are quoted in Rupnik (1989), 231.

Chapter 3

1. I am alluding to Lukács ([1954] 2021), where Nazi totalitarianism is seen as the outcome of the irrationalist side of bourgeois individualistic-solipsistic thought.

2. For the interpretation of totalitarianism in terms of political religions, see the important works collected in Maier 2004.

3. Many philosophers identify the explosion of totalitarianism in the intertwining of these dynamics. See, e.g., Camus ([1951] 2013); and Merleau-Ponty (2017).

4. Arendt to Henry Allen Moe, Jan. 29, 1953, Guggenheim Correspondences 012641.

5. Close to these positions is Lefort (2012).

6. All translations from *Die Antiquiertheit des Menschen* [The obsolescence of man] are mine and are based on the German edition.

7. I am alluding to Ernst Bloch's *Das Prinzip Hoffnung* (*The Principle of Hope*), a book published in three volumes during the 1950s.

Chapter 4

1. William E. Connolly's *Aspirational Fascism* (2017), a critique of Trumpism, resembles Wolin's diagnosis of the Bush administration's totalitarian aspirations.

2. Recently, many critiques of this kind have, in my opinion, continued and renewed the thesis of the "universe of domination" developed by authors of the Frankfurt School such as Adorno, Horkheimer, and Marcuse. For a wide-spectrum reconstruction see Ahmed (2019).

3. Didier Fassin stressed a fallacy within Foucault's position on biopower, as there is a difference between a biopolitics as government over population and the sacralization of biological life as absolute value on the altar of which anything can be sacrificed (Fassin 2018).

4. B. J. Fogg coined the neologism *captology* in *Persuasive Technology* (2003). As he explains in his introduction to that volume, the term is "an acronym based on the phrase 'computers as persuasive technologies,'" and "it describes the area where technology and persuasion overlap" (5).

5. Consider, for instance, Harcourt (2015). On the one hand, Harcourt warns us against the danger of digital technologies and their employment by Big Tech and intelligence agencies. On the other hand, he stresses our indifference toward the restrictions to our freedom, as well as our desire for continuing to expose our life to the visibility and transparency of technology, thereby nourishing increasingly the circularity between power and subjectivity.

References

Adorno, Theodor W. 2005. *Minima Moralia: Reflection on a Damaged Life*. New York: Verso.
Adorno, Theodor W., et al. 1950. *The Authoritarian Personality*. New York: Harper & Brothers.
Agamben, Giorgio. 1998. *Homo Sacer: Sovereign Power and Bare Life*. Stanford: Stanford University Press.
———. 1999. *Remnants of Auschwitz: The Witness and the Archive*. New York: Zone.
———. 2021. *Where Are We Now? The Epidemic as Politics*. London: Eris.
Ahmed, Saladdin. 2019. *Totalitarian Space and the Destruction of Aura*. Albany: State University of New York Press.
Almond, Gabriel A. 1956. "Comparative Political Systems." *Journal of Politics* 18, no. 3: 391–409.
Amendola, Giovanni. 1951. *La nuova democrazia*. Naples: Ricciardi.
———. 1960. *La democrazia italiana contro il fascismo, 1922-1924*. Milan-Naples: Ricciardi.
Anders, Günther. 1961. *Die Antiquiertheit des Menschen I: Über die Seele im Zeitalter der zweiten industriellen Revolution* [The obsolescence of man I: On the soul in the age of the Second Industrial Revolution]. München: C. H. Beck.
———. 1962. "Theses for the Atomic Age." *Massachusetts Review* 3, no. 3: 493–505.
———. 1980. *Die Antiquiertheit des Menschen II: Über die Zerstörung des Lebens im Zeitalter der dritten industriellen Revolution* [The obsolescence of man II: On the destruction of life in the age of the Third Industrial Revolution]. München: C. H. Beck.
———. 1984. "Mein Judentum." In *Das Günther Anders Lesebuch*, edited by Bernhard Lassahn, 234–51. Zurich: Diogenes. First published 1978.
———. 2009. "The Pathology of Freedom: An Essay on Non-identification." *Deleuze Studies* 3, no. 2: 278–310.
Arendt, Hannah. 1972. "Lying in Politics. Reflections on the Pentagon Paper." In *Crises of the Republic*, 1–48. New York: Harvest.
———. 1973. *The Origins of Totalitarianism*. New York: Harvest.

———. (1978) 1981. *The Life of the Mind.* Boston: Houghton Mifflin Harcourt.
———. 1994. "On the Nature of Totalitarianism." In *Essays in Understanding, 1930–1954*, 328–60. New York: Harcourt Brace.
———. 2002. "Karl Marx and the Tradition of Western Political Thought." *Social Research* 69, no. 2: 273–319.
Aron, Raymond. 1944. "L'avenir des religions séculières." Parts 1 and 2. *La France libre* 8, nos. 45–46: 210–17, 269–77.
———. 1954. "L'essence du totalitarisme." *Critique* 10, no. 80: 51–70.
———. 1969. *Democracy and Totalitarianism: A Theory of Political Regimes.* New York: Praeger.
Ash, Timothy G. 1986. "Does Central Europe Exist?" *New York Review of Books*, Oct. 9, 1986, 45–52.
Ayçoberry, Pierre. 1979. *La question nazie, les interprétations du national-socialisme, 1922–1975.* Paris: Seuil.
Baczko, Bronislaw. 1981. *Utopia.* In *Enciclopedia Einaudi.* Vol. 14, 856–920. Turin: Einaudi.
Baehr, Peter. 2009. "The Novelty of Jihadist Terror." *Society*, no. 46: 210–13.
Barber, Benjamin R. 1969. "Conceptual Foundations of Totalitarianism." In Friedrich, Curtis, and Barber 1969, 3–52.
Basso, Lelio, and Luigi Anderlini, eds. 1961. *Le riviste di Piero Gobetti.* Milano: Feltrinelli.
Bataille, Georges. 1970. *Œuvres complètes.* Paris: Gallimard.
Benjamin, Walter. 2005. *On the Concept of History.* Translated by Dennis Redmon. www.marxists.org/reference/archive/benjamin/1940/history.htm.
Berns, Thomas, and Antoinette Rouvroy. 2013. "Gouvernementalité algorithmique et perspectives d'émancipation." *Réseaux*, no. 177: 163–96.
Besançon, Alain. 1977. *Les origines intellectuelles du léninisme.* Paris: Calmann-Levy.
———. 1980. *Présent soviétique et passé russe.* Paris: Hachette.
Blanchot, Maurice. (1983) 1988. *The Unavowable Community.* New York: Station Hill.
Bongiovanni, Bruno. 1997. "Revisionismo e totalitarismo: Storie e significati." *Teoria politica* 13, no. 1: 23–54.
Bracher, Karl D. (1976) 1981. "Terrorism and Totalitarianism." In *Totalitarianism Reconsidered*, edited by Ernest A. Menze, 107–19. Port Washington, NY: Kennikat.
———. 1984. "Totalitarismo." In *Enciclopedia del Novecento.* Vol. 7. Rome: Istituto dell'Enciclopedia Italiana. www.treccani.it/enciclopedia/totalitarismo_%28Enciclopedia-del-Novecento%29.
———. 1987. *Totalitäre Erfahrung.* München: Piper.
Brossat, Alain. 1996. *L'épreuve du désastre. Le XXe siècle et les camps.* Paris: Albin Michel.
Brown, Wendy L. 2019. *In the Ruins of Neoliberalism: The Rise of Antidemocratic Politics in the West.* New York: Columbia University Press.
Brown, Wendy, Peter E. Gordon, and Max Pensky. 2018. *Authoritarianism: Three Inquiries in Critical Theory.* Chicago: University of Chicago Press.

Burleigh, Michel. 2010. *Blood and Rage: A Cultural History of Terrorism*. New York: Harper.

Burnham, James. 1941. *The Managerial Revolution: What Is Happening in the World*. New York: John Day.

Butler, Judith. 2004. *Precarious Life. The Powers of Mourning and Violence*. London: Verso.

———. 2022. *What World Is This? A Pandemic Phenomenology*. New York: Columbia University Press.

Camus, Albert. (1951) 2013. *The Rebel*. London: Penguin.

Castoriadis, Cornelius. 1973. *La societé bureaucratique*. Paris: UGE.

———. 1975. *L'institution imaginaire de la société*. Paris: Seuil.

———. 1981. *Devant la guerre*. Paris: Fayard.

———. 1986. *Domaines de l'homme: Les carrefours du labyrinthe*. Vol. 2. Paris: Seuil.

Chafarevitch, Igor. 1975. "Passé et avenir du socialisme." In *Des voix sous les décombres*, edited by Alexandre Soljénitsyne. Paris: Seuil.

Connolly, William E. 2017. *Aspirational Fascism: The Struggle for Multifaceted Democracy under Trumpism*. Minneapolis: University of Minnesota Press.

Cooper, Melinda. 2008. *Life as a Surplus: Biotechnology and Capitalism in the Neoliberal Era*. Seattle: University of Washington Press.

Curtis, Michael. 1969. "Retreat from Totalitarianism." In Friedrich, Curtis, and Barber 1969, 53–121.

Debord, Guy. (1988) 1990. *Comments on the Society of the Spectacle*. London: Verso.

De Felice, Renzo. 1977. *Interpretations of Fascism*. Cambridge, MA: Harvard University Press.

Deneault, Alain. 2023. *"Gouvernance": Le management totalitaire*. Paris: Lux Éditeur.

Derrida, Jacques. 1994. *Specters of Marx. The State of the Debt, the Work of Mourning and the New International*. London: Routledge.

Djilas, Milo (van). 1957. *The New Class. An Analysis of the Communist System*. London: Thames and Hudson.

Dumont, Louis. 1995. "The Totalitarian Disease." In *Rethinking the Subject: An Anthology of Contemporary European Social Thought*, edited by James D. Faubion, 176–92. New York: Routledge.

Esposito, Roberto. 2008. *Bíos: Biopolitics and Philosophy*. Minneapolis: University of Minnesota Press.

———. 2009. *Communitas: The Origin and Destiny of Community*. Stanford: Stanford University Press.

———. 2017. *Immunitas: The Protection and Negation of Life*. New York: Polity.

———. 2022. *Immunità comune: Biopolitica all'epoca della pandemia*. Turin: Einaudi.

Fassin, Didier. 2018. *La vie: Mode d'emploi critique*. Paris: Seuil.

Faye, Jean Pierre. 2003. *Introduction aux langages totalitaires: Théorie et transformations du récit*. Paris: Hermann.

Ferry, Luc and Pisier-Kouchner Evelyne. "Théorie du le totalitarisme." In Grawitz and Leca 1985, 117–59.
Finkielkraute, Alain. 2013. *L'identité malheureuse*. Paris: Folio-Gallimard.
Fogg, Brian Jeffrey. 2003. *Persuasive Technology: Using Computers to Change What We Think and Do*. San Francisco: Morgan Kaufmann.
Forsthoff, Ernst. 1933. *Der totaler Staat*. Hamburg: Hanseatische Verlagsanstalt.
Forti, Simona. 2006. *Hannah Arendt tra filosofia e politica*. Milano: Bruno Mondadori.
———. 2015. *New Demons: Rethinking Power and Evil Today*. Stanford: Stanford University Press.
Foucault, Michel. 2003. *"Society Must Be Defended": Lectures at the Collège de France, 1975–1976*. Edited by Mauro Bertani and Alessandro Fontana. New York: Picador.
Fraenkel, Ernst. (1941) 2006. *The Dual State: A Contribution to the Theory of Dictatorship*. Oxford: Oxford University Press.
Friedrich, Carl J. 1954. *Totalitarianism*. Cambridge, MA: Harvard University Press.
Friedrich, Carl J., and Zbigniew K. Brzezinski. 1956. *Totalitarian Dictatorship and Autocracy*. Cambridge, MA: Harvard University Press.
Friedrich, Carl J., Michael Curtis, and Benjamin R. Barber. 1969. *Totalitarianism in Perspective: Three Views*. New York: Praeger.
Fromm, Erich. 1941. *Escape from Freedom*. New York: Farrar & Rinehart.
Furet, François. (1978) 1981. *Interpreting the French Revolution*. Cambridge: Cambridge University Press.
———. 1995. *The Passing of an Illusion: The Idea of Communism in the Twentieth Century*. Chicago: University of Chicago Press.
Galli, Carlo. 1997. "Strategie della totalità: Stato autoritario, Stato totale, totalitarismo nella Germania degli anni Trenta." *Filosofia politica* 11, no. 1: 27–62.
Gauchet, Mercel. 1976. "L'expérience totalitaire et la pensée de la politique." *Ésprit*, no. 7–8: 3–28.
Gentile, Emilio. 2009. *The Italian Road to Totalitarianism*. London: Routledge.
Gentile, Giovanni. 1925. *Che cosa è il fascismo*. Florence: La Fenice.
Gessen, Masha. 2017. *The Future Is History: How Totalitarianism Reclaimed Russia*. New York: Riverhead.
Gleason, Abbott. 1995. *Totalitarianism: The Inner History of the Cold War*. Oxford: Oxford University Press.
Glucksmann, André. 2002. *Dostoïevski à Manhattan*. Paris: R. Laffont.
Gramsci, Antonio. 2007. *Prison Notebooks*. Vol. 3. New York: Columbia University Press.
Grawitz, Madeleine, and Jean Leca, eds. 1985. *Traité de science politique*. Vol. 2, *Les régimes politiques contemporains*, edited by Madeleine Grawitz and Jean Leca, 115–59. Paris: P.U.F.
Habermas, Jürgen. 2018. *The Philosophical Discourse of Modernity*. New York: Wiley.

Halévy, Élie. 1938. *L'ère des tyrannies: Études sur le socialisme et la guerre.* Paris: Gallimard.

Han, Byung-Chul. 2017a. *In the Swarm: Digital Prospects.* Cambridge, MA: MIT Press.

———. 2017b. *Psychopolitics: Neoliberalism and New Technologies of Power.* London: Verso.

Harcourt, Bernard E. 2015. *Exposed: Desire and Disobedience in the Digital Age.* Cambridge, MA: Harvard University Press.

Hartog, François. 2015. *Regimes of Historicity: Presentism and Experiences of Time.* New York: Columbia University Press.

Havel, Václav. (1978) 1985. *The Power of the Powerless.* New York: M. E. Sharpe.

———. 1988. "Stories and Totalitarianism." *Index on Censorship* 17, no. 3 (March): 14–21.

Hayek, Friedrich (von). (1944) 1976. *The Road to Serfdom.* New York: Taylor & Francis.

Heidegger, Martin. 2007. "The Question Concerning Technology." In *The Question Concerning Technology and Other Essays,* 3–35. New York: Garland.

Heller, Ágnes. 1989. "An Imaginary Preface to the 1984 Edition of Hannah Arendt's *The Origins of Totalitarianism.* In *The Public Realm,* edited by Reiner Schürmann, 253–67. Albany: State University of New York Press.

———. 2002. "9/11, or Modernity and Terror." *Constellations* 9, no. 1 (March): 53–62.

Hitler, Adolf. (1925) 1982. *Mein Kampf.* London: Hutchinson.

Hodge, Joel. 2016. "Terrorism's Answer to Modernity's Cultural Crisis: Re-sacralising Violence in the Name of Jihadist Totalitarianism." *Modern Theology* 32, no. 2 (April): 231–58.

Horkheimer, Max. (1938) 2020. "The Jews and Europe." In *Critical Theory and Society: A Reader,* edited by Stephen Eric Bronner and Douglas Kellner, 77–94. New York: Routledge.

———. (1942) 1973. "The Authoritarian State." *Telos,* no. 15 (Spring): 3–20.

———, ed. 1972. *Critical Theory: Selected Essays.* New York: Continuum.

Horkheimer, Max, and Theodor W Adorno. (1944) 2002. *Dialectic of Enlightenment.* Stanford: Stanford University Press.

Howe, Irving, ed. 1983. *1984 Revisited: Totalitarianism in Our Century.* New York: Harper & Row.

Huntington, Samuel P., and Clement H. Moore, eds. 1970. *Authoritarian Politics in Modern Society: The Dynamics of Established One-Party Systems.* New York: Basic Books.

Inkeles, Alex. 1969. "The Totalitarian Mystique: Some Impressions of Dynamics of Totalitarian Society." In Friedrich, Curtis, and Barber 1969, 88–107.

Isaac, Jeffrey. 2008. "Critics of Totalitarianism." In *The Cambridge History of Twentieth-Century Political Thought,* edited by Terence Ball and Richard Bellamy, 181–201. Cambridge: Cambridge University Press.

Jesse, Eckhard, ed. 1996. *Totalitarismus im 20. Jahrhundert. Eine Bilanz der internationalen Forschung.* Baden-Baden: Nomos.

Jonas, Hans. 1954. *Gnosis und spätantiker Geist*. Vols. 1–2. Göttingen: Vandenhoeck & Ruprecht.

Jünger, Ernst. 1993. "Total Mobilization." In *The Heidegger Controversy: A Critical Reader*, edited by Richard Wolin, 119–39. Cambridge, MA: MIT Press.

Kirkpatrick, Jeane J. 1982. *Dictatorship and Double Standards*. New York: American Enterprise Institute.

Kolakowski, Leszek. (1971) 1978. "Thèse sur l'espoir et le désespoir." In *La Pologne, une société en dissidence*, 77–92. Paris: Maspero.

———. 1983. "Totalitarianism and the Virtue of the Lie." In Howe 1983, 122–44.

———. 2005. *Main Currents of Marxism: Its Origins, Growth and Dissolution*. 3 vols. New York: Norton.

Kornhauser, William. 1959. *The Politics of Mass Society*. Glencoe, IL: Free Press.

Koyré, Alexandre. 2017. "The Political Function of the Modern Lie." *October*, no. 160: 143–51.

Krastev, Ivan. 2014. *Democracy Disrupted: The Politics of Global Protest*. Philadelphia: University of Pennsylvania Press.

Kundera, Milan. (1979) 1981. *The Book of Laughter and Forgetting*. London: Penguin.

Lacoue-Labarthe, Philippe. 1990. *Heidegger, Art, and Politics: The Fiction of the Political*. Oxford: Blackwell.

Lacoue-Labarthe, Philippe, and Jean-Luc Nancy. 1990. "The Nazi Myth." *Critical Inquiry* 16, no. 2 (Winter): 291–312.

Lasswell, Harold D. 1935. *World Politics and Personal Insecurity*. New York: McGraw-Hill.

Lederer, Emile. 1940. *State of the Masses: The Threat of the Classless Society*. New York: Norton.

Lefort, Claude. (1956) 1986a. "Totalitarianism without Stalin." In Lefort 1986c, 52–88.

———. (1972) 2012. *Machiavelli in the Making*. Evanston, IL: Northwestern University Press.

———. 1976. *Un homme en trop: Réflexions sur "l'Archipel du Goulag."* Paris: Seuil.

———. (1979) 1986b. "The Image of the Body and Totalitarianism." In Lefort 1986c, 292–306.

———. (1981) 1988a. "The Permanence of the Theologico-Political?" In Lefort 1988c, 213–55.

———. (1983) 1988b. "The Question of Democracy." In Lefort 1988c, 9–20.

———. 1986c. *The Political Forms of Modern Society: Bureaucracy, Democracy, Totalitarianism*. Edited by John B. Thompson. Cambridge, MA: MIT Press.

———. 1988c. *Democracy and Political Theory*. Cambridge: Polity.

———. (1999) 2007. *Complications: Communism and the Dilemmas of Democracy*. New York: Columbia University Press.

Leibholz, Gerhard. 1933. *Die Auflösung der liberalen Demokratie in Deutschland und das autoritäre Staatsbild*. München: Duncker & Humblot.

———. 1938. "Il secolo XIX e lo Stato totalitario del presente." *Rivista internazionale di filosofia del diritto* 18, no. 1: 1–40.

Levinas, Emmanuel. 1990a. *Difficult Freedom: Essays on Judaism*. Baltimore, MD: Johns Hopkins University Press. First published 1963.

———. 1990b. "Reflections on the Philosophy of Hitlerism." *Critical Inquiry* 17, no. 1: 62–71. First published 1934.

Linz, Juan J. 1997. "Totalitarian and Authoritarian Regimes. My Recollections on the Development of Comparative Politics." In Söllner, Walkenhaus, and Wieland 1997, 141–57.

Löwith, Karl. (1940) 1966. "The Historical Background of European Nihilism." In *Nature, History, and Existentialism, and Other Essays in the Philosophy of History*, edited by Arnold Boyd Levison, 3–16. Evanston, IL: Northwestern University Press.

———. (1949) 2011. *Meaning in History*. Chicago: University of Chicago Press.

Lukács, György. (1954) 2021. *The Destruction of Reason*. New York: Verso.

Lyotard, Jean-François. 1988. *The Differend: Phrases in Dispute*. Manchester: Manchester University Press.

———. (1988) 1990. *Heidegger and "the Jews."* Minneapolis: University of Minnesota Press.

———. 1991. *Lectures d'enfance*. Paris: Galilée.

———. 1992. *The Postmodern Explained: Correspondence, 1982–1985*. Minneapolis: University of Minnesota Press.

Macdonald, Douglas J. 2007. *The New Totalitarians: Social Identities and Radical Islamist Political Grand Strategy*. Carlisle, PA: US Army War College, Strategic Studies Institute.

Maffesoli, Michel. 1979. *La violence totalitaire: Essai d'anthropologie politique*. Paris: P.U.F.

Magyar, Bálint. 2016. *Post-Communist Mafia State: The Case of Hungary*. Budapest: Central European University.

Maier, Hans, ed. 2004. *Totalitarianism and Political Religions*. London: Routledge.

Marcuse, Herbert. 1934. "Der Kampf gegen den Liberalismus in der totalitäre Staatsauffassung." *Zeitschrift für Sozialforschung* 3, no. 2: 161–95.

———. 1964. *One-Dimensional Man: Studies in the Ideology of Advanced Industrial Society*. Boston: Beacon.

Mbembe, Achille. 2019. *Necropolitics*. Durham, NC: Duke University Press.

Merleau-Ponty, Maurice. 2017. *Humanism and Terror: The Communist Problem*. New York: Taylor & Francis.

Milosz, Czeslaw. 1953. *The Captive Mind*. New York: Vintage.

Mlynář, Zdeněk. 1983. *Crisis of the Soviet System 1953–1981*. Köln: Index.

Monnerot, Jules. 1945. *Les faits sociaux ne sont pas des choses*. Paris: Gallimard.

———. 1948. "Le totalitarisme: La droite et la gauche." *Le Nef*, April 1948.

———. 1949. *Sociologie du communisme: Échec d'une tentative religieuse au XXe siècle*. Paris: Gallimard.

———. 1968. *Sociologie de la Révolution: Mythologies politiques de XXe siècle*. Paris: Gallimard.

Monti, Augusto. 1924. "I liberali alla prova." *La rivoluzione liberale*, Jan. 22, 1924.
Mounier, Emmanuel. 1934a. "Anticapitalisme." *Ésprit* 2, no. 21 (June): 2–7.
———. 1934b. "Des pseudo-valeurs spirituelles fascistes." *Ésprit* 2, no. 16 (Jan.): 533–40.
———. 1934c. "Tentation du communisme." *Ésprit* 2, no. 21 (June): . 416–25.
———. 1961. "Les civilisations fascistes." *L'homme nouveau marxiste* (1936). In *Œuvres*. Paris: Seuil.
Mueller, Klaus. 1998. "East European Studies, Neo-totalitarianism and Social Science Theory." In Siegel 1998, 55–90.
Mussolini, Benito. 1932. "Fascism." In *Enciclopedia Italiana*. Vol. 14. Rome: Istituto dell'Enciclopedia Italiana.
———. 1956. *Opera omnia*. Vol. 21. Florence: La Fenice.
Neumann, Franz. 2009. *Behemoth: The Structure and Practice of National Socialism, 1933–1944*. Chicago: Ivan R. Dee.
Neumann, Sigmund. 1942. *Permanent Revolution: The Total State in a World at War*. New York: Harper & Brothers.
Nolte, Ernst. 1966. *Three Faces of Fascism: Action Française, Italian Fascism, National Socialism*. New York: Holt, Rinehart and Winston.
———. 1987. *Der europäische Bürgerkrieg, 1917–1945: Nationalsozialismus und Bolschewismus*. Berlin: Propyläen.
———. 1998. "The Three Versions of the Theory of Totalitarianism and the Significance of the Historical-Genetic Version." In Siegel 1998, 109–28.
Papaioannou, Kostas. 1967. *L'idéologie froide*. Paris: Pauvert.
Patočka, Jan. 1990. *Liberté et sacrifice: Écrits politiques*. Grenoble: J. Million.
———. 1996. *Heretical Essays in the Philosophy of History*. Chicago: Open Court.
Petersen, Jens. 1978. "Die Entstehung des Totalitarismusbegriffs in Italien." In *Totalitarismus: Ein Studien-Reader zur Herrschaftsanalyse moderner Diktaturen*, edited by Manfred Funke, 105–28. Düsseldorf: Droste.
———. 1996. "Die Geschichte des Totalitarismusbegriffs in Italien." In *"Totalitarismus" und "Politische Religionen,"* edited by Hans Mayer, 15–35. Paderborn: Ferdinand Schöningh.
Poliakov, Leon. 1987. *Les totalitarismes du XXe siècle: Un phénomène historique dépassé?* Paris: Fayard.
Popper, Karl. 1945. *The Open Society and Its Enemies*. Vol 1, *The Plato Spell*. London: Routledge.
———. (1944) 2012. *The Poverty of Historicism*. New York: Taylor & Francis.
Portinaro, Pier Paolo. 2003. *Il principio disperazione: Tre studi su Günther Anders*. Torino: Bollati Boringhieri.
Rauschning, Hermann. (1938) 1972. *The Revolution of Nihilism*. New York: Arno.
Reich, Wilhelm. 1933. *Mass Psychology of Fascism*. New York: Farrar, Straus and Giroux.
Richta, Radovan. 1969. *La civilisation au carrefour*. Paris: Anthropos.
Rizzi, Bruno B. 1939. *La bureaucratisation du monde*. Paris: Édité par l'auteur.

Rose, Nikolas. 2007. *The Politics of Life Itself: Biomedicine, Power, and Subjectivity in the Twenty-First Century*. Princeton, NJ: Princeton University Press.
Rouvroy, Antoinette. 2013. "The End(s) of Critique: Data-Behaviourism vs Due-Process." In *Privacy, Due Process and the Computational Turn: Philosophers of Law Meet Philosophers of Technology*, edited by M. Hildebrandt and E. De Vries, 143–68. London: Routledge.
Ruocco, Giovanni, and Luca Scuccimarra. 1996. "Il concetto di totalitarismo e la ricerca storica." *Storica* 2, no. 6: 119–59.
Rupnik, Jacques. 1984. "Le totalitarisme vu de l'Est." In *Totalitarismes*, edited by Guy Hermet, Pierre Hassner, and Jacques Rupnik, 43–71. Paris: Economica.
———. 1989. *The Other Europe: The Rise and Fall of Communism in East-Central Europe*. New York: Pantheon.
Schmitt, Carl. 1940. *Positionen und Begriffe im Kampf mit Weimar-Genf-Versailles 1923–1939*. Hamburg: Hanseatische Verlagsanstalt. First published 1931.
———. 1958. *Verfassungsrechtliche Aufsätze aus den Jahren 1924–1954: Materialien zu einer Verfassungslehre*. Berlin: Duncker & Humblot.
———. 2001. *State, Movement, People: The Triadic Structure of the Political Unity (1933)*. Corvallis, OR: Plutarch.
———. 2016. *Der Hüter der Verfassung*. Berlin: Duncker & Humblot. First published 1931.
Serge, Victor. 1937. *Destin d'une révolution: Urss 1917–1936*. Parsi: Plon.
Shapiro, Leonard. 1972. *Totalitarianism*. London: Pall Mall.
Siegel, Achim, ed. 1998. *The Totalitarian Paradigm after the End of Communism*. Amsterdam: Rodopi.
Simecka, Milan. (1979) 1984. *Restoration of Order: Normalization of Czechoslovakia, 1969–76*. London: Verso.
Söllner, Alfons, Ralf Walkenhaus, and Karin Wieland, eds. 1997. *Totalitarismus. Eine Ideengeschichte des 20. Jahrhunderts*. Berlin: Akademie Verlag.
Soljénitsyne, Alexandre, et al. 1975. *Des voix sous les décombres*. Paris: Seuil.
Souvarine, Boris. 1939. *Stalin: A Critical Survey of Bolshevism*. New York: Longmans.
———. 1985. *Écrits, 1925–1939*. Paris: Denoël.
Spiro, Herbert J. 1968. "Totalitarianism." In *International Encyclopedia of the Social Sciences*, edited by David L. Sills. 27 vols. New York: Macmillan / Free Press.
Stawar, Andre. 1963. *Libres Essais Marxistes*. Paris: Éditions du Seuil.
Stiegler, Barbara. 2021. *De la démocratie en pandémie: Santé, recherche, éducation*. Paris: Gallimard.
Stiegler, Bernard. 2015. *La société automatique: 1. L'avenir du travail*. Paris: Fayard.
Strauss, Leo. 1941. "German Nihilism." *Interpretation* 26, no. 3 (Spring 1999): 353–78.
———. (1948) 2000. *On Tyranny*. Chicago: University of Chicago Press.
———. (1953) 1965. *Natural Right and History*. Chicago: University of Chicago Press.
———. 1959. *What Is Political Philosophy? And Other Studies*. Chicago: University of Chicago Press.
Sturzo, Luigi. 1924. "Spirito e realtà." *La rivoluzione liberale*, Jan. 22, 1924.

———. 1926. *Italy and Fascismo*. London: Faber & Gwyer.
Talmon, Jacob Leib. 1952. *The Origins of Totalitarian Democracy*. London: Secker & Warburg.
Ternon, Yves. 1995. *L'État criminel: Les génocides au XXe siècle*. Paris: Seuil.
Tibi, Bassam. 2007. "The Totalitarianism of Jihadist Islamism and Its Challenge to Europe and Islam." In *Totalitarian Movements and Political Religions* 8, no. 1 (Feb.): 35–54.
Traverso, Enzo. 2019. *The New Faces of Fascism: Populism and the Far Right*. London: Verso.
Tucker, Robert C. 1961. "Toward a Comparative Politics of Movement-Regimes." *American Political Science Review* 15, no. 2: 281–89.
———. 1983. "Does Big Brother Truly Exist?" In Howe 1983, 89–102.
Urbinati, Nadia. 2014. *Democracy Disfigured: Opinion, Truth, and the People*. Cambridge, MA: Harvard University Press.
Vaidhyanathan, Siva. 2021. *Antisocial Media: How Facebook Disconnects Us and Undermines Democracy*. Oxford: Oxford University Press.
Voegelin, Eric. 1956. *Order and History*. Baton Rouge: Louisiana State University Press.
———. 1959. *Wissenschaft, Politik und Gnosis*. München: Kösel.
———. 1990. *Anamnesis: On the Theory of History and Politics*. Columbia: University of Missouri Press.
———. 2000a. *Modernity without Restraint*. Vol. 5. Edited by Manfred Henningsen. Columbia: University of Missouri Press.
———. 2000b. "The New Science of Politics: An Introduction." In Voegelin 2000a, 75–242. First published 1952.
———. 2000c. "The Political Religions." In Voegelin 2000a, 19–74. First published 1938.
Waldemar, Gurian. 1969. "Totalitarianism as Political Religion." In Friedrich, Curtis, and Barber 1969, 119–40.
Walzer, Michael. 1983. "On Failed Totalitarianism." In Howe 1983, 103–21.
Weil, Simone. 1962. "The Great Beast: Some Reflections on the Origins of Hitlerism." In *Selected Essays, 1934-1943: Historical, Political, and Moral Writings*, edited by Richard Rees, 89–144. London: Oxford University Press.
———. 2004. "Reflections Concerning the Causes of Liberty and Social Oppression." In *Oppression and Liberty*, 36–117. London: Taylor & Francis.
———. 2014. *On the Abolition of All Political Parties*. New York: NYRB Classics.
Wipperman, Wolfgang. 1997. *Totalitarismustheorien: Die Entwicklung der Diskussion von den Anfängen bis heute*. Darmstadt: Primus.
Wolin, Sheldon S. 2008. *Democracy Incorporated: Managed Democracy and the Specter of Inverted Totalitarianism*. Princeton, NJ: Princeton University Press.
Ziegler, Heinz Otto. 1932. *Autoritärer oder totaler Staat*. Tübingen: Mohr.
Zinoviev, Alexander. 1979. *The Yawning Heights*. New York: Random House.
———. 1984. *The Reality of Communism*. New York: Schocken.

Žižek, Slavoj. 2001. *Did Somebody Say Totalitarianism? Five Interventions in the (Mis)Use of a Notion*. London: Verso.

Zuboff, Shoshana. 2015. "Big Other: Surveillance Capitalism and the Prospects of an Informative Civilization." *Journal of Information Technology* 30, no. 1 (March): 75–89.

———. 2019. *The Age of Surveillance Capitalism: The Fight for a Human Future at the New Frontier of Power*. London: Profile.

Index

Adorno, Theodor, 71, 80, 96–98, 102, 138, 140, 148n2
Agamben, Giorgio, 118–20, 124–27, 138, 142
The Age of Surveillance Capitalism (Zuboff), 128
Amendola, Giovanni, 9–10
Anders, Günther: anthropocentrism and, 102–3; *Die Antiquiertheit des Menschen,* 100, 102–6; apocalyptic times and, 98, 104; atomic bomb and, 98–109; background of, 99; climate change and, 108; eschatology and, 104–6; evil and, 105; freedom and, 97, 101; Heideggerian aspects of thought of, 62, 99–103; human condition for, 100–101; imperative of responsibility and, 104–5; Jewish origins of, 100–101; little attention received by, 99; *The Man on the Bridge,* 100; *The Moral Implications of the Atomic Age,* 106; name of, 100; nihilism and, 98, 104–5, 107; *Pathology of Freedom,* 100; philosophical anthropology of, 100–104; philosophical background of, 100; promethean gap and, 103, 107–8; shock of the contingent and, 101; technology and, 98, 102–4, 130; theses for the atomic age of, 106–8; world without human beings and, 104
Angelus Novus (Klee), 99
Die Antiquiertheit des Menschen (Anders), 100, 102–6
Arendt, Hannah: biopolitics and, 118–19; construction of models and, 37; definition of totalitarianism and, 32; deterioration of social bonds and, 125; extermination camps and, 96, 118, 120; ideological supersense and, 57; imperialism and, 120; influence of, 37, 77; Jew as symbolic figure for, 101; lies and, 138; *The Life of the Mind,* 76; Marxism and, 76–77; plural action and, 74; politics that reevaluates the ontological of, 74; radical evil and, 6; terror and, 76; *Totalitarian Elements in Marxism,* 76; Western thought and, 74–76, 96. *See also Origins of Totalitarianism*
Aron, Raymond: construction of models and, 38; democracy and, 38–40; detotalitarianization of Soviet Union and, 39; influences on, 38; Nazism compared to Stalinism by, 38–39; political parties and, 38–40; secular religions and, 40, 57; totalitarian syndrome and, 38

atomic bomb, 98–109
Atti del Congresso dell'Unione Nazionale (Amendola), 9
Auschwitz, 75–78, 81, 91, 96, 119
"Authoritarian State, The" (Horkheimer), 71–72
authoritarianism: authoritarian syndrome, 29; characteristics of, 46–49; communism and, 54; conservative nature of, 47; construction of models and, 45–59; development of totalitarianism and, 32–33; ideology and, 54; masses and, 47; mentality and, 47–48; obedience and, 47; political parties and, 46–47; residual pluralism of, 46–47; routinization of charisma in, 49; totalitarianism's relation to, 4, 16, 27, 32–33, 45–49, 54, 110; tradition valued in, 48; transitions to and from, 46

Barber, Benjamin, 41–42
Basso, Lelio (pseudonym Prometeo Filodemo), 10–11
Bataille, Georges, 21–23, 68, 142
Benjamin, Walter, 99, 104
Besançon, Alain, 43–44, 57
biopolitics, 91–96, 118–27, 134–35
biopower, 74, 91–96, 118–20, 122, 124–27, 134–35
Bloch, Ernst, 101–2, 105
Bolshevik Revolution, 4, 17–18, 23, 41, 88–89
Bolshevism, 18, 55, 84–85
Bracher, Karl D., 42
Brzezinski, Zbigniew, 37–38, 40
Burnham, James, 18
Butler, Judith, 119–22, 135

camps. *See* concentration camps; extermination camps
Castoriadis, Cornelius, 83, 89–91

characteristics of totalitarianism, 4–6, 26, 37–38, 42–56, 58, 111. *See also* construction of models
Charter 77 movement, 55–56
communism: authoritarianism's relation to, 54; construction of models and, 40–41, 49–56; democracy and, 83, 85, 88; development of totalitarianism and, 9–10; discrediting through totalitarianism accusations of, 4, 111; fascism's relation to, 9–10, 18–19, 88; French Revolution and, 83; historicism and, 64, 70; ideology and, 54; Nazism's relation to, 51, 53, 63; new man of, 90; objectivist metaphysics and, 55; philosophy in the face of extremes and, 63–64, 66, 83; power and, 24; as secular religion, 20–24; state's role and, 22; totalitarianism's relation to, 4, 6, 9–10, 20–24, 40–41, 49–56, 72, 111–12; unity affirmed in, 6; Western thought and, 63. *See also* Marxism; Soviet Union; Stalinism
concentration camps: annihilation of individual identity through, 33–34, 44; atomic bomb and, 98, 107; construction of models and, 44; extermination camps distinguished from, 33; as laboratory of total domination, 33–34, 111; paradigm of political evil and, 142; philosophy in the face of extremes and, 75, 98; as suspension of law, 44
The Conceptual Foundations of Totalitarianism (Barber), 41
conformism, 52, 133
construction of models: acceptance of compromises and, 39; adjective use of 'totalitarian,' 36; analyses of political science and, 36–45; applicability of models and,

37–38; attempts on distinctions and, 45–56; authoritarianism distinguished from totalitarianism and, 45–59; banality of evil and, 52; characteristics of totalitarianism and, 4–6, 26, 37–38, 42–56, 58, 111; communism and, 40–41, 49–56; concentration camps and, 44; conformism and, 52; crisis as nurturing totalitarian regimes and, 47; definition of totalitarianism and, 2–6, 9, 10–14, 20, 27, 32, 37–38, 41–43, 89, 141–45; democracy and, 38–41, 46; dissent practices and, 55–56; distinctiveness of totalitarianism and, 37–45, 54–55; Eastern European perspectives and, 49–56; elimination of totalitarian concept and, 41–42; essentialist approach and, 37, 41, 51; freedom and, 39–40, 48, 52–54; ideology and, 44–47, 54; initial attempts at, 37–38; Italian fascism and, 38; language and, 51–52; lies and, 52; masses and, 39, 47; memory and, 51–53; metaphysics and, 55–56; Nazism and, 38–39, 41, 45, 55; need to monitor revival of totalitarianism and, 37–38; overview of, 36–45; phenomenological approach and, 41, 51; pluralism contrasted with total domination and, 44–47; political legitimacy and, 44–45, 54; political parties and, 38–40, 46–47; post-totalitarianism and, 49, 51–52, 54, 56; rationality and, 55; reconsideration of totalitarianism in, 41–42, 48; respect for competition and, 39; retroactive application of totalitarianism and, 36–37; revolution of all social values and relations in totalitarianism and, 47–48; search for a typology in, 36–45; secret police and, 44; secular religions and, 40; spatial and temporal expansion of use of 'totalitarian,' 36–37; Stalinism and, 38–39, 41, 45; state's role and, 40, 43, 45–47; sub-types of totalitarian systems and, 43; terror and, 43–45; totalitarian syndrome and, 38, 40, 42; truth destroyed in totalitarianism and, 52; typographical theory and, 42–43

control: hypercontrolled societies, 127–37; *Postscript on the Societies of Control* (Deleuze), 134

COVID-19 pandemic, 120–27

Davanzati Forges, Sergio, 11

death camps. *See* extermination camps

definition of totalitarianism, 2–6, 9, 10–14, 20, 27, 32, 37–38, 41–43, 89, 141–45. *See also* construction of models

Deleuze, Gilles, 128, 134

democracy: acceptance of compromises and, 39; communism and, 83, 85, 88; construction of models and, 38–41, 46; COVID-19 pandemic and, 120; definition of, 84–85; development of totalitarianism and, 9, 12–13, 20–22, 28, 38–40, 82, 85, 124–25; fascism and, 72; foundations of, 9; inverted totalitarianism and, 116–18; mysticism and, 82; as only possibility of opposition and resistance, 39; philosophy in the face of extremes and, 72, 82–98; political parties and, 23, 39–40; postdemocratic phenomenon, totalitarianism as, 85–86; power and, 84–87; radical indeterminacy of, 85; rationality and, 22; respect for competition and, 39; revolutions and, 86–87; socialization and, 85; specters of totality and, 110–18;

democracy (*cont.*)
　surveillance capitalism and, 128, 132, 137; true community as basis of, 25
Democracy Incorporated (Wolin), 113–16, 118
Derrida, Jacques, 101, 126
Devant la guerre (Castoriadis), 89
development of totalitarianism: adjective use of 'totalitarian,' 8–13, 16; antifascist opposition and, 8–13, 16; authoritarianism's relation to totalitarianism and, 32–33; Catholic critique of totalitarianism and, 25; communism's relation to, 9–10; community of the people and, 15–16; continuist interpretation and, 24; debate of the 1940s and, 26–29; definition of totalitarianism and, 9, 10–11, 13–14, 20; democracy's relation to, 9, 12–13, 20–22, 28, 38–40, 124–25; extermination camps and, 33–35; fascism's relation to, 8–13; international reception of totalitarianism and, 12–13; Italian fascism and, 4, 8–13, 38; law and, 33–35; masses and, 28–29; modern tendency to dissolve and, 17; Nazism and, 13–17, 26–27; nostalgia and, 22; noun use of 'totalitarianism,' 10–13; origins of a neologism and, 8–13; *Origins of Totalitarianism* and, 29–35; overview of, 8–13; Parisian laboratory and, 17–25; permanent revolutions and, 28, 33; political parties and, 23; power and, 24–25; radical evil and, 34; religion and, 22, 25; Soviet Union and, 17–24; state's role and, 12–15, 22, 24, 26, 31; total dimension of politics and, 13–17; transcendence and, 22; use of totalitarianism by apologists and, 11–12; war as required state and, 28; Weimar Republic and, 13–15; Western thought and, 21, 26; World War I and, 14, 20
Dialectic of Enlightenment (Horkheimer and Adorno), 72
dialectic of reason, 69–81
The Double State (Fraenkel), 60

Eastern European perspectives, 49–56
Eatherly, Claude, 100
Engels, Friedrich, 61
Enlightenment thought, 66, 72, 82, 91
eschatology, 104–6
Esposito, Roberto, 119, 122, 126
essentialist approach, 6, 37, 41, 51, 58, 65, 144
extermination camps: concentration camps distinguished from, 33; development of totalitarianism and, 33–35; final solution and, 94, 96; Jew as symbolic figure and, 78; Nazism and, 78; nihilism and, 78–79; *Origins of Totalitarianism* and, 33–35, 75; philosophy in the face of extremes and, 75–79, 96; rationality and, 35; terror and, 75; third industrial revolution and, 108; tragicomic equality realized in, 34; uniformity and identity fully realized in, 77–78

fascism: communism's relation to, 9–10, 18–19, 88; COVID-19 pandemic and, 124; democracy and, 72; development of totalitarianism and, 8–13; freedom and, 124; French Revolution and, 83; ideology and, 11, 88–89; Marxism and, 41; masses and, 72; rationality and, 73; religion and, 22; secret of power and, 24; unity affirmed in, 6. *See also* Italian fascism
Fassin, Didier, 148n3
final solution, 94, 96. *See also* extermination camps

Fogg, B. J., 148n4
Forsthoff, Ernst, 15–16
Foucault, Michel: biopower and, 93–96, 119–20, 135; Enlightenment and, 91; governmentality and, 128; modernity and, 91; Nazism and, 94–95; panopticon and, 134; power and, 91–96, 119–20, 135, 145; racism and, 91–95, 120; state socialism and, 94; technology and, 91–92, 128; thanatopolitics and, 118
Fraenkel, Ernst, 26–27, 32–33, 60–61
Franco, Francisco, 4, 19, 36
Frankfurt School, 13, 16, 18, 72–74, 99
freedom, 39–40, 48, 52–54, 68, 97, 101, 124
French Revolution, 63, 82–83, 120
Friedrich, Carl J., 37
Fromm, Eric, 28–29
Furet, François, 82–83

Gauchet, Marcel, 88–89
Gentile, Giovanni, 11–14
Germany. *See* Nazism; Weimar Republic
Gleason, Abbott, 111–12
Glucksmann, André, 112
Gnosis und spätantiker Geist (Jonas), 64
Gnosticism, 64–65, 105
Gobetti, Piero, 10
Gramsci, Antonio, 11
The Great Beast (Weil), 23
Great Replacement, 2
Gulags, 51, 83, 96

Habermas, Jürgen, 73, 90
Halévy, Élie, 20
Han, Byung-Chul, 133–36
Harcourt, Bernard, 136–37, 148n5
Hayek, Friedrich von, 71
Hegel, G. W. F., 12, 21, 60, 63, 67, 70, 76
Heidegger, Martin, 62–63, 65, 67, 73, 79, 98, 100, 102–3

Heller, Agnes, 112
historicism, 19, 62, 64, 66, 69–71
Historikerstreit, 41
Hitler, Adolf: freedom and, 68; *Mein Kampf,* 16, 61; nihilism and, 62–63, 68–69; pathological romanticism of, 19; rise to power of, 15; *Some Reflections on the Philosophy of Hitlerism* (Levinas), 68; state's role for, 16, 27; total and totalitarian interchangeable due to, 15; 'totalitarian' use by, 15
Hobbes, Thomas, 28, 36, 77, 116
Homo Sacer (Agamben), 118
Horkheimer, Max, 71–72, 96
hypercontrolled societies, 127–37

ideology: authoritarianism and, 54; communism and, 54; construction of models and, 44–47, 54; fascism and, 11, 88–89; golden age of, 54; ideocracy, 52, 54, 57, 89–90; institutions and devices for actualization of, 44–45; language and, 51; Marxism and, 88–89; mentality distinguished from, 47; philosophy in the face of extremes and, 57–58, 72–76, 88–90; pivotal role of, 33, 37, 111; post-ideology state, 54; praxis and, 57; reality recreated according to, 33; terror and, 3, 34, 43–45, 72–73, 130; voluntarism and, 11
In the Swarm (Han), 133
Information Fatigue Syndrome (IFS), 137
inverted totalitarianism, 114–18, 129
Italian fascism: authoritarianism of, 4, 13, 33; construction of models and, 38; development of totalitarianism and, 4, 8–13, 38; language and, 13; state's role and, 22; totalitarianism's relation to, 4, 13

Jew as symbolic figure, 78, 80–81, 94, 96, 101
Jewish question, 30–31
Jonas, Hans, 62, 64–65, 102, 104
Jünger, Ernst, 13–14

Khrushchev, Nikita, 50
Kirkpatrick, Jeane, 48–49
Kojève, Alexandre, 21
Kolakowski, Leszek, 52

Lacoue-Labarthe, Philippe, 77–79
language, 13, 51–53, 90, 111–12, 138–40
law, 27, 31, 33–35, 44, 53, 59–62, 70
Lefort, Claude, 83–87, 89–90
Leibholz, Gerhard, 15–16
Levinas, Emmanuel, 68–69
lies, 51–52, 138–40
The Life of the Mind (Arendt), 76
Linz, Juan J., 42–43, 46
Löwith, Karl, 66–67
Lukács, György, 148n1
Lyotard, Jean-François, 77–78, 80–81, 83, 96–98

Machiavelli, Niccolò, 60, 84
The Man on the Bridge (Anders), 100
Manicheanism, 3, 19, 111–12
Marcuse, Herbert, 62, 73–74
Marx, Karl, 76–77
Marxism: deconstruction of, 19; fascism and, 41; ideology and, 88–89; philosophy in the face of extremes and, 70, 71–72, 82, 88–89; power and, 24; praxis primary in, 77; secular religions and, 20; Soviet Union and, 17–19; Stalinism and, 76; totalitarianism's relation to, 55, 76–77, 111. *See also* communism
masses, 14, 19, 28–29, 31, 39, 47, 72, 133
materialism, 60, 63, 69, 81
Mbembe, Achille, 119–20
Meaning of History (Löwith), 66

Mein Kampf (Hitler), 16, 61
metaphysics, 55–56, 58, 62, 67, 69–70, 74–75, 77, 79, 90, 100, 102–3
Milosz, Czeslaw, 52, 57
Mlynář, Zdeněk., 50, 53
model construction. *See* construction of models
Monnerot, Jules, 22–23
Monti, Augusto, 9
The Moral Implications of the Atomic Age (Anders), 106
Mounier, Emmanuel, 25
Mussolini, Benito, 8–9, 11–12, 19
mysticism, 57, 61, 82

Nancy, Jean-Luc, 77–78, 97–98
natural law, 31, 60–61, 70
Nazism: antifascist opposition to, 16; arbitrary tribunals in, 27; biologism of, 61; body's role in, 68; civilization questioned by, 68; communism's relation to, 51, 53, 63; communitarian basis of, 15–16, 61; construction of models and, 38–39, 41, 45, 55; cultural roots of, 60; development of totalitarianism and, 13–17, 26–27; extermination camps and, 78; *Führerprinzip* in, 27; Gnosticism and, 64–65; Hegel's influence on, 60; hubris of, 78; Jew as symbolic figure for, 80; mysticism of, 61, 79–80; natural law and, 60–61; nihilism and, 59–62, 67–69, 78–79; objectivist metaphysics and, 55; onto-typology and, 79–80; originality of, 94; philosophy in the face of extremes and, 58–62, 66–67, 70, 72, 78–82, 94; political-judiciary structure of, 26–28; polycentric disorder of, 27–28; power and, 94; racism and, 79; rationality and, 72; salvation and, 70; socialism's relation to, 95; Stalinism compared

to, 30, 32–35, 38, 110; state's role in, 13–16, 22; as total revolution, 15; Western thought and, 60–61, 69, 72, 78–80
necropolitics, 119–27
neoliberalism, 73, 112, 114–17, 121–23, 133–35
Neumann, Franz, 26–28, 32
Neumann, Sigmund, 28, 33
The New Class (van Djilas), 50
Nietzsche, Friedrich, 21, 63, 67, 79, 90
nihilism: concrete possibility of total nihilism, 98–109; extermination camps and, 78–79; Nazism and, 59–62, 67–69, 78–79; philosophy in the face of extremes and, 57–59, 78, 98–109
1984 (Orwell), 51
Nolte, Ernst, 41

On Democracy in America (Tocqueville), 116
On the Abolition of All Political Parties (Weil), 23
On the Concept of History (Benjamin), 99
One-Dimensional Man (Marcuse), 73
Open Society and Its Enemies (Popper), 70
Origins of Totalitarianism (Arendt): authoritarianism's relation to totalitarianism in, 32–33; concentration camps in, 75; development of totalitarianism and, 29–35; essentialist approach influenced by, 35; extermination camps in, 33–35, 75; human nature in, 75; human rights critiqued in, 31; ideology in, 74–75; imperialization in, 93; influence of, 29–35; innovations of, 29–35; Jewish question in, 30–31; law in, 33–35; metapolitics of totalitarianism in, 74–75; methodological approach of, 29–30; Nazism and Stalinism compared in, 30, 32–35; people lacking homeland in, 31; permanent revolutions in, 33; phenomenological approach influenced by, 35; power in, 32–33; radical evil in, 34; reception of, 30; state's role in, 31–35; structural traits of totalitarian regimes in, 32; teleology rejected in, 30–32; terror in, 75; totalitarian mentality in, 74–75; Western thought's relation to totalitarianism in, 74–76
Orwell, George, *1984*, 51

Pathology of Freedom (Anders), 100
Patočka, Jan, 55–56
Permanent Revolution (Neumann), 17, 28
permanent revolutions, 28, 33, 35, 59–60
phenomenological approach, 35, 41, 51
philosophy in the face of extremes: aestheticism and, 79; apocalyptic thinking and, 65–66; atomic bomb and, 98–109; autonomy of the political and, 74; biopolitics and, 91–96; body's role and, 68; characteristics of totalitarianism and, 78; communism and, 63–64, 66, 83; concentration camps and, 75, 98; concrete possibility of total nihilism and, 98–109; cultural basis of totalitarianism and, 60; definition of totalitarianism and, 89; democracy and, 72, 82–98; dialectic of reason and, 69–81; Enlightenment thought and, 66, 72, 82, 91; essentialist approach and, 58, 144; ethnic community and, 61; experience of time and, 66; extermination camps and, 75–79, 96; falsehood of the whole and, 71–72;

philosophy in the face of extremes (*cont.*)
first philosophical interpretations of totalitarianism, 58–59; forclusion and, 80; Frankfurt School and, 72–74; French Revolution and, 63, 82–83; globalizing projects and, 80–81; Gnosticism and, 64–65; Hegelian thought and, 60, 67, 70; Heideggerian thought and, 62, 67, 73, 98; historicism and, 66, 69–71; ideology and, 57–58, 72–76, 88–90; Jew as symbolic figure and, 78, 80–81; Marxism and, 70, 71–72, 82, 88–89; mass society and, 72; materialism and, 60, 63, 69, 81; metaphysics and, 55–56, 58, 62, 67, 69–70, 74–75, 77–80, 90, 96, 100, 102–3; metapolitics and, 58, 74–75; modernity and, 55, 57–69, 82, 91–94; mysticism and, 61, 66, 82; natural law and, 60–61; Nazism and, 58–62, 66–67, 70, 72, 78–82, 94; new human nature and, 75; nihilism and, 57–59, 78, 98–109; ontology and, 68–69, 74, 79–80; onto-typology and, 79–80; overview of, 57–69, 142–45; permanent revolutions and, 60; philosophy of history and, 65–67; Plato's *Republic* as first totalitarian project and, 70–71; pluralism and, 79; political evil and, 57; postmodernism and, 81; power and, 57–69, 84–87, 91–96; racism and, 70, 79, 91–95; rationality and, 59–64, 67, 69–82, 89–92; resistance and, 97–98; salvation and, 70–71; secularization and, 65–67, 69; socialization and, 84–85; soft totalitarianism and, 81, 98–99; Soviet Union and, 83–84; Stalinism and, 58, 62–63, 78, 80–81; statocracy and, 89–90; subjectivity and, 69, 73–74, 79; technology and, 73–74, 98–109; terror and, 72–73, 75, 82–98; totalitarian mentality and, 74–75; transcendence and, 66; Western thought's relation to totalitarianism and, 59–63, 68–82, 144

Plato, 36, 55, 70–71, 77, 79, 96
pluralism, 2, 5, 14, 20, 44–47, 50, 79, 110
The Political Function of the Modern Lie (Koyré), 138
political parties, 23, 38–40, 46–47
The Political Religions (Voegelin), 65
Popper, Karl, 70–71
postmodernism, 80–81, 116
Postscript on the Societies of Control (Deleuze), 134
power: biopower, 74, 91–96, 118–20, 122, 124–27, 134–35; communism and, 24; cultivation power, 94; democracy and, 84–87; development of totalitarianism and, 24–25; fascism and, 24; Marxism and, 24; Nazism and, 94; philosophy in the face of extremes and, 57–69, 84–87, 91–96; place of power, 84, 86–87; racism and, 91–95; secret of, 24; sovereign power to kill, 94; specters of totality and, 118–27, 134–35; Western thought and, 91
practice of dissent. *See* construction of models
Prague Spring, 50–51
Prison Notebooks (Gramsci), 11

The Question Concerning Technology (Heidegger), 102

racism, 31, 70, 79, 91–96, 121–22
radical evil, 6, 34
rationality: construction of models and, 55; democracy and, 22; dialectic of reason, 69–81; extermination camps and, 35;

fascism and, 73; historicism and, 89; instrumental rationality, 19, 33, 35, 65, 73; irrationalism and, 61, 67, 77–78; modernity and, 65; Nazism and, 72; nihilism and, 62; philosophy in the face of extremes and, 59–64, 67, 69–82, 89–92; technical rationality, 55; Western thought and, 60, 62, 71–73

Rauschning, Hermann, 33, 59–60, 63

reason. *See* rationality

Reflections Concerning the Causes of Liberty and Social Oppression (Weil), 23

Reich, Willhelm, 28–29

Remnants of Auschwitz (Agamben), 118

Republic (Plato), 36, 70–71, 96

The Revolution Betrayed (Trotsky), 17

The Revolution of Nihilism (Rauschning), 59

Rizzi, Bruno, 18

The Road to Serfdom (Hayek), 71

Rousseau, Jean-Jacques, 23, 36, 77

Russia. *See* Soviet Union

Schmitt, Carl, 14–15, 27, 60–61

secret police, 33, 38, 44, 111

secular religions, 20–24, 40, 57

Serge, Victor, 18

Shapiro, Leonard, 42

Šimečka, Milan, 52

Socialisme ou barbarie (journal), 83–84

Society Must Be Defended (Foucault), 91

soft totalitarianism, 74, 81, 98–99, 133–35

Soljénitsyne, Alexandre, 51, 86

Some Reflections on the Philosophy of Hitlerism (Levinas), 68

Souvarine, Souvarine, 19, 21–22

Soviet Union: anti-Stalinism and, 19; bureaucratic collectivism and, 17–19, 23; detotalitarianization of, 39; development of totalitarianism and, 17–24; as ideocracy, 89; limited pluralism of, 50; Marxism and, 17–19, 41; philosophy in the face of extremes and, 83–84; socialism's relation to, 83–84; Stalin/Lenin break and, 18, 50; as statocracy, 90–91; totalitarianism associated with, 50–51, 83–84. *See also* Stalinism

specters of totality: algorithmic governmentality and, 128; axis of evil and, 112; biopolitics and, 118–27, 134–35; biosecurity and, 125; colonialism and, 120; conformism and, 133; COVID-19 pandemic and, 120–27; crisis of the real and, 136–40; democracy incorporated and, 110–18; digital culture and, 136; governance and, 117; *homo sacer* and, 118; hypercontrolled societies and, 127–37; identity of information and being and, 137; inverted totalitarianism and, 114–18, 129; Islamic totalitarianism and, 112–13; language and, 138–40; lies and, 138–40; to make live and let die and, 118–27; Manicheanism and, 111–12; mass culture and, 136; necropolitics and, 119–27; neoliberalism and, 112, 114–17, 121–23, 133–35; overview of, 110–18; power and, 118–27, 134–35; psychopolitical turn and, 134–35; racism and, 121–22; revival of totalitarianism and, 112; September 11 attacks and, 115–16; social imaginary and, 123; soft totalitarianism and, 134; state's role and, 124–25; surveillance capitalism and, 128–32; technology and, 127–32; terror and, 124–25; thanatopolitics and, 118–27; US totalitarianism and, 113–17; war on terrorism and, 125; Western thought and, 119–23

Spiro, Herbert, 41

Stalin, Josef, 17–19, 33, 50, 54, 89
Stalinism: construction of models and, 38–39, 41, 45; ending of, 51; Leninism's relation to, 50–51; Marxism and, 76; Nazism compared to, 30, 32–35, 38, 110; philosophy in the face of extremes and, 58, 62–63, 78, 80–81
state's role in society, 10, 12–16, 22, 24, 26, 31, 40, 43, 45–47, 124–25
statocracy, 89–90
Stiegler, Bernard, 128, 135
Strauss, Leo, 62–64
Sturzo, Luigi, 10–11, 13
subjectivity, 69, 73–74, 79
surveillance capitalism, 128–32, 136

Talmon, Jacob, 82–83
technology, 73–74, 91–92, 98–109, 127–32
terror: construction of models and, 43–45; democracy and, 82–98; extermination camps and, 75; health terror, 124–25; ideology and, 3, 34, 43–45, 130; philosophy in the face of extremes and, 72–73, 75, 82–98; specters of totality and, 124–25
thanatopolitics, 118–27, 135
Totalitarian and Authoritarian Regimes (Linz), 42
Totalitarian Dictatorship and Autocracy (Friedrich and Brzezinski), 37
Totalitarian Elements in Marxism (Arendt), 76
totalitarian mentality, 74–75
totalitarian syndrome, 38, 40, 42
totalitarianism, 1–7, 141–45; characteristics of, 4–6, 26, 37–38, 42–56, 58, 111; definition of, 2–6, 9, 10–14, 20, 27, 32, 37–38, 41–43, 89, 141–45; emergence of, 3–5; inverted, 114–18, 129; methodological approach to, 4; as new category of political thought, 4; organizational approach to, 5–7; ostracizing judgment in use of, 3; philosophy in the face of extremes, 142–45; political use of, 4–5; reconsideration of, 144–45; revival of, 1–3; rhetorical use of, 2–5; shattering of limits in relationships between power and life, 141–43; totalitarian regimes distinguished from totalitarianism, 143; twentieth century as unified by concept of, 4–6. *See also* construction of models; development of totalitarianism; specters of totality
transcendence, 21–22, 25, 56, 65–66, 68
Trotsky, Leon, 17–19, 23

USSR. *See* Soviet Union

violence. *See* concentration camps; extermination camps; terror
Voegelin, Eric, 57, 62, 64–66

Walzer, Michael, 48–49
Weber, Max, 49
Weil, Simone, 19, 20–21, 23–24, 68
Weimar Republic, 13–15
Western thought: communism and, 63; development of totalitarianism and, 21, 26; Enlightenment thought in, 66, 72, 82, 91; evil and, 68; Jew as symbolic figure in, 80; Nazism and, 60–61, 69, 72, 78–80; philosophy in the face of extremes and, 59–63, 68–82, 144; power and, 91; rationality and, 60, 62, 71–73; specters of totality and, 119–23
Wolin, Sheldon, 113–18, 125, 129

Ziegler, Heinz Otto, 15
Zinoviev, Alexander, 53
Zuboff, Shoshana, 128–33

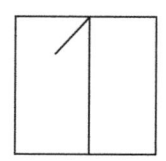

SQUARE ONE
First-Order Questions in the Humanities

Series Editor: **PAUL A. KOTTMAN**

PHILIPPE HUNEMAN
Why?: The Philosophy Behind the Question

ROY BEN-SHAI
Critique of Critique

RICHARD VAN OORT
Shakespeare's Mad Men: A Crisis of Authority

DAVIDE TARIZZO
Political Grammars: The Unconscious Foundations of Modern Democracy

AMIR ESHEL
Poetic Thinking Today: An Essay

PETER MURPHY
The Long Public Life of a Short Private Poem: Reading and Remembering Thomas Wyatt

JON BASKIN
Ordinary Unhappiness: The Therapeutic Fiction of David Foster Wallace

PAULA BLANK
Shakesplish: How We Read Shakespeare's Language

PAUL A. KOTTMAN
Love as Human Freedom

ADRIANA CAVARERO
Inclinations: A Critique of Rectitude

Printed and bound by CPI Group (UK) Ltd, Croydon, CR0 4YY
11/01/2024
08221105-0001